365 Days to Crazy Web Traffic

Month 1 – Getting Started

By

C. J. Oakes

My Guarantee

98% of all websites never get more than a few visits per month.

Do what I describe in this book and you will get that, and much more. If after a year, you do not get such traffic, I will provide you with a free analysis of your website. If I have found that you have done what I have taught, I will provide you with a full refund of your purchase price.

Regardless of the case, I will also provide you with a detailed road map to get your website on track.

Just write to me at cjeffoakes@365crazywebtraffic.com

ISBN-13:
978-1497584952

ISBN-10:
1497584957

Contents

Introduction

Building a website is easy. Getting traffic is…well, easy too. The only reason getting traffic is not-so-easy for many is that the Internet is so full of advice that most newbies to the Web become inundated and experience information overload. Deciding between what works and what does not can be tough. What is even tougher is knowing where and how to start.

The goal of this book is to take the mystery away and teach you step-by-step what you need to know and do to build a successful website, a website that gets crazy amounts of traffic. I am going to show you just how easy it is to build a website that can get crazy traffic in only a year…365 Days to be exact.

If you have been researching websites for any amount of time, you know that traffic is the life of a website. Without traffic, a website is like a book on a shelf collecting dust. So I am going to simplify the matter for you.

I have built several websites. One was a support site for a series of books I wrote (Survive and Thrive After the Collapse of the Dollar – http://collapseconsultants.com); one for my own self-interest (http://criminaljusticelaw.us); another for my wife as sort of training for this book (http://wallysweirdstuff.com); and others so that I could experiment with the concepts I was learning years ago (including http://jeffoakes.me which is now shut down for reasons explained in the final chapter. In some ways however, all the sites I have built have been experiments. Years ago I decided I wanted to understand how the Internet works so that I could build websites whenever and for whatever purpose I decided. In this book I'll teach you what I know.

Over the course of the last year or so, I have been ghostwriting for clients worldwide as well as self-publishing books in my own name. In the past several months, many of my clients and friends have sought my advice in setting up their own websites. One, Jason Hudson, author of the recent book, *Hard Knocks: The Method and the Madness*, suggested I put what I know into a book for others (although I think part of his suggestion is more to reduce the number of calls to me for advice). Jason is both friend and boss. I formerly worked for him in Public Relations for Woodbridge Home Exteriors where he has been supervising and honing his own expertise in canvassing for many years. If you want to learn how to locate leads for your business the traditional way, I strongly recommend his book. His website, which he recently began building in support of his book is http://hardknockscourse.com.

A third reason for breaking the material into chunks is that some readers of this series will want to follow each book whereas others may choose to skip some. The reason is that many reading these books may already be websperts in certain areas of website development whereas others may be complete novices. Thus, as each book is published, a reader can check out the Introduction of each and decide if he or she even needs to read it. If you are completely new to building a website or simply want to learn how to build in a simple step-by-step manner, then follow the whole series. If you already know some things, you can skip some of the books and know which to skip simply by reading the Introduction to each.

Moving into subsequent books, I will build on the foundation of Month One so that by the end of the year, you will not only have crazy traffic going to your site (and likely a good stream of revenue), but more importantly, you will be a Webspert in your own right (A Webspert is a Web Expert – someone who knows how to build a website that gets traffic).

This will be a relatively short book (though the completed version will be quite lengthy). The reason is that I am not going to add a bunch of extraneous information simply to add filler material. I am only going to tell you what you need to know, as you need to know it. Think of it like getting an education. In the first grade, you gain a foundation of knowledge upon which to build. What you learn in the first grade is not all that complicated, but to grow to the point of the second grade, you must master what you learn in the first. By the time you graduate the 12th Grade, you will have gained a body of knowledge that you can use throughout your life. Then, should you wish, you can continue to University so as to specialize in a particular field. This series is like the 1st through 12th Grades. You will learn what you need to know to be successful in your weblife.

That said, you can always go to the website http://356CrazyWebTraffic.com to get the extraneous information. Also, this book can stand alone. That is, I will provide all you need to build a website and if you continue with just one particular step in the process, you will be able to build a website that gets lots of traffic (hint: that single step is discussed in the last chapter of this book).

About Month One (This book)

Starting with the first week, you will learn the basics of the Internet…how it started, how it functions, how search engines work, and so forth. The object is to give you a good overview of the Internet itself from the standpoint of someone wanting to do more than simply use the beast. Once you understand how it works, building within the rules established by the pioneers of the Internet will be much easier. For this reason, much of week one will seem useless to those who want to "get rich quick" using the Internet. To be clear: NO ONE has gotten rich "quick." Success may have followed years of hard work not seen by the public eye, but "quick" was not the case. That said, the speed at which a person may excel online is quicker than traditional paths, but time, dedication, and yes, hard work are involved. If you are not ready to put in the work necessary to make your website a success, put this book down now. Get a refund and stick to your 9-5 job.

But if you are willing to put in the time and effort, you can and will have a website that is getting tons of traffic in only one year—365 days. I guarantee it.

The secret to website traffic is actually no secret. Thousands of individuals have created websites that get so much traffic, they make a living just from the ad revenue alone. Many more are selling products they never touch and making a substantially better living than they were in their professional careers. Still others have found great ways to build sites that millions love—in some cases, they have rode a wave to financial success in keeping their website and in others, they have sold the website to major players for millions. We have all heard these stories.

The key to it all is traffic.

To clarify. What if you owned a billboard alongside a highway? If you had no traffic on that road, you would not likely be able to get an advertiser for the billboard. If you had a hundred people a day traveling that road, you could get something. But if you had thousands of people a day traveling that road, you would be able to sell that billboard space for still more. And the amount you can get increases as the traffic increases.

Likewise if you had a store. To make sales in the store, you need people. Traffic. The more people who enter your store, the more sales you will make…unless you run a really crappy store. Still, the law of averages will ensure that you will make more sales with more traffic.

Websites are the same.

But you need to understand why people go to websites and how they get there. That will be the goal of week one.

Moving into Week 2, you will prepare to build your website.

We will be building in WordPress. For those who are unfamiliar, WordPress is the #1 site building tool in the world. It is a blogging platform, but that is good because blogs have become an essential element of most websites today. However, the principles applied in this book work for any website, not just a WordPress site so anyone can learn from this book.

There are numerous advantages to using WordPress, especially for those new to building websites, and these will be explained early in Week 2.

In getting ready to build, you will learn how to make the choices that will affect your website for years to come. Too often, website builder's start without any planning and the website that results shows it. Like having any goal, you need to know where to aim. If shooting at a target with a bow, you need to be able to see the target if you are to hit it. The goal of Week 2 is to help you visualize the target and prepare you for firing at it.

Week 3 is when you actually begin to pull the bowstring back and ready for firing.

In Week 3, you will begin actually building your website. You will learn how to write for the TWO audiences of the Internet. You will learn about SEO, Search Engine Optimization, and how to ensure that what you write will get the results you want.

Writing for the Internet is quite different from writing for other forms of media. You need to know how to write in such a way that both the search engines and your visitors will like what you have written. But don't fear. Even if you are not a writer, you can learn to do this. I have developed a technique that anyone can learn and in this book, you will learn the basics of this technique. If you do what I tell you, this alone will account for copious amounts of traffic to your website.

Moving into Week 4 you will come to understand content. The Internet is "content driven." This is to say, that people go online looking for "content." Understanding what content is and how to best use content is the key to getting people to visit your website repeatedly. Just like a store, you want people to return again and again. Just like a billboard, you want traffic to continue, to grow, and much of this comes from having the same people traveling that road daily.

A website is no different. The best traffic is repeat traffic. This is because repeat traffic permits your website to continue to grow, which permits you to either sell more products or advertising.

Finally, we will wrap up with you learning how to tie it all together. Once you complete this first Month, you will know all you need to know to build a successful website. You will know enough that if you want, you can continue learning more elsewhere and further hone your ability to capitalize on the traffic you will gain after only a year. You can stop reading with this book, or pick up the next one and learn how to start super-charging your website so that you can grow it to CRAZY levels.

What you will learn here is not a big secret. The only difference between this book and others is that for the first time, here is a book that will concisely put what you need to know in the order you need to know it. In this way, you will build a solid foundation for future success. If you follow the entire series, after one year you will not only have a successful website, but will be an Internet Guru yourself.

Note for those reading this book in print:

Where links appear in the text, the complete and proper URL/web address will be placed in parentheses (http://URL.com). I do this because this book is simultaneously appearing in both book and electronic form. If reading this in Kindle, you may naturally click on the links to be taken to a website.

With that said, I know you are eager to get started, so let's jump in.

Regards,

C. Jeff Oakes

October 2013

"Content is King"
> ➤ Bill Gates

Day 1: Decide on a Site Type

This may seem like a no brainer, but you would be surprised at how many people want to start a website, but simply don't know what type of site they want to build. When I started my first website, I was as clueless as some reading this book right now. My interests are varied and eclectic, so my first website, http://jeffoakes.me, was just as varied and eclectic as I. I had stories, poetry, essays, screenplays, and tons of other things I had written over the years on it. I had no clue about how to draw traffic from the search engines and even less about how to build links to get traffic from elsewhere. I had no advertising and so made no money.

But I knew one thing when I started that website years ago: I wanted to understand what works in getting traffic and what does not. I wanted to experiment and I did. What I have learned, I share in this book.

One thing I learned is that all websites can be broken into three primary categories.

1. Sales sites
2. Support sites
3. Entertainment/Educational sites

These can be further subdivided, but essentially, every website fits into one or a combination of these three types. Depending on your goals for building a website, you will want to know and understand which type you will build, for this will determine every choice thereafter.

So the first thing you need to ask yourself is, "What is my goal for building a website?"

If your answer is to add to an existing business, then you will have **a Support site**. Even if your business is in direct sales of a product, your website is a supportive extension of your primary business. Of course, in some cases, business owners have managed to build such a strong website that they were able to close their traditional brick-and-mortar business to focus solely on their web business. In this case, the site transformed from a support site to a sales site.

If your goal is to help other websites and web businesses, then you also will be building **a support site**. If your goal is to provide a way to show a particular population what you can offer in the way of expertise, you have **a support site**. If your goal is to help people locate useful resources, get help for a problem, or find information, then you have **a support site**.

Of course, if your goal is to only sell online (without a traditional real-world business), then the website will be **a Sales site** from the start.

Finally, if your goal is simply to entertain or teach something, whether you plan on monetizing the site or not, then your website is **an Entertainment/Educational site**. Even such websites as Facebook and MySpace are in reality nothing more than Entertainment sites, for people go to these sites to socialize and thus, be entertained…much like going to a party. Yet, in a very real sense of the word, the social media sites are at the same time **Support sites**, for they are often used to support or add value to other websites and businesses.

As you may have guessed therefore, most websites are in fact support sites of some form. For instance, the largest website in the world, Google, is **a support site,** for the purpose of Google from the start was to help people locate useful and accurate information. Google has expanded into many other functions, but the overall goal is the same: to support the efforts of other users of the web.

This makes perfect sense, for as you will learn on Days Three and Four, the primary purpose of the Internet is the spreading of information easily.

Hence, you must know your goal for building a website before you get started. Think of it like shooting a gun or throwing a ball to a friend. You must know where you are aiming if you are to be successful.

So decide right now what type of website you will build. Will it be a support site, a sales site, or an entertainment/educational site? If you are not sure, give it careful thought for the answer will determine how you build.

That's it for Day One. Easy day.

Day 2: Set up a Google Account

Open your web browser and type in http://mail.google.com

You are going to set up a Google account and the best way to do this is to first set up a gmail account.

Now, some may chafe at this for as the big boy on the Internet, some are beginning to fear Google. Don't. Like Google or not, the simple fact is that if you want to have the most successful website possible, you need to learn to use Google and its myriad of services for webmasters.

The simple reality is that Google established the first truly useful search engine and as such, it remains the leader of the Internet. All other search engines follow the lead of Google and because of this, Google remains the best source of useful information for anyone wanting to build a strong website (more on this on Days Three and Four). This could all change in a few years, but for now, like it or not, Googling is vital for websperts.

So for now, simply set up your Gmail account. I recommend choosing a Gmail account using your name for although you will later set up a dedicated email account for your website, there will be times when you will use this email for your business. Though cutsie names may be fine for networking with friends, you want something more related to your business for this.

Of course, if you are planning a cutsie website and have absolutely NO plans for ever having another website, go for it. Also, if you are planning a website whereby you don't want your name associated with the site in any way, you want something more anonymous. But other than these two exceptions, I recommend using some form of your name.

This does a couple of things.

First, it helps your website be more credible from the beginning. Next, if you are going to write in your name for your site (and thus establish yourself as an expert – more on this in Month Four), this helps Google build your authorship, which is one of the parameters used by its search engine crawlers.

This was part of the reason you determined what type of website you are planning before this step. If you are building a support site, you want your name out there to establish your credibility and expertise. If you are selling something, you also want credibility and expertise, which build trust and higher conversion rates. If you are an educational website, you likewise want to establish these elements from the start. The only instance whereby you may want to keep your name out of the mix is if you are building an adult site of some sort (including gambling) or running some sort of illegal or unethical activity. I will not be addressing these forms of websites in this book directly, although the principles I teach will still apply.

The primary intent of this book is to teach people who want to build a credible and ethical website, so I recommend using your name for the Google account.

In addition, your Gmail account will be the login for most of the other services provided by Google, which I will teach you about in this and future books. Google provides many useful tools and services, but to access most of them, you need an account.

So log in now and create your Gmail account. Once you have done this, play around with it and learn how to use this email service. Here is what your Gmail dashboard will look like once you have created and accessed your account.

Like most email services, this is pretty simple. If you want to write an email, click the red "compose" button in the upper left corner (it will be gray in the printed version and is located just below the Google logo and the words "Gmail". Your inbox is split between "Unread" and "Everything else."

If you look at the image shown, just to the right of the "compose" button is an ad for an SEO Consultant and below this is the "Unread" mail. Just below this, you will see a square box, a star, and a sort of arrow box. If you want to place a star beside an email for sorting purposes, simply click the blank star and it becomes yellow. It is now starred. Likewise with the arrow box to the right of the star. This is for using special folders like any other email sorter system, but Gmail "learns" where to place these as you create folders (it just takes a step out of the process).

Your contacts, as you add them, will appear on the left just below the "search people" box. The gray bar at the top simply lets you toggle between various Google functions. On the far right near the top, you will see what looks like a gear. This is where you can adjust settings, themes, and other functions of your Gmail account.

Just play around with this and learn your way around for now.

That is all for Day Two.

Day 3: Understanding the Internet

The Internet is much older than many today know.

The Internet was actually started in the 1950s when researchers at UCLA created a wired network with researchers at Stanford University and sent the first message. In time, University researchers worldwide would use

Tim Berners-Lee, The True Father of the Internet, courtesy of cellanr, flickr

the network initially developed to exchange and compare research with each other. By the early 1980s, the first standard protocol (TCP) was developed to make the sharing of research documents easier. This was then called the Internet, but it was not until 1989 that a researcher named Tim Berners-Lee developed the Hypertext Transfer Protocol (HTTP), which created the Internet as we know it.

The hypertext, or hyperlink as we now call it, is what made the transfer of information as revolutionary. No longer did the average person need to know and understand complicated computer languages in order to transfer information across the web. Virtually overnight, the real "Internet" was born.

But to really understand how to build a website that gets traffic, a webmaster must understand the importance of these hyperlinks (links for short).

A link is nothing more than an address where certain information is stored. Think of it like a filing system. On your computer, you have programs. In these programs, you have files. Within each file, are subfiles and likely more subfiles within these.

Look at the example on the next page from my computer showing the Word Documents leading up to this book.

Notice that in the address line, it reads "BOOKS IN PROGRESS" then "Crazy Web Traffic" then "Month1." Then in the box below, there is a folder with "images" and a Word Document titled "month1."

 See the two little arrows to the left of "BOOKS IN PROGRESS" in the address line (<<)?

This indicates that there are additional folders prior to this which also make up the address, or link, for that particular file location. Hyperlinks work in this exact same way.

By breaking the World Wide Web into decreasingly smaller "file" locations, we are able to direct anyone to any file containing any information we desire. To illustrate, here is the complete file location for this book. Compare it to the image which only shows a portion of the file location information.

You can see that the complete file location reads first "F:" which is my jump drive. Then within that drive is a file called "JOEPub" which is the name of my publishing arm. Then the next folder is named "Books by Cjeffoakes" (me) followed by "BOOKS IN PROGRESS" then "Crazy Web Traffic" then "Month1." This makes up the complete address so that I can locate and access this file in my computer.

In the same way, hyperlinks help us find information on the Internet. For instance, go to http://criminaljusticelaw.us right now. On the main menu, choose "Demo Page." Once on that page, click on the link for the "Next Page." Then click on the link for "Final." You have just navigated to where I wanted you to via links, but look at the address line. It should read (with or without the http://) 365crazywebtraffic.com/demo-page/next-page/final/. Do you see that?

See, it doesn't matter the format chosen, all a link does is point the user from the wider picture (the whole website as in 365crazywebtraffic.com) to the desired page further in, using directional tools much like road signs. Had those who programmed the web wanted, this could have just as easily been written as 365crazywebtraffic.com>>>demo.page>>>next.page>>>final. Any system would have worked as long as it was simple and understood by computers and people worldwide.

Can you see the similarities between links on the internet and the method of accessing files on your computer?

If you are old enough to remember filing cabinets (which are rapidly disappearing), the system is the same. If you wanted to find a file on a particular client, you would go to the file cabinets and choose the correct cabinet, then a particular drawer, then the files within the drawer would (ideally) be in a particular order which made it easy to find that client. Then most companies would have a particular order for the information contained within the file folder. This system made it easy to quickly locate information about any client quickly.

File/folder systems on PC's are the same system as are the hyperlink protocol developed by Tim Berners-Lee. In other words, hyperlinks or links, are nothing more than simple ways to point people to the information they are seeking—a sort of filing system map. The Internet is simply a network of links which help guild people to locations. Web Addresses are the links.

The Internet is really that simple, but having a firm understanding of this simple concept is vital to knowing how to build websites that get traffic.

Play around with your computer. Go to files and notice the pathways created to get to where you want to go. Pay attention to these and understand how they work. Building links is the same process and if you want to have a successful website, you need to understand how links work. Links are like nerves connecting various parts of our body to other parts. If there is a disconnect in our nervous system, we will likely need to visit a Doctor. If there is a disconnect in links we create to our website, people will not be able to find us. We need to be able to be found if we are to get traffic.

So take some time to study how "links" are built even now on your computer automatically. This way, when we start building links on your website, you will grasp the material better.

That's all for today.

Day 4: Understanding Search Engines

With the average website, traffic from search engines accounts for between 30% and 40% of all traffic. A website that is built properly therefore, can receive large amounts of traffic from search engines. But what is a search engine and how can you learn to make these work for, rather than against you?

Simply put, a search engine is nothing more than a special program that helps people find what they are looking for quickly. A good search engine provides accurate results, while one less-than-good will provide terrible results. For instance, in the days just prior to Google, a person could enter the search terms "riding horses" if looking for information on riding horses. The results would be as varied as horses for sale to pornography involving horses. If your daughter or son were the one doing the search, you may shudder to think of what they would find.

At the time, the Internet was a hodge-podge of websites with few ways to locate useful information. Some of the early solutions were Directories. Directories were (and remain—more on this in Month 3) effective ways of locating websites that many found useful for a variety of subjects. For instance, if you were looking for information about riding horses and not in the sexual way, a Directory would have a section on Animals, then a subsection on Horses, then perhaps a subsection on Riding. This would point you in the right direction, though you would then likely have to search through numerous sites to find the specific information you were seeking.

Needless to say, Directories were useful, but time-consuming.

The idea behind search engines was to develop a program (an algorithm) that could search websites for information, then as people entered keywords to describe what they were seeking, the search engine could quickly and conveniently locate that information regardless of the page of the website on which it was located. It was a great idea, but in the early phases as already mentioned, search engines failed to return useful information at best and offensive information at worst.

Google Changed Searching

Two Stanford University students named Sergey Brin and Larry Page developed an algorithm that searched for information and returned very accurate results. They took their program to Sun Microsystems in San Diego and the CEO, seeing the results, provided them with the seed capital to launch their company. Google did not advertise in the early years and the search engine grew rapidly just through word of mouth. It was that good.

I was one of the people who learned of Google through word-of-mouth for at the time, I was bouncing between Yahoo search and Compuserve. Neither was very effective for my research and a friend recommended Google. I was hooked from the first search for I literally cut my research time by 80%!

But why was Googles algorithm (search engine) so much better than the others?

Although the exact programming remains a closely-guarded secret (much like the formula for Coca-Cola), careful research since that time along with numerous experiments, indicates that the secret lay in quality writing.

Page and Brin set out to develop a search engine that would help them in their PhD studies and lest we forget, the Internet was established for research purposes between Universities. Thus, it stands to reason, that these two developed their search engine in such a way that it would seek out quality documents of a nature similar to college essays, dissertations, and research papers.

The evidence bears this out for most SEO experts will tell you that headings are important (more on this later) and that any web page must contain a header, a footer, and a body. Contained within these must be the subject of the page. And should the page not be written in such a way that the subject is clearly understood, the page will be fairly ignored by the search engine. In other words, just as Google claims, its search engine seeks quality content.

Thus, keywords (or subjects) are important. Headings (to divide the content into easier-to-read sections) are important. Clear, understandable language is important. Relevant links (to help locate related material, a.k.a. References) are important. Descriptions (tags) are important. A table of contents is important as is some form of index (page tabs and a sitemap). Finally, because a website is used by humans to locate useful and reliable information quickly, ease of navigation is important, along with certain credibility factors.

All of these concepts will be covered during this month. Don't feel overwhelmed by this for by the end of this book, you will understand how to implement each of these concepts into whatever website you build.

The important thing to understand for now is that after Google set the pace, all the other search engines then followed suit. So if you want a site with traffic, especially traffic derived from the search engines, you must do these things. There are no magic formulas and no shortcuts (more on this on Day 8).

Search engines simply seek the best information according to the search terms entered by humans and the Google search engine remains the best at doing this quickly and accurately. Understanding and accepting this is vital to building a website that will get good traffic results.

How Search Engines Work

Search engines work by assigning values to words called "keywords." Keywords are simply the terms used to define a search. We all have used search engines by typing in some words that define what we are looking for. The search engine then uses a complex algorithm to assign value to the words and order in which we placed the words. If these appear as common phrases, for example, there is one value. If the words do not make a common phrase, there is another value or even a set of values.

These values are numeric.

Unseen, in the background, the search engine, the search crawlers to be more specific, have already crawled the web and millions of websites and pages. Those which have passed certain guidelines are indexed according to the parameters written into the algorithm. Those which have not passed these guidelines are ignored for the sake of speeding future searches and conserving computing time and energy. Thus, the first goal of any website is to pass the initial "guideline" test.

Once the crawlers have indexed information, it can then create matches to what you have entered into the search bar. It then returns the matches based again on a complex mathematical score derived from previous scans and indexing. This appears as your results.

Those results with the highest scores appear first, which subsequently lower scoring pages appearing lower and lower on the results.

Hence, one key in building a website that gets traffic from search engines is to learn what the search engines want and give it to them. Considering that since Google set the pace that all others have subsequently followed (for instance, Yahoo now buys results from Google), all one needs to do is understand what Google wants and results will flow from other search engines as well.

So what does Google want in a website?

What does a webmaster need to do to create a website that the Google search engines will like?

How can we be sure that what we are building is what the search engines want?

All good questions and answered soon. For now, play around with various search strings. Choose odd combinations of words and look at the results. Go to some of the websites provided and compare what you entered to what you find. This will help you get a feel for how the search engines will index your own site and how you can create content that will get found. I will give you specifics on doing this later in this book, so for now, just play around a bit.

See you tomorrow.

Day 5: Elements of a Good Website

Google created the definition of a "good" website with their Page Rank. In the early years of the Google Search Engine, the Page Rank was a method for rating websites according to certain elements in the search algorithm, while providing webmasters a goal for creating sites that Google would like. This system worked fine until some webmasters and programmers managed to find ways to cheat the search engines and the system. So in 2009, Google changed their algorithm in such a way that the Page Rank system would no longer carry the weight it formerly did.

However, while the changes were not welcomed by most webmasters, especially those who were making a good living from Search Engine Optimization (SEO—to be discussed tomorrow), the changes were needed and useful.

For instance, one change made required that websites provide fresh, original content. At the time this change was made, many webmasters had developed the habit of optimizing a single page, then loading that page onto several locations in the site. This method tricked the search engines into believing that the site carried considerable relevant material; the site thus ranked higher in search results. But because the content was duplicated on page after page, the website was really not very relevant for most searchers. This was most commonly used in aggressive sales sites that bordered on cons. There were numerous other methods used and the changes allowed the search engines to identify these abuses; thus was performed the infamous Google "Slap Down" whereby a website which formerly had strong ranking in the search results was penalized and often completely eliminated from search results.

Of course, Google recognized that the system was not perfect, but simply better, so it further enhanced their search engines with the Penguin and Panda updates. These continue to be updated as needed so that the Google search engines continue to return great results.

In light of these changes, what elements would a website need to be considered credible in the eyes of the Google search engines (and others as well)?

Certainly all the elements that were required of credible websites during the Page Rank phase would be a good thing for a webmaster to include. Whereas the algorithm changes may have made this ranking system fairly obsolete (but not done away with entirely), it only stands to reason that Google would keep the same elements that identified a website as credible. Thus, the changes only added to the elements required. So here are the elements needed for your website to be counted as credible or "good" in the eyes of the search engines.

- About Page
- Contact Page
- Terms & Conditions Page
- Privacy Policy
- Networks
- Fresh, Relevant Content
- Clear Navigation
- Sitemap

I should pause to note here, however, that even if your site does not have all of these elements in place, it can attain considerable ranking with the search engines. This is because of the Panda updates.

One key aspect of the Panda updates is to place emphasis on websites that are engaging readers, getting them to return, and move through the website rather than hit a single page and leave. This update observes traffic patterns of websites and learns from these patterns; it is a form of AI, or artificial intelligence. Websites that clearly hold value based on the returning visitors and their habits while on the site, can gain strong search engine juice even without having all these elements in place.

However, websites that do so AND have these elements in place, still get better results than those without, so having them is still important.

Before the month is up, your website will have these in place and in subsequent months, you will learn how to get visitors to return, be more active on your website, and spend more time with you.

For now, I would like you to start using Google Chrome if you don't already. If you are not, you need to. Chrome is simply a web browser like Firefox or Internet Explorer, but really, that is an understatement. For the webmaster serious about developing traffic on their website, Chrome is an indispensable tool. So get it now.

Simply type "Google Chrome" into your web browser and after going to the site, download Chrome. It is free from Google (like all of their apps).

Once you have done this, you are going to adjust your settings so that you can have access to certain useful web tools. These will be used tomorrow and throughout the duration of your web building.

Look at the above image. Once you have accessed Chrome for the first time,

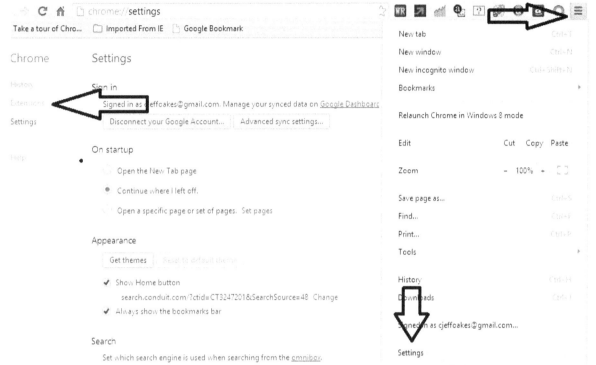

you will notice an icon in the upper right-hand corner of the browser with three short horizontal lines as shown by the arrow pointing right in the image. Click on this and a drop-down menu appears. Near the bottom, as shown by the arrow pointing down, you will find settings. Select this and you will be taken to a screen that looks just like the one in this image. On the left, you will notice an arrow pointing left to the word, "Extensions."

Choose this.

After choosing the Extensions, the next screen will look like the image on the next page…

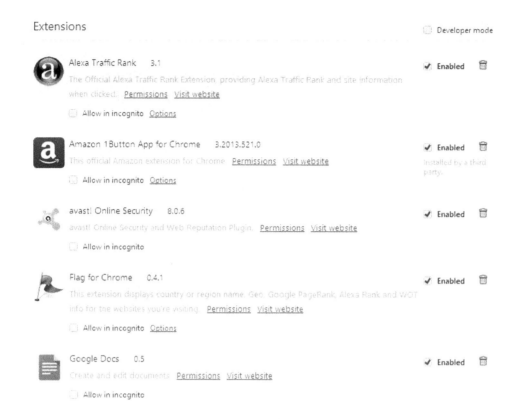

Extensions — Developer mode

Alexa Traffic Rank 3.1 — ✔ Enabled
The Official Alexa Traffic Rank Extension, providing Alexa Traffic Rank and site information when clicked. Permissions Visit website
☐ Allow in incognito Options

Amazon 1Button App for Chrome 3.2013.521.0 — ✔ Enabled
This official Amazon extension for Chrome. Permissions Visit website Installed by a third party.
☐ Allow in incognito Options

avast! Online Security 8.0.6 — ✔ Enabled
avast! Online Security and Web Reputation Plugin. Permissions Visit website
☐ Allow in incognito

Flag for Chrome 0.4.1 — ✔ Enabled
This extension displays country or region name, Geo, Google PageRank, Alexa Rank and WOT info for the websites you're visiting. Permissions Visit website
☐ Allow in incognito Options

Google Docs 0.5 — ✔ Enabled
Create and edit documents. Permissions Visit website
☐ Allow in incognito

This is just a partial showing of the extensions on the Chrome Toolbar, but it will suffice to show you what to do. You will notice that I have them all enabled. This is because I like to compare and use many different extensions depending on my research and purpose. Notice too, the previous image. Where the arrow is pointing right in the upper right-hand corner is where these will appear once enabled.

For now, simply choose the first, which is the Alexa Traffic Rank (shown) and the SEO Status Pagerank/Alexa Toolbar (not shown as it is further down the list). With these two extensions in place, you will be able at a glance to understand what will be discussed in the next chapter.

With that said, I'll see you on Day 6.

Day 6: Understanding SEO

SEO, or Search Engine Optimization, is the process of tweaking, or fine-tuning a website such that the search engines will find it attractive. In doing so, a website builder must also ensure that the content is attractive to human visitors as well.

Thus, one of the most important things to remember when seeking to develop a strong stream of website traffic is:

You are Writing for Two Audiences:

The first is a program called a search engine algorithm

and the second is human.

In writing for the search engines, you must write according to their rules of good writing; the rules that these programs look for—there are no shortcuts. The Google algorithm has been modified to seek out any website which appears to break the rules by using "shortcuts" and when it finds these, the site is blacklisted, sometimes permanently. In writing for human readers, there are also rules which will either make people want to read more or cause them to leave the site, never to return. The trick is writing in such a way as to satisfy BOTH.

Hence, writing for websites is a completely new form of writing, unlike any before.

I will get into the rules of writing for the web which will engage human readers so that they return on Day 15. This will happen AFTER you have written your first page and learned some foundational concepts. For now, I will teach you the rules of writing SEO content. Later, you will learn the specifics of each element in this form of writing, but for now I want you to get a foundational understanding of this process. (NOTE: A future book will examine writing for the Internet in much greater detail, but in this book, you will learn enough to avoid the most common mistakes and write in such a way that you will get plenty of traffic.)

Also, I want you to understand that writing SEO content is not difficult, but with anything different, it takes some getting used to. It also helps if you have the right tools and these will be provided. On Day 13, I have you put some special plugins into your WordPress site and one of these in particular will prove most valuable in teaching you this concept.

What is Search Engine Optimization, in writing content?

First, recall that earlier I explained how Google set up their algorithm in such a way as to locate good writing and that this naturally follows academic formats such as College essays and papers. Now, I am not saying that you need to write as an academician; no, you simply need to know the rules that surround such writing and apply these such that the search engines view your writing as valuable.

These rules are:

1. **Don't Plagiarize**: Plagiarism occurs when five or more words are repeated without being quoted and cited as belonging to a certain author, even if that author is you. Thus, you can plagiarize your own writing. The search engines view duplicate content in the same light that a College Professor will view copying someone else's material without giving them credit. You must even credit yourself if the content was previously published. NOTE: Writing a web page IS publishing, hence, a duplicate web page not cited is plagiarized.

2. **Proper Format:** The content must have an Introduction, a Body, and a Conclusion. All web pages will either have this in the body of the content or created as a Header, Body, and Footer—or some combination. Essentially, the opening of the material will comprise 5-15% of the total content, the conclusion will be about the same, and the body (the middle) will be the rest. Plays, movies, and novels are no different—all have a beginning, middle, and an end, with the majority making up the middle, the body of the content. This is also college essay format.

3. **Clear Subject**: The subject of the page must be clear. This is best accomplished by choosing good keyword combinations that clearly describe or define the content created. Then be sure that that keyword combination is presented at least once in the title, the first paragraph (preferably the first sentence or better, the first words of the sentence),

and in the last or next to last sentence of the concluding paragraph. Also, it would make sense if that specific subject, as described through that keyword combination, is presented throughout the body of the material. Just remember that keywords are subjects and descriptions of those subjects.

4. **Tied to Site Theme:** If you have a website that is all about Dogs, there should be a very good reason for writing a page or blog about cats. Be sure to include your website keyword combination at least a couple of times in the content on this subject in such a way that makes sense (I will teach you about choosing your Primary Website Keyword combination on Day.

5. **Don't Overdo Keywords**: One of the "tricks" some used in the past to gain weight with the search engines yet not make human readers think they were nuts was to "stack" or "stuff" keywords. I will discuss this more fully on Day 7, but the thing to know and remember now is that you don't want to put too many keywords on a page. Although Google is tight lipped about what would be an optimal use of keywords, most SEO experts agree that between 1% and 3% concentration of keywords is ideal. Don't worry if you are unclear about keywords at this point for all will be made clear on Day 8 and discussed more fully on Day 17.

6. **Word Count**: Just as College essays have a minimum word count, so too the search engines seek a minimum. For blogs, the minimum word count is generally 300 and for pages, generally 500 words. Thus, to get the attention of the search engines, you must actually present information, useful content, not just brief snippets of jargon.

7. **Subheadings**: Just as a College essay would contain subheadings to break up the material into logical, easy-to-read segments, a website should do the same. And the keywords should ideally be contained in at least one of these. On Day 17, you will learn all about this.

8. **Keywords in Page URL**: The URL, or Uniform Resource Locator, is the address that the search engines and humans use to find that page. To be fully optimized, the keyword combination chosen for that page must be included in the URL. Days 7, 8, and 17 will clarify this.

9. **Keywords in Meta Description:** Later, you will learn all about Meta Tags and Meta Descriptions. It is important that the keyword combinations be included in these for this is how many search engines determine what the page is about. These then compare what you have said the page is about to what is found in the content. If there is a mismatch, the page is penalized. Google today claims not to use these tags any longer, but the description remains important so it is best to

simply comply.

10. **Image/Video Alt Tags**: Days 23 and 24 will teach you how to properly add images and video to your website. The Alt Tags are labels that the search engines use to determine what is contained in the image or video because facing facts, these are not able to "view" images and video as a human can to determine content—at least not yet. To optimize a page, these must also contain the keyword combinations chosen for the page.

11. **Fresh/Original:** As previously mentioned, never duplicate content from one page to another and be careful to avoid plagiarizing even yourself. Be sure that each page is fresh and original. It also helps to add references to date the material, such as event calendars and specials.

I know this seems like a lot to remember, but don't worry. I am going to have you put that plugin that I told you about earlier into your website on Day 12. This wonderful tool will teach you how to optimize each page of your website. Very quickly, you will be able to write a page or blog without even thinking of how. It only seems difficult, but in reality, Search Engine Optimization is really very simple. All that is required is some guidance and time.

Of course, if you have chosen to build your website in a platform other than WordPress, you will need to refer to this page often and the subsequent lessons I will teach you. If you are using WordPress however, you will have one of the best cheat sheets ever created, a plugin you will install.

Task for Today:

Go to several of your favorite websites and take a look at the pages and blogs written. Then compare these to the rules mentioned above.

Do they comply?

If not, how does the site differ?

In the case of some of the larger, established websites, these rules are not as necessary. This is because these sites developed strong enough traffic to ignore the rules. Still, such sites likely do not get much traffic from search engines. For example: Facebook gets less than 1% of its traffic from search engines and Yahoo gets only between two and three percent. Why so little?

In the case of Facebook it is because there is not true "content" that the search engines would find relevant and most people do not search for Facebook because the domain is known by name. Just type it in and you are there.

The same is fairly true of Yahoo. As an email client, Yahoo developed enough traffic pre-Google that most people just go right to it. The search engine traffic it does get is from the news articles posted on the front page (mainly) of the site and its archives. Still, because the site gets so much traffic from other sources, search engine results are a negligible portion of its traffic.

If you have added the Alexa tool to your Chrome as instructed, you can also compare the Alexa Rating to websites. You will often find that websites which comply with these rules will have better ratings than those which do not.

Now the caveat: In looking at these rules and various websites, bear in mind that sometimes the rules do not apply. Case in point: YouTube. YouTube is all video, so it would appear that the rules do not apply here. In reality, they apply more. Notice that there is generally a description below the video. This description need not be as long as a blog, but the search engines do use this to help people find videos, so it is important. In looking at these descriptions, you will notice that whereas not all of the rules apply, enough do so that the search engines can direct people to the videos. As time brings greater competition in videos, these rules will take on greater import.

This brings us to the last aspect of these rules you need to remember. These rules are in place to separate the good from the bad, the better from the best. If there is no competition, the rules matter little. If there is much competition, the rules matter much. So if you are planning a website based on some other really popular websites already in place, you really need to pay attention to these rules.

Finally, try this. Type in a string of keywords, any words, and check the results provided. Go to the websites returned on the first couple of pages, then head to say, page 20 and check a couple there. Can you see a difference? Also, in a reverse of this, go to some of your favorite websites, read an article, then using what you guess to be the subject/keywords, see if you can locate that same page using a search engine results page (SERP). If the SERP's do not return the website, what do you think could be the reason? Could it be that the Search Engines do not recognize the subject as clearly as you? Or could the subject actually be something different? If the site does return in the results, can you see why it did?

Keep surfing and checking out the different pages and comparing these to the traffic ratings you see on the Alexa toolbar. Your goal is to get a better understanding of how using these rules can help you write better content and be found by the search engines.

That's all for today.

Day 7: Determine Primary Keywords

NOTE: As of this writing, the Keyword Tool was in the process of changing, though just what these changes will entail, is not yet known. If the changes have occurred by the time you read this, simply go to my companion website, http://365crazywebtraffic.com for updates.

NOTE #2: To illustrate just how rapidly Google changes things to prevent cheating, as of the date of publication, yet another change had taken place. This required some editing to this and a couple other chapters prior to publishing. The change is that the Keyword Tool is no longer available to anyone who is not an Adwords account holder. Even then, the tool is not as useful for the kind of research originally presented in this chapter. The modified chapter will refer to how it was once done, and what can be done now. It does not get into using Adwords for this is out of the realm of most new site builders. Learning to use Adwords is reserved for a future book.

As you may have gathered from the previous chapter, keywords are very important to a website. Keywords help both the search engines and your human visitors find the information you present for keywords form a sort of 'connect' between the two viewers. Keywords tell both humans and non-humans what your website is about; what your pages are about.

You have no doubt used a search engine once or twice. When you enter certain words that describe what you are seeking, the search engines compare these words to what is in their database and return results. Thus, the more accurate you are with your choice of keywords, the more likely that someone searching for information you have placed on your website will find you.

Now, in the early years of search engines, only the keywords you put into the tags and repeated on individual pages returned results, but Google is changing all that. The Google web crawlers "read" your entire website and catalog all important words. The only words not included are prepositions such as "a" "an" "the" "and" and so forth. Pronouns, unless they are important to particular subjects are also not cataloged. Thus, if you are searching for "Jack and Jill" you could just as easily search "Jack Jill" and get the same results. In other words, the only words that actually matter are nouns and adjectives; occasionally pronouns and verbs IF these are important to identifying the subject more clearly. (BTW. You could also search Jack and Jillian on Amazon to find my erotic novella,)

Remember this as you choose your primary keywords for your website, which is what we are about to do. There is no need to include useless terms in your keyword combinations unless doing so simply makes it easier for you when writing. Including these will neither help, nor hurt your optimization efforts. However, the plugin I will have you add to your WordPress site, will tell you that you have failed to match some terms if you include these in some places and not in others. There is no need to worry about that now; you will see what I mean. I just wanted you to be aware of this.

At this point, you likely already have some idea of what you want your website to be about. We have not set up the website URL (address) yet, because it is best to choose a good keyword combination for the website first. Once you know the keywords you will use, you can then try to get the URL to match. You want to determine a good focus for your site; you can either find a keyword combination that clearly shows what your website is about or choose some innocuous term which you can build into a brand—this second choice is fine, but know that it is far more difficult to grow such a site and far more time-consuming.

At one time, we would have gone to the Google Keyword Tool to check the results of various keywords and keyword combinations. Today, that is not an option. Google has eliminated this tool for use by the general public. It is available via the Google Adwords program, but as use of this program is out of the realm of the basics presented here, I am going to offer an alternate approach. In a later book, you will learn how to advertise using Google Adwords and in that book, you will learn about this handy tool.

Task for Today:

You can get an understanding of what keywords are best by doing some searching yourself. Think about what your website is going to be about. In the following spaces (if reading this in print—if in electronic form, get out some paper), write all the words you can think of that describe your website. Separate the nouns from the adjectives and verbs for now. I will explain why later.

NOUNS   ADJECTIVES/VERBS

_____   _____

_____   _____

_____   _____

_____   _____

_____   _____

_____   _____

_____   _____

_____   _____

_____   _____

_____   _____

_____   _____

_____   _____

Brainstorm as many as you can, adding to the sides of the page and on a separate sheet of paper if need be. Just get as many key nouns and key descriptors as possible. Now take a look at your list. If you are not sure which words to use as key words for your website, don't worry, all will be made clear.

The first thing you are going to do is type one word from each list into a search engine. The following is the list for my CriminalJusticeLaw.us website. After showing you this list, I am going to show you how to use it to narrow the best words for inclusion in the name of your website. Note too that these are all keywords that you will use at some point on your website. You are only trying to narrow the best to use as the overall theme, which will also be used in the site name.

Criminal Justice Law US Keyword List

NOUNS

Criminal

Law

Justice

Police

Crime

Corrections

Judge

Lawyer

Attorney

Prison

State

Federal

Legislature

Juvenile

US

United States

Drugs

Criminal justice

Penitentiary

Cop

Defendant

Plaintiff

Sheriff

Deputy

Officer

Drug war

Bill

Supreme Court

Amendment

Constitution

Court

Organized crime

<u>ADJECTIVES/VERBS</u>

Justice

Criminal

Crime

Correctional

Legislation

Legislative

Legalistic

Punitive

Penalize

Punishment

System

Race

Injustice

Rights

Intent

Principles

Intent

Motive

Theory

Theories

Now, take one word from each list and type it into a search engine. In the first example, I am going to use the terms, "police" and "rights." Notice the results.

Google | police rights

Web   News   Images   Videos   Shopping   More ▾   Search tools

About 1,870,000,000 results (0.38 seconds)

Know Your Rights: What To Do If You're Stopped By Police ...
https://www.aclu.org/...rights.../know-you... ▾ American Civil Liberties Union ▾
We rely on the **police** to keep us safe and treat us all fairly, regardless of race, ethnicity,
national origin or religion. This card provides tips for interacting with ...
Know Your Rights - Racial Profiling - Elon James White: What To Do ...

How to Flex Your Rights During Police Encounters
www.flexyourrights.org/ ▾ Flex Your Rights ▾
Flex Your **Rights** is an educational nonprofit dedicated to educating the public about
understanding their **rights** during encounters with law enforcement.
Traffic Stop - Popular Myths - 7 Rules for Recording Police - At Your Door

Police Brutality Harassment Know My Rights never talk to th...
www.policecrimes.com/police.html ▾
Police brutality, **police rights**, police harassment, know my rights police, never talk
police, abuse, misconduct, brutality, remain silent, student rights, traffic stop, ...

Do you see anything here about "police rights? Actually, no. Why not? Is that not what we entered? The reason for this anomaly of sorts is because the search engine returned results based on the most commonly understood meaning of those two keywords strung together. Thus, if my website were about the rights of police, I may need to find some other way to put it. So these two keywords together do not yield the results I would want in that case.

Let's try another, but this time, let's be more specific. Let's use three words together. How about "Organized crime" and "theory." This will provide two keyword terms, but three total keywords and hopefully zero in on the actual topic. On the next page are the results.

What do you know? Does the second result look familiar? That is an article from my website criminaljusticelaw.us. But note that the other articles are also spot on about the intended subject. Why?

Part of the reason is because when we enter strings of three or more keywords, the intended subject becomes much clearer to the search engines. Thus, if you want to get noticed, it would be best to choose a name which uses at least three keywords. You could even use four, even more. Just be careful not to make a site name/domain name that is too wordy for people to remember or type in correctly.

Something this tells me is that I could have started a website called OrganizedCrimeTheory.com and it would likely get great results. Perhaps someday I will. Indeed, I choose the site name I did because the search strings rang to my intent with the site. The site itself is about criminal justice law. But because there is so much competition for these keywords, typing these words into a search engine places me a few pages into the results. Still, because of the content contained on my site, I get plenty of traffic and make a few bucks to boot. In the Index, I provide site stats to give you an idea of the traffic this site got after just a year.

Something else to take from this is that look too at the "Sponsored Results." There are none in either case. What this tells us is that there are no other websites advertising these search strings. Thus, competition for these key words is minimal. It could also mean that few people are searching these terms as well, which would not be good. How can we tell how many searches are performed for these words?

At one time, we could use the Google Keyword Tool, but those days are no more. Instead, we have to be a tad more intuitive.

Notice that the returned results for "organized crime theory" is "About 11,600,000 results." This seems to imply that this string of keywords returned this many results but in reality, it only means that 11,600,000 websites use these three words in some combination therein. Still, that is strong so if planning to use these terms for your primary keywords, you could not go wrong.

To test this, try typing in the term "organized crime."

The result is "About 62,700,000."

Now try "crime theory."

The result is "About 178,000,000."

Now "Crime."

"195,000,000."

Now, to get some useful meaning from this information, subtract 178 million from 195 million and we get 18 million. This means that only 18 million of the total articles that mention crime leave out any mention of theory. This also tells us that we can tie various strings of keywords together and compare results to determine the approximate strength of the keywords. Thus, we can be confident that the terms "organized crime theory" would be fairly strong search terms to use. These would be strong keywords for a website. Build a website all about Organized Crime Theory and chances are good you will grow great traffic.

So play around with your list. What you want to do is narrow the terms to the best you think would both return results AND well define what you want your site to accomplish. Remember too that you will use all of the keywords at some point or another in your website. All you are trying to do at the moment is determine the PRIMARY keywords, the ones which will be incorporated into your domain name.

There is one more thing you want to do. Let's check out the competition.

For this, I am going to use my wife's website, WallysWeirdStuff.com. This website is just a fun site developed to teach her a few things and explore weird stuff.

Using the keywords "weird stuff" we are going to type these into the Google Search Engine. This will give us an idea of the competition for this keyword combination. You will get results similar to the following.

Scroll past the sponsored results (the paid search results) to the natural results

WeirdStuff - Resellers of surplus computer hardware and software ....
www.weirdstuff.com/
WeirdStuff.com online provides new, used, excess, refurbished, surplus computer hardware and software. We also provide services for asset management and ...
Sunnyvale Store - Contact Us - E-Recycling - Directions
You visited this page on 5/1/13.

Weird Stuff - Mashable
mashable.com/category/weird-stuff/
We all have **weird** hobbies. Some of us collect pins or stamps or maybe we like to post fake signs on the subway or do parkour. How about slashing water bottles ...
You visited this page on 5/1/13.

Images for weird stuff - Report images

Weird Stuff | eBay
www.ebay.com/sch/Weird-Stuff-/1466/i.html
Visit eBay for great deals in **Weird Stuff**. Shop eBay!

Weird Stuff: photos of strange people, places and things - Bit of Fu...
www.bitoffun.com/weird_stuff.htm
What you will find in this section can be described as **weird stuff**, strange stuff, and generally offbeat. Or, if you prefer, try our fun stuff section.

and the first item is for a website called weirdstuff.com. Not surprising since that is exactly what I searched for. However, I can tell that this website is not a competitor for the Meta Description reads,

> "***WEIRDSTUFF***.com online provides new, used, excess, refurbished, surplus computer hardware and software. We also provide services for asset management and."

Google boldened the keywords I chose, namely, WeirdStuff, but only there does the term show up in the description. In checking out the website, I discovered that it does not get very much traffic and has nothing really weird on it (I did this by checking the Alexa Rating, which was in the millions, which means very little traffic). But it does provide some good deals on electronics. Cool. I like electronics, especially when these do not compete with me.

The next one is Mashable, which is an awesome website. If you have never checked it out, go on, have fun. I'll be here when you get back.

Mashable has a category for weird stuff, but that is only a portion of their website, so this is not a direct competitor either. Also, given that none of the remaining searches actually have weird stuff in the name of the website, in a short time, I should be able to dominate the searches for those keywords. Then there is ebay and bitofun, both which do not focus on weird stuff, but have categories for weird stuff, like Mashable. So I have found a keyword combination which should allow me to eventually dominate the search results with little effort. Notice too that image results also appear. This is a clue to me to include "weird stuff" on all my image alt tags; I will also want to find great weird images to place on the website. This will help bring more traffic when searchers are seeking weird images.

Can you sort of get an idea how to use the keyword tool to first find great keywords to use in your website name and then actually do a search using that keyword combination to understand what kind of competition you will face in using it?

If you find that you have strong competition, maybe you would like to keep thinking of better keywords to use. If the competition is weak, then you have either found a great set of keywords or terrible, there is seldom any in between. These are great if plenty of people are searching for these keywords, but if not many people search for these, then the keywords are not good. With the demise of the Google Keyword Tool, it has become more difficult, but not impossible, to determine the popularity of keywords.

Fortunately, there are other such tools on the web. http://www.wordstream.com/keyword-tools is one such. Another is http://keywordeye.co.uk/ Still another is http://www.keywordspy.com/ And another is found at www.semrush.com.

There are many more, some paid, some free, but the big thing to remember in all cases is that the keyword results represent just a small slice of the overall traffic of the Internet. To date, no company has managed to get an aggregate total. The Google Keyword Tool available with a Google Adwords account still only represents about a quarter of all Internet traffic. In general, all you need to do to know if a keyword is strong is look at the number of searchers presented by any such tool and multiply by 4. This will give you a pretty good idea of the total traffic for that set of keywords.

Another way to know whether site competition is strong is to first notice how many sites used the keywords directly in their primary URL (name of the site, like weirdstuff.com) and how many use it in a subdomain (such as mashable). Then visit the site to find out if the website is actually presenting what they claim. If not, then the site is not that strong in competition.

Another tool to use in doing this is to look at the traffic rating. When you use Chrome and have activated the extensions as instructed in Day 8, you will notice a bar just below the Meta Title ("WeirdStuff – Resellers of surplus computer hardware and software") and just to the left of the actual web address. In the case of Weirdstuff.com, there is not much filled in, but in the case of Mashable, you will see that there is a ¾ filled line of blue. This reveals the rough Alexa Rating of the site, which gives an idea of the traffic.

If you place your cursor over that bar, you will see in the case of weirdstuff.com (as of 5/23/13) an Alexa Rating of 1,026,232. This means that of all websites in the world, this is the ranking of that site. Basically, the higher the number, the less traffic; the lower the number, the more traffic. Mashable, by contrast has an Alexa Rating of 365. Clearly, Mashable gets LOTS of traffic and rightfully so, it is a super website.

Finally, you will have a symbol at the top of your toolbar (if you set up the

extensions) that looks like the above.

When you visit a competitor's website, you can click on that icon for more information. To illustrate how to use this feature, visit http://wallysweirdstuff.com now.

By placing your cursor over that icon, you can get the Alexa Traffic Rank for Wallys Weird Stuff. As of 5/23/13, the ranking is 1,321,137, which is not bad considering the site has only been live for 23 days. Now click on the icon. A dropdown box like the one following will appear.

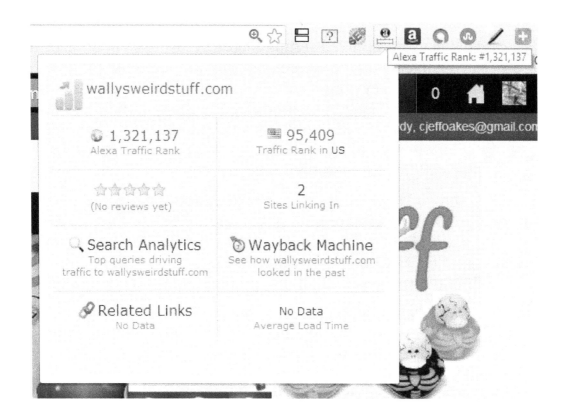

You will notice that there is little information here for the website is less than three months old. After three months, there will be more information. But as you can see, there are only 2 sites linking to Wallys, which is correct, for my wife has done no link-Building as of now (remember, she is learning from my book and I have yet to write month 2, which focuses on link-building). I have checked and found that two other sites have already linked to Wallys.

Do you see where it reads "wallysweirdstuff.com" at the top of this dropdown box?

If you click on this, you will be taken to the Alexa website where there is plenty of information on a website, provided it is at least three months old. I am not going to go into detail here about the information found there for I do not want to overload you, but you are free to explore. The information that Alexa provides is fairly easy to understand and if you go there when checking out a competitor, you'll find that you can learn much about their website. But what I have explained so far should be enough for you to decide whether to use a certain combination of keywords for your website or not. You will learn much more about this tool in a future book in this series.

The best way is to brainstorm ideas based on the keywords you search and compare to a live search. By doing this, you can narrow your focus until something stands out most.

One other thing to do is try to get a combination of at least three keywords for your website (four is great too). I chose Wallys and weird and stuff in combination because I want to build a brand and the name Wallys just seemed to add to the weirdness of the site. Somehow it just sounded weird. But the keywords that drive traffic are simply, weird stuff and although using only two can be weak, I decided to go with it. Two is ok, three are better. Be warned, however, a single keyword is death for a website for it will usually take years to get traffic based on search engines. To achieve this requires considerable effort and perhaps large sums of advertising dollars (or pounds or euros or whatever). Just try to find three keywords used by many people for your site name with low competition and you can rank quickly. If you have to settle for two, that will be ok as well, but it will take a little longer to draw strong traffic results.

Finally, remember that the keywords you choose will not only be used for your website name (which will be discussed tomorrow) but also feature prominently in your website on pages and blogs. This is how you will get traffic, so choose wisely.

Day 8: Choose a Site Name

You should now have a list of keyword combinations from which to decide a website name. Now you want to figure out if these are taken by anyone else. What we are going to do is simply narrow the list and decide on just a few possibilities. The reason you are not now going to decide on a site name is because if you do, you may discover that the name is taken when you sign up with a host.

In narrowing the list, you will eliminate any obvious website name choices and at least see where there may be problems. In addition, when you start to narrow the list, you may come up with an alternative choice you had not considered before. If this happens, you can do some quick keyword research, check out competition, and perhaps find a site name that is even better than any on your first list.

Ready to get started?

Using your list of keywords you are going to decide on a site name/URL (this is also known as your Domain Name).

The URL, to give you an example in case you don't already know, is http://yourwebsite.com (or .net, .org, .us, etc.). To create the URL for your website then, you are going to use the keyword combination along with anything else you consider important to the site name. For instance, for weird stuff, we added Wallys to brand the site name. Had we chosen to narrow the items on the site, we could have called it Wallys weird pizza recipes (which is currently a page on WallysWeirdStuff.com). In that case, rather than http://wallysweirdstuff.com, we would have done something like http://wallysweirdpizzarecipes.com or simply http://weirdpizzarecipes.com .

So all you are going to do is take the keywords, place them after "**http://**" and add either .com, .org, .net, .me, .us, or any of literally hundreds of possibilities. In case you don't know what these mean, .com is commercial, .net is a network, .org usually denotes a non-profit—though not necessarily; the others are simply alternatives operated by various countries. These are available through the host you choose and some may not be available through all hosts. In short, as we check on some of the possibilities, if you cannot find a .com to your liking (someone has it already, that is), you may decide to call it .org, .biz, .me, or whatever.

For my personal website whereby I taught some of what is found in this book, I chose a ".me," which is the country code for Montenegro. That site is http://jeffoakes.me. I graduated in criminal justice and still have an interest in this field, so when I set up my site for that purpose, I used http://criminaljusticelaw.us. For promoting my series of survival books, I set up http://collapseconsultants.com. The point is, there are a number of designations you can use, depending on availability and purpose. In setting up the domain name (web address or URL) for the website to accompany this book, I chose http://365CrazyWebTraffic.com. This one was tricky because I initially wanted to simply call it Crazy Web Traffic, but the appropriate web address was taken—it is parked, which means that no one is actually using it, but taken is taken. In any case, this forced me to consider other options and I think adding the "365" to the domain works better, especially considering that is the title of the book. The point is, no matter how clever you think you are with your choice of domain name, don't get too stuck on it because chances are fairly good that someone has beaten you to it. There are many clever people out there.

So brainstorm a list of possible domain names. Then you need to narrow the list.

Task for Today:

The best way to narrow your list is to start trying out website names simply by typing these into the address line of your web browser. For instance, suppose you have the keywords, "large dog breeds" and your website is going to be about that subject. Type http://largedogbreeds.com into the address line of your browser. Hit enter and see if a website comes up. In this case, the domain host company DomainMarket.com comes up and informs you that the site is for sale. This means that someone already owns it but is not doing anything with the domain. Thus, you may inquire about a purchase, but I recommend against this for often people either will not sell or want far more than it is worth—you will simply waste a lot of time trying. If your entry turns up a working website, then you must choose something else. If you get a page that reads, "site not found" or something similar, then the website *should* be available. Make a note of it.

Just keep trying different possibilities, altering the end or perhaps the name itself, but keeping the order of the important keywords used. The proper order is important for SEO purposes. Once you have narrowed the possibilities of a domain name to three or more, you are ready to choose a web host.

Day 9: Choose a Web Host

The reason I had you just narrow the choices is because after you have chosen a website hosting company (host) and begin the process of obtaining your Domain Name (your URL, or web address), you may still find that the name you have decided on is not available. Thus, you need to have some options. In addition, many hosts will provide a list of possibilities from which to choose should your first, second, or third preference not be available.

For instance, with BlueHost or HostMonster, which I use and strongly recommend, when you seek a particular Domain name, a large number of

Choose a domain: weirdstuff   com ⌄

Check

Standard Domains*	.com	.org	.net	.us	.info	.biz
	~~14.99~~	~~14.99~~	~~14.99~~	~~14.99~~	~~14.99~~	~~14.99~~
	11.99	8.99	9.99	11.99	11.99	11.99
MyWeirdStuff		☐	☐			☐
TheWeirdStuff		☐	☐			☐
WeirdStuffGroup	☐	☐	☐			☐
WeirdStuffOnline	☐	☐	☐			☐
NewWeirdStuff	☐	☐	☐			☐
WeirdStuffInc	☐	☐	☐			☐
AllWeirdStuff		☐	☐			☐
WeirdStuffShop		☐	☐			☐
FreeWeirdStuff	☐	☐	☐			☐
WeirdStuffStore		☐	☐			☐

Show more suggestions...

alternate choices are provided automatically. Look at the following image.

For this example, I chose to show you what appears for a check of "Weirdstuff.com" which I already know is taken. See the check boxes in the chart? If I wanted "MyWeirdStuff" I still could not get a .com though I could choose .org, .net, or .biz. Notice that .us and .info are also not available. Then notice that I could also obtain WeirdStuffOnline.com, .org, .net, or .biz. And if these suggestions are not to my liking, at the bottom I can select "Show more suggestions" and I will be taken to a much larger selection.

This should suffice to give you a good idea about how to check your options should your primary choices either not be available or should you see an option that catches your eye such that you may decide to go with something else. Just try to get something that has the keywords you chose and has the ring you seek. If you look through enough choices, when you see the one that fits, you will know it. If you don't find something right for you and your site, then perhaps you need to take another look at both the keywords you chose and/or your goal for the site.

Now that you know how to choose your Domain name, you need to begin looking for a web host.

Some of the most popular web hosting companies today are...

1. BlueHost
2. HostMonster
3. HostGator
4. GoDaddy
5. JustHost

Of these, I **strongly recommend against** only one: GoDaddy (Notice that I don't even link to them—if you want GoDaddy, that is your choice—not my recommendation). The reason is because although you can get a Domain through GoDaddy for only 99 cents, there are many other features you are going to need for your website and these add-ons will soon have you paying far more than most web hosts. In addition, experience has taught me that the customer service at GoDaddy is terribly lacking. Some people love the host, I do not. The choice is yours.

HostGator is pretty good and I have some friends who use it, though I did not find their offering to my liking. It was not that the company is not good, it is.

I just preferred the features and customer service of HostMonster and BlueHost over them.

As for JustHost, I cannot really say much other than many people use it. I never have, nor have I tried it, but it is a popular choice. They offer reasonable rates and great customer service from what I hear.

Now, for HostMonster (which I use) and BlueHost, these are sister companies and everything from customer service to the dashboard you will use are identical. I signed up initially with BlueHost, but had some problems with my website initially. The problems were not related to BlueHost and I decided to return to my free hosting through WordPress (more on this in a moment). One thing that really impressed me however, was that on canceling my account, my money was returned to my bank in less than five minutes. They did not sit on my funds like some I have heard about. They promise satisfaction or an instant refund and they delivered on that promise.

After some additional research (and a few emails to friends), I decided to give self-hosting another chance. Self-hosting simply means that I am using a paid host rather than a free host as I will explain in a moment. When I called BlueHost, I was told that I would not be able to receive the introductory special I had previously received because the system no longer recognized me as a "new" customer. However, the CSR told me that I could sign up with HostMonster and get the same offer through that division. I did.

Initially, I had the same problems with my website that I had previously, but this time, rather than panic and leave self-hosting, I got with the CSR and Tech support to find out how to resolve the issues. They were incredibly patient and helpful and in time, the issues were resolved. Since that time, I have contacted Tech support many times with many questions and have always found them very helpful and courteous. I cannot say enough how much I have enjoyed the superior customer service of BlueHost and HostMonster. They are excellent to work with.

Part of the reason I tell you this story is because when I began looking into self-hosting, I came across some less-than-reputable companies with terrible customer service. Most offer fairly similar rates, but service is really the distinguishing difference and BlueHost or HostMonster really blew me away. All of my websites are hosted with them and I suspect that barring some really radical changes in the company, I will be with them for life. As long as they keep treating me the way they do, they will keep my business.

I recommend BlueHost or HostMonster highly, but naturally, you are free to choose any host you desire. Just understand that this is the only one I recommend personally because this is the host I have found to provide the level of service I expect. To sign up with BlueHost, follow this link. Or if reading this in print, just go to http://www.hostmonster.com/track/cjeffoakes. The link will take you to a special page whereby you can get the same great deal I did, which is only $5.95 per month if you sign up for a year. If you sign up for longer, you can get an even better deal. Either way, you'll pay less than their normal rate.

Now to be honest, you will notice that my name is in the link. This is because I am an affiliate with the company. This means that when you sign up with them using my link, I get paid a small sum. Keep this concept in mind as you build your own website for there are plenty of affiliate opportunities on the web promoting services you have found useful yourself. The one thing I will strongly recommend against, however, is promoting anything you either do not, or would not use or try yourself. Your reputation and the reputation of your website are on the line. You want people to return and only by earning and keeping their trust will they.

After you have signed up with your web host, you can either get with either customer service or tech support to walk you through setting up your Domain and site building platform (more on this in Day 10) by calling their toll-free number or follow the instructions for setting up the website in the Appendix. Also, tomorrow I will walk you through setting this up as well.

For now, you need to understand the difference between self-hosting and free hosting. On Day 10 I will explain the differences in Platforms for building a website but for now, let us assume you are going to follow my recommendation to build in WordPress.

Free WordPress Hosting

WordPress began as a building platform for blogs. Through WordPress.com, you can obtain free blog hosting. It costs you nothing unless you choose to sign up for some of the additional functions such as special themes or other premium services. The drawback is that you will be very limited in your ability to make money from your website. For instance, you will not have the ability to place ads, you cannot link to certain websites such as Clickbank or Amazon (or eBay, though I strongly discourage using them because of their useless "guarantee" policy). You may even find that if you are promoting your own book or some other business, there could be problems.

For this reason, I recommend self-hosting.

Of course, you could build your website using the free platform first and go to self-hosting later, which is what I did. But there can be some problems with this approach.

When you switch to self-hosting after free hosting, there is a lag time between when the search engines locate your website and the pages contained therein. Thus, for about two weeks, you can expect traffic from search engines to drop to nil until the web crawlers find your new site location. Changing hosts changes the address. Think of it like moving a traditional business across town or even to another city. You have to submit a change of address and do considerable advertising for your customers to find you again. And this brings up the other drawback.

If anyone has linked to your site while you were with the free host and you change, it is unlikely they will find you again or even try. Then, they would have to manually change the links on their website. If they do not change these links, anyone clicking these links will receive a message that the page does not exists (an error 404 – page not found message will appear). Thus, it will look like your website has been shut down to most people and you will lose those links. I lost nearly 1000 links when I switched and my traffic plummeted.

For this reason, I recommend that you self-host from the start if you have any plans for using the website to earn income from any sources. If the website is just for fun and will remain so forever, use the free WordPress.com.

Otherwise, go to BlueHost. You can host unlimited domains (websites) and build in a WordPress platform. Simply follow this link to receive your special rate for signing up with BlueHost then move on to Day 12 http://www.hostmonster.com/track/cjeffoakes

Task for Today:

Decide which web host to sign up with. Explore them, look at what each offers, then decide. You will notice that there are few real noticeable differences between hosts. Really, it all comes down to service. If you find a host without live customer support, I recommend staying away. If you find one with multiple methods of customer support, such as live, chat, and/or email, good option. Just remember to take note of their guarantee and how long you have to back out without cost to you. This way, even if you don't like the host after a few days or weeks, you can always switch to another.

Day 10: Choose a Platform

By saying you are going to choose a platform, what I mean is that you need to decide how you are going to build your website. If you are reading this book, I believe I can safely assume you know neither HTML nor CSS design languages, for if you did, you would likely already have a running website and know most of the basics I am teaching.

So that leaves you with certain web-building programs and templates, of which there are many.

If you simply do a search for "website platforms," you will find plenty of options. Some of the more popular scripts are Weebly, Hub, and Yahoo site builders. These are all good and come with a number of different perks and options.

In the realm of blogging, you will find WordPress, Bloggit, and Blogger to name just a few.

Personally, I prefer WordPress and what I teach in this first book applies primarily to that format, though the principles are the same no matter the site builder you choose. The only difference is that WordPress has grown to become the most popular choice and as a result, literally thousands of plugins have been developed by devotees. These plugins can perform so many functions automatically for you (which you would otherwise have to perform manually), that this platform simply continues to grow in popularity—this despite the terrible customer service from WordPress.

And believe me, WordPress customer service IS terrible, actually, pretty much non-existent. But when we consider that it is a completely FREE platform AND the biggest, most popular, and easiest to use, who needs customer service—they are forgiven. Instead, there is a huge forum of users ready to help anytime and a growing number of books (such as this one) to help newbies to WordPress.

To make that clear, WordPress began as a free or file-sharing platform, otherwise known as open source software. In many ways, it remains such and thus really does not provide customer service per se. However, the millions of users will answer your questions via the forum and various chats that are available. Just be sure to be courteous and clear when asking questions and people will respond and help. Look for tutorials on 365Crazywebtraffic.com to help you in navigating the WordPress forums or write me any time with questions at cjeffoakes@365crazywebtraffic.com. In addition, if you build using BlueHost as your hosting company, their tech support is great at helping resolve any WordPress issues—hence, you really don't need customer service from WordPress.

Now, the differences between a standard web building platform and a blogging platform at one time were considerable, but now the two are virtually the same. The only real difference is in appearance, which can be mitigated using the right theme plugins if using WordPress (which I strongly advise). In other words, websites look like websites and blogs tend to look like, well, blogs. There is a visual difference. This difference causes some to view a blog as a not-so-serious website, though that bias is changing rapidly given the enormous popularity and financial revenues of many pro bloggers. In addition, because the search engines pay special attention to blogs, most websites are adding blogs and in some cases, the costs to do this are considerable. By comparison, a blog is inexpensive to set-up and maintain, yet can contain all the features of a traditional website.

To me, the choice is a no-brainer for anyone starting on a shoestring budget. Build in a blog platform and WordPress is hands down the best in the market.

Following is the step-by-step way of setting up your BlueHost account and Website (I also include these instructions in the Appendix for easy reference.

Sign Up with BlueHost and Installing WordPress

Go to http://www.bluehost.com/track/owc5

You will see a screen that looks like this, though instead of "Hostmonster" you will see "BlueHost"...

Click on "Sign Up Now."

The next screen will look like the following image...

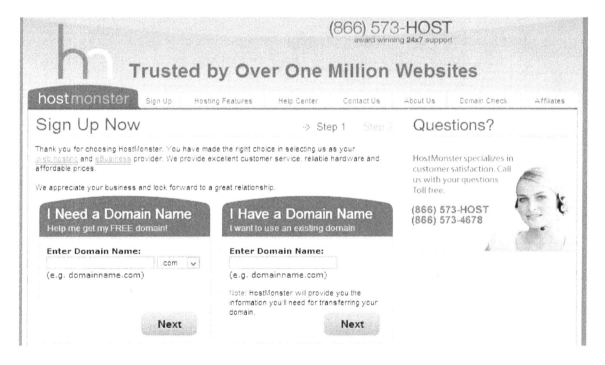

Simply enter the domain name you have chosen in the left option and choose either .com, .org, .net, etc from the dropdown menu to the right of the domain you seek. If you already own a domain, use the choice on the right. If you have a free website you are transferring to self-hosting, you will use the right option. After entering the desired domain information, click "Next."

If the domain you have chosen is not available, you will be sent to a screen similar to the one shown earlier which will prompt you to choose an alternative from a grid-listing. Once you decide, you can move on.

The next screen you will go to will ask for your personal information such as name, address, email, and so forth. Scroll down and there will be a special offer. This offer chances from time to time and whether you choose it or not is up to you, but generally speaking, if you are just starting out and are uncertain whether to go with an offer or not, just refuse for you can always add it later. The only difference being that if you add it later, you will pay a little more. In some cases, the offers you may choose can be had by obtaining free or very inexpensive plugins. Many of which you will learn about in this book.

For instance, the current offer is a special rate on the Power Pack, which to be honest, I am considering adding myself for the higher rate, so you may consider it. Much depends on your personal finances at this point, for this extra is not vital, but nice.

Scroll further down and you will find package choices as well as various security options. Personally, I opted out of the extra security functions for I did not feel I needed them for my kind of websites, but you can read about these by clicking "More information" and decide for yourself.

Finally, you will enter your billing information and choose "Next" at the bottom of the screen.

After choosing "Next," you will be given additional instructions and receive an email from BlueHost. When I first signed on, I had to enter the password information sent to me in an email, but a friend has informed me that he was allowed directly into the control panel. Whichever method is in operation when you sign up, just be sure to make a note of any user name and password information for you will need it for logging in to the control panel.

To log in, you will simply go to either Bluehost.com or HostMonster.com and enter your login information. You will then arrive at a screen that looks like the original screen from which you first entered the site. But at the top right-hand corner, you will notice a blue button which reads,

(866) 573-HOST
award winning 24x7 support
Control Panel Login

"Control Panel Login."

Click on this blue button and you will arrive at a screen that looks like the following...

Just below the HostMonster (or BlueHost) logo, you can see a tab in green that reads "Hosting." Just to the right of that is a blue tab which reads "Domains." We are now going to assign your domain.

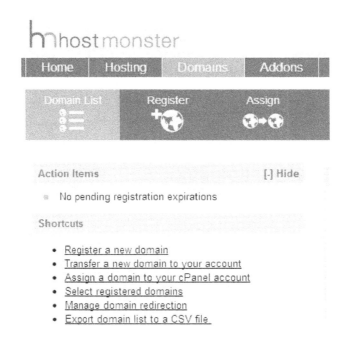

Under "Shortcuts" choose "Assign a domain to your cPanel account. The next screen will look like...

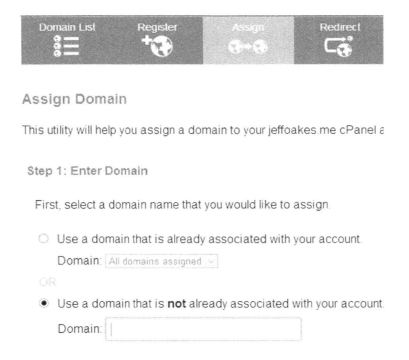

There are 4 steps here. Some choices will be pre-populated so you may need to change them. In **Step One** as seen, choose the first option, "Use a domain already associated..."

You can likely skip **Step Two** as it relates only to websites previously owned and transferred. If your website is completely new, you should be able to just ignore this step.

Step Three will ask you to choose the location of the new domain. Since you are setting up your primary web address (domain), choose the second option, "Parked domain." Later, if you add another domain to the first website and want the two linked in some way, you can connect them using the other options. I recommend phoning support if you do this so you can get it the way you want it. For now, because this is your only website and your primary one, park it.

Finally, **Step Four** asks for the directory location. Again, as this is your primary website, you will choose the first option, "use an existing directory" and ensure that the proper site is chosen in the dropdown box (there should only be one if this is your only website—otherwise, get with support for detailed instructions).

The click the green "assign this domain" button at the bottom.

Your domain is now assigned.

Next, you are going to choose the platform in which to build your website.

Go to the tab at the top which reads, "Hosting."

Here you will face a control panel with numerous options. At first, this will seem quite intimidating, but don't worry, it is really fairly simple.

Scroll down until you see a section called "Site Builders." It will look like this...

Recall that I said you could build with a variety of site builders, depending on your own preferences and needs? If you want a strictly mobile website, which is growing in popularity, though seems counter-productive to me considering it is easy to make a standard website also mobile, you can choose the "goMobi" builder. Weebly and Simple Scripts are also here, which are standard website builders, but considering that you are going to want to add a blog anyway, I recommend just starting with a blog site, WordPress. The choice is yours, but I am going to explain the WP way, since that is all I use.

After choosing the site builder, you will be taken to a screen that allows you to upload this builder program into your server space. After doing this, all your building will occur from your website control panel and you will only need to come here for adding things such as email and other special features (explained in another book/month).

At the top of the screen, you will see an image/set of choices which look like this...

This is very simple. Scroll down to where you see the following "Script List."

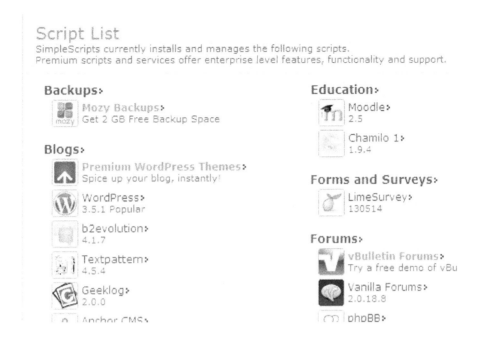

Script List

SimpleScripts currently installs and manages the following scripts.
Premium scripts and services offer enterprise level features, functionality and support.

Backups

Mozy Backups
Get 2 GB Free Backup Space

Blogs

Premium WordPress Themes
Spice up your blog, instantly!

WordPress
3.5.1 Popular

b2evolution
4.1.7

Textpattern
4.5.4

Geeklog
2.0.0

Anchor CMS

Education

Moodle
2.5

Chamilo 1
1.9.4

Forms and Surveys

LimeSurvey
130514

Forums

vBulletin Forums
Try a free demo of vBu

Vanilla Forums
2.0.18.8

phpBB

Choose the one you want, namely WordPress, and click on it.

On the next screen, scroll down until you see "Install WordPress" as follows...

Install WordPress
By clicking Install/Import below, you accept the SimpleScripts Term

Install   Location   Script
a brand new version   & Options   Installed

Article: Creating a Website using SimpleScripts›

Next, you will be taken to a screen which asks you to enter location and preferences.

See the following image.

Step 1: Installation Preferences

Preparing to install WordPress version 3.5.1

Where would you like WordPress installed?

http://jeffoakes.me/   ▾ /

Access URL: http://jeffoakes.me/
Server Path: //home4/jeffoake/public_html//

Step 2: Advanced Options

Site Name or Title

My Website / Blog

These options include administrative privileges, database configuration, and more. Changes are optional.
Click here to display›

Step 3: Plugins and Themes

We can automatically install additional plugins and themes.

☑ Mobile by UppSite Inc.›   ☑ SmallBiz Theme by Expand2Web›   ☑ SiteWit by S

UppSite   Make your WordPress site mobile in 2 minutes. With UppSite you can easily turn your site into fully functional and customizable native apps for iPhone, iPad, Android & Windows Phone. You also get a native-style HTML5 mobile web app, so we got you mobile-covered all around.

SmallBiz   Create your website in minutes including unlimited Pages, Blog, Facebook and Mobile!

Activate under Appearance -> Themes.

SiteWit

☑ Cashie Commerce by Cashie Commerce›

Sell on your WordPress site   The easiest way to sell on your WordPress site! Compatible with any theme, can be managed entirely from your WordPress admin, accept both credit cards

Step One will ask for the location. Since this is your only website/domain currently with BlueHost, there will only be a single option and it should populate. If not, just choose the domain from the dropdown menu. Later, if you add more domains, you will have to choose which to install to. This allows you to have some websites in WP, others only mobile, and others in Weebly or Simple Scripts. Or you can have them all in WP as do I. The choice is yours.

In **Step two,** you will change the site name from "My Website/Blog" to the actual name of your website. In the case of wallysweirdstuff.com, I entered Wallys Weird Stuff for this is the proper name of the site.

Step three allows you to automatically install certain useful plugins from the get-go. These change from time to time so just read them and if you think you may like to use them, leave them checked. If you are uncertain, just leave them checked for all this does is add them to your plugin list. To use them, you would still need to activate them later (This is discussed fully on Days 14 and 15 of this book).

Finally, **Step four** is the boring legal stuff. Read the Terms and Conditions, check the box, and click complete.

Now, after you have done this, you will likely be taken to a screen which informs you that you are about to overwrite your website. It will ask you to verify this choice and you want to confirm. If you'd like to understand why this is happening, simply open a new tab in your browser now, enter your domain name in the address line, then hit enter. Your website will open but you will notice the BlueHost/HostMonster logo and a bunch of links for ads. This is the default of your website until you install a script/platform and begin building. Since you don't want your website to look like this, you overwrite the script. After you do so, you will be informed of success and you are now ready to begin building your website.

If the tab with your website is still open, refresh it. If not, reopen it. You will then be taken to a fairly blank screen that looks like this (if using WordPress)...

(W) WORDPRESS

You are now logged out.

Username

admin

Password

•••••••••

☐ Remember Me   Log In

Lost your password?

← Back to Criminal Justice Law

This is the login screen for your website. To enter this whenever you want to access your site as an administrator, you will type into an address line "yourwebsitename.com/admin." Notice that I even used Admin for my username. Remember earlier I told you to keep track of your login information? If you did not choose (or were even given an option to choose) a username, enter the email address you signed up with and the password you either chose or were given. The click on the blue "Log In" button to the lower right. (If you have forgotten this, just phone or go to the online chat with your host and they will help you.

From here, you will be taken to your WP dashboard and this ends this tutorial. Tomorrow, we will explore your WP dashboard together, for understanding how to use this is the foundation for building your website properly. In subsequent days, you will learn how to write posts and pages, how to optimize, and how to add really cool features to make your life online much easier and productive.

See you tomorrow.

Day 11: Set Up Your Website/Theme

Today we are going to explore your WordPress dashboard. If you have chosen to build using another platform/script, this information can be skipped, but of course, since every dashboard contains pretty much the same elements, you will still find this information useful. The only thing that will be different will be the exact terms used for various features and the locations of these.

Virtually every website builder comes with a pre-loaded theme. But often, the themes provided are not exactly what someone building a website necessarily wants. For this reason, we will also explore themes and how to decide what to choose. This is the process of setting up your website.

After logging into your website (http://yourwebsite.com/admin) you will be taken to your dashboard.

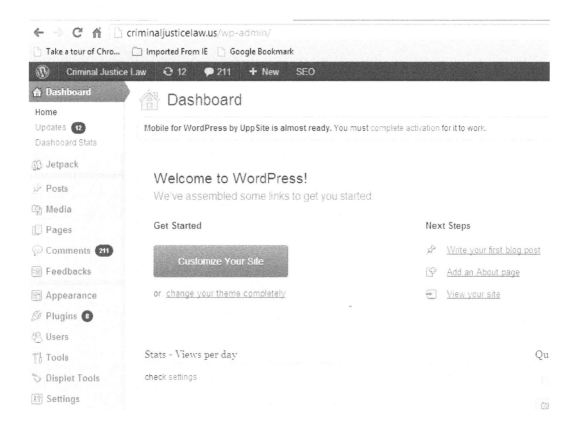

This is the dashboard for my criminaljusticelaw.us website. Remember the site name you chose when setting up your site in BlueHost? In the upper left-hand corner, you will see your site name. If ever you are somewhere other than your dashboard while in admin mode, you can find your dashboard simply by placing your cursor over the site name here and a dropdown will allow you to access your dashboard. If you are in the dashboard when you place your cursor over this, you will have the option to "visit site" which means you will be taken to your home page. Just below the name, you will see the word "Dashboard" to indicate that this is where you are located.

Also, I should inform you that your dashboard will not necessarily contain everything that mine does at this point. As you add certain plugins, these will appear on the dashboard; you can see "Dashboard Stats" on mine. This will not likely be on yours, at least not yet.

Running down the left hand side of your dashboard, you will see "Updates." If there is a number beside this in gray, this is the number of updates that are available for various features of your website, most often plugins. As you can see, there are 12 updates for this site at the moment. The updates are not incredibly important, but often there are useful features added so you will want to check and update these from time to time.

"Jetpack" is another that either is or will be on your WP site once we have put in the basic plugins you will need on Day 14. This is the plugin that provides you with a quick view and expanded views of your stats in real time.

Continuing down, you find the "Posts" access, which will be discussed on Day 16. These are your blogs and they will appear on your home page. If you put your cursor over this, you will see a menu pop out that allows you to view "all posts" in a separate listing, add a new post, view categories for posts (like an index), and view the tags used for posts. If you click on the word Posts, the same menu will appear below the word.

Next you will find "Media," which is a quick way of adding images and video for use on your website. Days 25/26 will fill you in on how to add these. Here you can either access your existing library or add new items either by clicking and placing a new menu below or by placing your cursor over the word to view a popout menu just as with the Posts. In fact, you can access any of these features in the same way. Simplicity of navigation is one of the benefits of building in WordPress.

Next are pages, which are different from blogs/posts in that these are sections of the website reserved for specific functions. Pages appear as tabs at the top navigation of your website and Days 27 through 29 will explain how to implement and use various pages. Again, you can view all pages in a list or choose to add a new page with the menu choice by either clicking on the word or placing your cursor over it to get a popout menu.

Then there is a "comments" section. If you want to see how many comments you have, just look at the number beside the word in gray. As you can see, I have 211 comments awaiting moderation on this site. This is because I do not have spam filters on this particular site and receive copious amounts of spam mail. This is only 2 days' worth. I left it like this so you could see the importance of a good spam filter plugin. Without a good spam blocker, you will spend more time sorting through useless emails than you will actually working on your website. Another reason I leave it without a filter is because again, this is still an experimental website. One of the things I am doing with this site is putting together a compendium of spammers. I am not going to let on how I am going to use this information, but the spammers are going to love it—really.

Next, you will see "Feedbacks." This is part of an experimental plugin and you should not have this on your dashboard. It is for a form I have in place. If by some odd chance you do see this, then you have a plugin on your site which came as part of your chosen theme. Explore it.

"Appearance" is an important feature of your dashboard, at least in the early stages and whenever you want to change your site up for freshness. The submenu for this provides changes to Themes, Widgets, Menus, Theme Options, CSS Editing, Header, Background, and a general Editor. Not all of these options will be available for every theme and some themes will have different choices, but all appearance features will be found here. We'll be working in this element further in this chapter. Note: Anytime you find an Editor function, don't play with it unless you understand what you are doing. You can access these if you are curious about what is there, but make no changes or you may have problems. For instance, if you edit your theme CSS, you will have to delete that theme by replacing it with another, then reinstall that theme again unless you know how to correct the mistake.

Next you will see the "Plugins" function. The submenu provides a list of Installed Plugins, the ability to Add New plugins, an Editor feature, and after you have installed a sitemap generator, access to this. More on Plugins in the next two days.

Then you will see "Users." This is a feature that allows you to permit access to other people who may be writing directly to your website. You can view All Users, Add New Users, and View Your Profile from this location. If you are working alone or with a family member and don't mind them having full access to the site, no need to bother with this feature. This is only for when you reach a point where you start to hire writers and other workers to do things on the site and want to restrict access or provide them with online credit for their work.

Next is the "Tools" function. There is available tools, which change per the theme chosen but are basically the Press This feature, which allows you to quickly and easily grab interesting pages for use on your own and often a Categories/Tag conversion tool, which I never use. As long as you categorize and tag your material properly, this need not be used and I will teach you how to do this. In addition, there is an import and export feature here. These are simply ways to either import your pages (if you change your server/host) or export your website as an XML file as a backup. I recommend doing this once a month for should anything ever happen to the host, you may lose the data. If you have a backup, you can simply upload (import) the file and continue on. Of course, today, this may not be an issue for most information is kept on cloud servers in many different locations and most hosts, including BlueHost, keep multiple servers online. Still, better safe.

Next you will see on my dashboard (though not yours, yet), "Displet Tools." Ignore that for now. I will explain this on Day 15.

Last you will see "Settings." The menu that pops out for this allows you to choose from General Settings such as day/time configuration, Writing Settings, Reading Settings, Discussion, Media, Permalinks, and other features available through plugins. In time, we will discuss all these settings. For now, just access them an see what is there. You can change some if you like because frankly, there is nothing you can "mess up" that cannot be fixed easily enough in WP. This is another reason I like it.

Your Theme and Appearance

Your site comes pre-loaded with a basic WP theme which you likely will not want. You may, however, because the theme provided will be crisp, simple, and clean—all the things that a modern website should be. But maybe you want a bit more panache for your site.

Take a look at http://criminaljusticelaw.us

Scroll to the bottom of the home page and you will see the words "Proudly powered by WordPress/ Theme Academica. If you like this theme, it is free through the WordPress themes options which we will go to here shortly. I chose this theme because this is a more academic/educational type of website and this theme well-portrays that idea. The header image I created on my simple, little old paint program. I will teach you this shortly.

Now look at http://collapseconsultants.com

Scroll down the page and notice the difference. This was created using a very common WP theme called Twenty Ten. It is a simple, no-nonsense theme which allows readers to view multiple blogs and other elements quickly and easily. The purpose of this site was to promote a series of survival books I wrote and I felt that this style accomplished that goal best.

Now take a look at http:wallysweirdstuff.com

In this case, we chose a theme called EvoLve. It is a more complex theme, allowing for a multitude of options. We are not yet using all the features, but this is a theme that is well-suited to commercial sites.

I share these websites with you to help you appreciate what to consider when choosing a theme. Now for the best part. If you choose a theme and don't like it, just choose another. Or another even. The point is, even after checking out a live preview of a theme, often it just doesn't seem right, so just change it. Of course, you are unlikely to find one that you will like perfectly, but get one that comes close and check back from time to time for new ones. If you find one you like better, there is nothing wrong with changing it. Just be warned that once you get a lot of stuff on your site, changing the theme is likely to alter some favored elements, so you may find yourself returning to the previous theme until something better comes along.

Also, know that some themes are for sale. Not all are free. You can buy a premium theme or even paid upgrades to some of the free ones if you like, but I have yet to find this necessary. The choice is all yours.

Themes for Sale

One of the best places to buy themes if you don't find what you like among the free or paid themes through WordPress is themeforest. Themeforest is a veritable, well, forest of themes. The company has put together one of the largest libraries of pro themes I have found and the prices are very reasonable. On average, expect to pay between $20 and $50 for a great theme, no matter the purpose of your website. In fact, one of the greatest features of themeforest is that you can search for themes according to the type of website you are building. And if you want exclusive rights to the theme, there is an option for doing this—it costs more, of course, but if you want it to be all yours, it can be.

Buying and adding a theme from themeforest is simple. You buy it, download it to your computer, and then upload to your website using the "Install Themes" option which will be explained shortly.

Now, let's find you a theme.

From your dashboard, go to "Appearance" then "Themes."

You will see at the top the current theme, which is a default. Scroll down. Just below the image of your current theme, you will see the words, "Available Themes." This is where any themes you upload to your site will appear, though inactive. For now, you may have one if it loaded when setting up your account. As you add themes, you can keep them here as sort of a library of themes or delete them if you are never going to use them. You will accumulate themes here every time you upload one.

So let's locate some themes.

Scroll back to the top of this page. Notice two tabs. The first is "Manage Themes" and the one to the right of this is "Install Themes." You will also notice an icon to the immediate left of these. This is what you would use if you were to obtain a theme from some source outside of this site which you have saved on your computer. You would click on that and follow the prompts to upload the theme you have saved. So select "Install Themes."

The page will then look something like this...

Search | Upload | Featured | Newest | Recently Updated

Search for themes by keyword.

[   ] [Search]

Feature Filter

Find a theme based on specific features.

Colors

☐ Black   ☐ Blue   ☐ Brown

☐ Pink   ☐ Purple   ☐ Red

☐ Yellow   ☐ Dark   ☐ Light

Notice that you can search by keyword. If you wanted one of the themes I mentioned or a friend recommended a theme by name, enter it and search. Or you can browse themes by Featured, Newest, or Recently Updated. You can also search according to filtered requirements.

For instance, if you only want Pink and Black themes, choose Pink and Black from the Colors and scroll to the bottom of this page. You will find a button which reads, "Find Themes." Click it and only themes featuring the colors pink and black will appear.

Or maybe you only want to view themes with a certain number of column possibilities (for instance, if setting up an online newspaper, you may want four columns; if an online magazine, perhaps three). You can further filter according to column width, features (which you know little of at the moment I'm sure), or even subject. One common favorite these days are the Photoblogging Themes, which come pre-loaded for thumbnails and galleries.

For now, choose "Featured."

This will take you to a small selection of themes that currently trending. In other words, these are the themes that many are choosing now. Naturally, this is subject to change so every time you check this, you may find different choices.

Now choose "Newest." These are the latest themes which have been developed by advanced users of WordPress. Again, this list changes in both themes listed and length of list as new themes come out. This is a great way to find the freshest themes for use, but also a good way to get themes that may have some bugs to work out. Personally, I hold off on these until they are updated. If I find one I think I will like, I install it but don't activate until at least one update has been created (remember the updates I told you about earlier? A theme update will show up there. You just go to it and choose to install the update.).

Finally, you can check out the "Recently Updated themes.

Look around at the different themes. Below each, you have the choice to Preview the theme or read details about it. If you think you will like it, click on "Install Now."

You will then be taken to a screen that looks like this...

 Installing Theme: Alexandria 1.0.4

Downloading install package from http://wordpress.org/themes/download/alexandria.1.0.4.zip...

Unpacking the package...

Installing the theme...

Successfully installed the theme **Alexandria 1.0.4.**

Live Preview | Activate | Return to Theme Installer

Notice that I have just installed the Alexandria Theme. It has "Successfully installed." Just below this, I can now preview this theme "Live" or "Activate" it, or return to the "Theme Installer" screen so I can choose others. Note that until you get content on your site, a Live Preview will be fairly useless. Also, I like to wait to Activate until I have checked out some other themes. So go look at some more. Choose three or four (or more, it's up to you) and once you have, we can resume. For sake of teaching you, be sure to add the Twenty Ten.

Ready to resume?

Once you have added a few themes, you can then click on the "Themes" from the menu on the left (just below "Appearance." This will bring you to the screen where your current theme is located and if you scroll down, there is your theme library.

Now you can look at the various themes side-by-side and decide which you would like to try out the most. There is no wrong choice here, just pick the one you think you will like working in and will best represent your site (for now, activate the Twenty Ten so that we can be on the same page as I am teaching you. You can change it after and will have a good grasp on how to do things with the theme of your choice. Of course, every theme has different options, but many are standard.). Remember too, if you don't like a theme you choose, you can change it any time.

Welcome to Twenty Ten

Return to the Manage Themes area and notice that your Twenty Ten is now the active theme. Don't worry much about how it looks for now, as you will change it when you feel comfortable. I only want to use this one so that we will be in synch.

Notice that there are a number of options below the description paragraph. Go first to "Customize."

Once you choose Customize, you will be taken to a screen similar to this one.

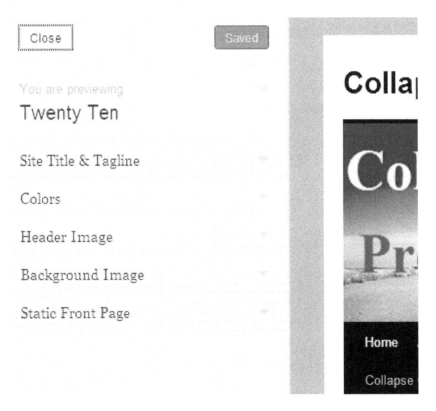

Notice that each element here has a small arrow to the right. This is a dropdown menu. In the case of the first, "Site Title & Tagline," the menu allows you to enter those two items. For this website, the title is "Collapse Consultants" and the tagline appears (on the site) to the far right and reads, "See What Lies Ahead." If you go to http://collapseconsultants.com, you will see what I mean.

Next, you can choose your color scheme. This is simply the background color of the page, that which appears around the border. On this site, it is a faint blue/gray.

Then you can add a header image. Just open, click on the preloaded image, and add your own. However, you can also add the header elsewhere. Notice on the image prior to the above where it reads "Header?" If you go to this selection on virtually any of the themes, you will even be given either dimensions for the header so you can build it in Paint or Photoshop, then upload it in without any changes. For some themes, you add the header then crop it. If you are not given the dimensions, you then have to experiment to get it right. That is just the drawback of some themes, but it is easy to get the hang of.

Next, you can add a background image. This generally will replace the background color so really you simply need to choose one or the other.

Finally, most themes provide for either a "Static Front Page" or a page with the latest posts. In the case of this website, I chose to have my latest posts. The difference is that if you choose static, then what you place on the front page is all that is there and it does not change. This is only a good option for websites that are seeking strong conversions such as obtaining leads through a good landing page. For all other uses, an ever changing front page is advisable. In addition, under the "Static Front Page" section, some themes offer other options. Just play with these until you know the difference and decide what you want. The way to do this is to simply make a choice, then go to your home page to see how it looks. The easiest way to do this is to open your site in a second browser tab. Then when you make the changes, you simply go to the other tab, hit refresh, and see the results in real time. Just remember to click on the blue "Save" button each time or you may think it is not working right.

After saving your choices (by clicking the blue save button), you can hit "Close" and return to the Manage Themes screen. Check out the "header" selection now. Just look at it, unless you already know what to put there. You will notice that this theme comes pre-loaded with some header options. You can use these, or create and upload your own. Save any changes by using the Save button at the lower left and return to the Manage Themes screen.

You will also notice that again, you can alter your background from this screen as well. You have the same options, just in a different layout. You can alter the background color or upload a image to use. Some themes allow you to tile the images, add movement to the images, center, or any manner of other possibilities. I recommend against doing anything to the background which will detract from the main content and focus of your site.

Returning to the Manage Themes screen, you notice the "Edit CSS" and "Menus" options. Ignore CSS for now unless you know CSS. The "Menus" is an option that allows you to create customized menus to place on the side bars, header, footer, or anywhere the theme option will allow. You often see custom menus in the footer of a website, especially when the theme only allows for a single space there. But you need content before you can create such menus, so for now, ignore this option. Later, on Day 26 you are going to learn how to use Widgets. Pay close attention to these handy tools for these are the things which can make the difference between an average website and one with distinction. Widgets add user friendly elements to your site, but because you need some other elements in place before seeing many of the results, these will be discussed much later,

For now, get ready for Day 14. We are going to add some basic plugins which will be very useful as you begin to write pages and build your website.

Day 12: Add Basic Plugins (WP Site)

One of the key advantages to building a website in WordPress over other platforms is that the millions of long-time users of WP have developed and share tens of thousands of plugins. Plugins are simply programs that will function within the WP platform to create many of the great effects and elements we find on websites. If you want a function to gather email addresses for you, get a plugin. If you want an easy way to build newsletters, get a plugin. Want to merge the two? Yep, there's a plugin. If you know nothing about SEO yet still want your website and pages optimized, there are numerous plugins...the one you will upload in this chapter will even teach you how to optimize pages so that should you ever build in another platform, you will know what you are doing.

So with that, I am going to have you upload some of the more basic plugins that you should have on your website if you want to make the most of it and get that crazy traffic I promised. These are just the basics that you need, but there are many more. In the next Chapter/Day, I will recommend some advanced plugins. The ones covered here are essentials and none of the cost a dime. So let's get started.

From your dashboard, put your cursor over the "Plugins" option then choose "Add New."

You will then be taken to a screen like the image on the following page...

```
                    NOTES
    _____
    _____
    _____
    _____
    _____
    _____
    _____
    _____
    _____
    _____
    _____
```

Popular tags

You may also browse based on the most popular tags in the Plugin Directory.

admin AJAX buddypress category comment comments
link links login media page pages photo photos plugin

Notice first that there is a search function. This is useful if you have some idea of what you are seeking. For instance, if you were to type in SEO and hit the "Search Plugins" button, you would be given a list of SEO plugins that is quite long. No need to worry about this though, shortly, I am going to turn you on to the best one I have found yet.

There is also Featured, Popular, Newest, and Favorites if you would like to simply browse and see what's out there. Finally, notice the "Popular tags" section. This will allow you to browse certain plugins according to how their creators have tagged them.

For now, I am simply going to tell you what plugins to seek so all you need to do is enter the terms in the search and select them from the choices. I will give you the exact title so you need only install and activate when it appears. However, in some cases, there could be updates or older versions appearing so be sure to choose the newest version.

Also, some of these will come automatically with your WP installation. To know which, simply access "Installed Plugins" from the "Plugin" menu option on your dashboard. If a plugin is already installed and you look it up, it will even be listed as installed. For instance, if I search for Askimet then scroll through the list of options, I will find this one down the list, which shows it is already installed.

Akismet   2.5.7   ☆ ☆ ☆ ☆ ☆

Details | Installed

The basic Plugins you need for your website are:

1. **Acurax Social Media Widget**: This is a social media sharing Widget that will make it easy for you when you begin to build your social media presence. For now, install it, but do not activate. To activate a plugin, all you need to do is access the "Installed Plugins" and click on Activate. If you accidentally activate a plugin or decide you no longer want to use it, you simply click "deactivate." If you are not going to use it again, you can uninstall it as well. And if you change your mind later, simply look it up and install again. See, there is nothing with WP that you do that cannot be simply undone or redone. Before using this Widget, however, you will need to configure it. Once it is installed and activated, the Settings option will appear on your left menu of your dashboard near the bottom. You will first need to create accounts for each social media button you wish to include when using this plugin for you will need the address for each. Then it is a simple matter of telling the program where in your site to place the social media buttons you have activated. You have a choice of themes (button styles) and even a premium upgrade (paid) if you choose. The free version provides sharing buttons for Twitter, Facebook, Google+, Pinterest, YouTube, LinkedIn, and an RSS feed.

2. **Akismet**: Remember earlier when I told you about Spam protection? This is it. Unless you want countless bogus messages coming in from all over the web (and doing nothing for your traffic), you want this little baby in place. That said, there are additional filters you will want to implement from your regular settings menu (be sure to explore this, especially General Settings and Discussion Settings) to add further protection against spam. When adjusting these settings, just limit links in a comment to one or two max and that will filter much of the spam out. Also set the comments such that you must moderate and you could even require comments be previously approved before posting automatically. Of course, there will still be some that will get by, but these two measures will reduce spam immensely. Activate this as soon as it is installed.

3. **Editorial Assistant by Zemanta**: This little puppy is excellent. Activate

now and when we get to Day 16 when you write your first post, I will explain how to use this feature.

4. **Google Site Verification Plugin**: Activate now. This will be used more fully later (and explained in a future book). This is the means by which you authorize Google to provide Analytics for your website. Let it get to work immediately, even though learning how to read these analytics must wait for a more advanced course. In so doing, you will have stats to read when I do teach you that information so it will all make better sense.

5. **Google XML Sitemaps v3 for qTranslate**: Every website must have a sitemap and this function provides a sitemap automatically. However, if you read about the plugin, it claims to serve the sitemap to Google automatically—not true. I will teach you in the last chapter how to submit your sitemap properly. This will not be necessary at the moment, for you don't have content on your site yet, but later you will want it done. Go on and activate it now though, for it does submit to some of the other search engines automatically and really, Google does not even much need a sitemap anymore to find your pages—but the sitemap does help for SEO and analytics purposes.

6. **Jetpack by WordPress.com**: This is one of two stats plugins I am having you install. This one provides at a glance site stats at the top of your admin bar no matter which page you are on as well as excellent stats on searches and pages visited. Activate it once installed.

7. **Related Posts by Zemanta**: This is another great plugin from Zemanta. It allows you to provide related links/posts by other bloggers but by way of extension, you also make your own available to others for their use. This is a great way to share links and gain added exposure over time. Activate it once installed and as you write your first post, I will show you how to use it to the greatest advantage.

8. **UppSite – Go Mobile**: Once installed and activated, this will automatically transform your website into a mobile site so that when people access your site via their cell phone, it is in the format which is easiest to read in that media. Activate immediately.

9. **Social Media Auto Publish**: You will use this later, once you have set up your social media accounts so install, but don't activate just yet.

10. **WP-Stats-Dashboard**: This is the second stats plugin. This one provides a bunch of useful stats information related to activity on your site, conveniently located right on your dashboard. It can help you ensure that you are reaching your social media goals and staying on target with your site. Go on an activate it once installed, though you will not be actually using it much until later. Still, having it there will

help you get used to what it can do for you and teach you in time how to grow your site through social media.

11. **WordPress SEO version 2.9.4 by Joost de Valk**: I saved the best for last for good reason. One of the key reasons websites fail to get traffic from search engines is because the site is not optimized. If we consider that 30-40% of all traffic to a website comes from search engines, this accounts for a good deal of lost traffic. In addition, consider too that Social Media likewise accounts for around this figure, and good links and strong email/newsletter campaigns the remainder. But an interesting thing happens when all these elements are functioning in synch: There is an exponential element to growing traffic such that the search results become far more important in the early stages of building a website, though less so once established. For instance, if you were to compare a relatively unknown website to one known, such as Yahoo, you would find that the unknown gets far more traffic as a percentage than Yahoo, which only gets around 3% from searches. This is because Yahoo does not need search traffic because of how well-known the site is. Yet, if you were to search virtually anything, Yahoo appears somewhere in the results. Fame breeds strong search results, but immense fame does not require them. To grow your website strong, you need to rely on search results at least until you become as big as Yahoo. Activate this as soon as installed and in Chapter/Day 18, I will teach you how to use it.

Get these plugins onto your website and begin thinking about what you want to write about for your first post on Day 16. For now, take a break. Tomorrow we will discuss and install some plugins which you will use later. The reason we install them now is so that you can explore the websites that have created them, go to the forums to learn about them further should you want, and generally understand what you have to look forward to as you build your website. See you tomorrow.

Day 13: Advanced Plugins (WP Site)

The list of plugins you can get to help you build your website is literally endless. Part of the reason that blogs are now on a par with websites is because of these plugins. Things which were once reserved only for website owners with either the skill or the cash to develop cool add-ons are now in the grasp of anyone willing to take a few minutes to explore the possibilities.

For instance, if you would like to add a video player to your website, ala YouTube style or any other, you do not need a webmaster with special skills and prices—you can do it yourself.

If you'd like to put an image gallery into your site, there is a plugin. You can even get a plugin which will allow visitors to upload any kind of content you allow. They can upload videos, still images, MP3, MP4, whatever.

Maybe you would like a good tool for collecting email addresses to use in your Newsletter campaign. Or perhaps you would like the ability to easily translate your website into other languages. Maybe you would like to be able to _____ (fill in the blank). If you can think of it, there is likely already a plugin for doing it.

So here I am going to go through some of the plugins I have tried. Some I continue to use on various sites and others I found to be no use to me, but none-the-less useful to someone. I'll tell you a little about each and you decide if it is something you may like on your site.

Also, these are the one's I have found and tried. If you go exploring, you will likely find others that you prefer. Also, I should tell you a little about how to check these out should you be curious about how to use them. Look at the following image.

Tumblr Importer 0.8 Imports a Tumblr blog into a WordPress blog.
Details | Install Now Correctly handles post formats
Background importing: start it up, then come back later to see how far it's gotten
Duplicate checking: will not create duplicate imported posts
Imports posts, drafts, and pages
Media Side loading (for audio, video, and image posts) By wordpressdotorg

In this example, I simply browsed Featured plugins and found this one for the Tumblr Importer. To the right of the name of the plugin is the version, in this case 0.8 and it is rated 4-Stars by users who have rated it, which tells me it is pretty good overall. The information to the right of this rating, tells me roughly what the plugin will do for my website, but I would like to know more.

To find out more about this plugin, there are two things I can do. The first is to click on the "Details" link. The image above displays the popup window

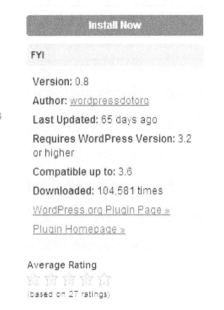

Description   Installation   Changelog

Description

Imports a Tumblr blog into a WordPress blog.

- Correctly handles post formats
- Background importing: start it up, then come back later to see how far its gotten
- Duplicate checking, will not create duplicate imported posts
- Imports posts, drafts, and pages
- Media Side loading (for audio, video, and image posts)

Install Now

FYI

Version: 0.8
Author: wordpressdotorg
Last Updated: 65 days ago
Requires WordPress Version: 3.2 or higher
Compatible up to: 3.6
Downloaded: 104,581 times
WordPress.org Plugin Page »
Plugin Homepage »

Average Rating

(based on 27 ratings)

that will fill me in better.

Here I get the same description, but notice the tabs at the top. There are installation instructions in case I download the plugin using means other than through the dashboard installer and information related to accessing the plugin once installed. The Changelog will tell me what is different from previous versions, should I care to know. If I have not updated my WP version, I should for the box to the right informs me of the minimum version needed to run this plugin (updating the WP version should always be a priority when updates arrive). I can see that over 100,000 people have used this plugin and that the rating is based on 27 reviews. Most important, however, I can access the Plugin Homepage via the link contained just above the rating on the right. This is often very useful for the homepage will often provide many useful details, FAQ's, and forums for getting help should it be needed.

Just remember that after you have installed the plugin, the "Details" link remains available so if you have trouble with the plugin, you can get help. I should note, however, that not all plugin homepages are created equal and sometimes they are in a foreign language. This is because the plugins are often developed by people completely independent of WordPress and by people from around the world.

If you install a plugin and find that you cannot figure out how to use it and cannot get help through this means, there is also the WordPress forum. This can be accessed through the "WordPress.org Plugin Page" link just above the plugin homepage link. There you can search for answers to your questions or ask other users. Just be mindful that if you ask a question in a rude way, you are likely to get a rude response. Ask in sincerity and clarity and the WordPress community will come to you aid, should anyone have the answer.

If you still don't get an answer to your problem, simply uninstall the plugin and seek another. There are always alternatives.

One more thing. To get rid of the popup window with this information, simply click to either side of the box and it will go away.

Now, on to some recommended plugins.

- **FlexyTalk:** Free Live Chat Widget: This is a plugin that I have on WallysWeirdStuff.com but have yet to implement. The reason has to do with scheduling and the fact that I do not yet have the traffic goals reached that I want for using it. But it allows you to build a Live Chat Widget to place anywhere on your website so that if anyone would like to ask you a question (or a moderator if you'd like to have one), they can do so live. Nice.

- **Frontend Uploader**: This is a plugin that allows visitors the ability to upload ANY format of content I permit. I can adjust the settings, create the page, and let the fun begin. I have plans for this little baby on WallysWeirdStuff.com and cannot wait to see what people send in.

- **Wysija Newsletters:** This one is very new and really cool. I have been playing with it and cannot tell you much other than it will be an immense time-saver when building newsletters. The widget allows you to add subscription forms to any page, post, or widget area and this alone makes it great. I am currently using the next one I will tell you about and may use them both, but at this point am not sure. All I do know is that this one is awesome when you start your newsletter campaign I will teach you about in a future book.

- **Displet Pop:** Set this how you'd like. After some time and pages on your site, a popup message will appear to encourage visitors to sign up for your newsletter. I have mine on JeffOakes.me set to 20 seconds after visiting the third page. You have likely seen these and sometimes the site builder will set it to pop as soon as someone enters the site. This is fairly useless for who really knows if they want to sign up before even seeing if the site is worthwhile or not. Be patient and let them check out the site a bit then ask for their subscription. However, in order to use this, you must also have...

- **WP Email Capture:** or a similar plugin. The way it works is that you first must set up the WP Email Capture and place it into a Widget. Then when you set up the Displet Pop, you link the two (just follow the instructions on the Displet Pop setup page or Homepage and you will do fine). You can even use this as a stand-alone email capture plugin by placing various forms around your site. If you visit http://jeffoakes.me, you will find one in the footer and another on the right sidebar of any page except the home page if you want to see what it looks like. Visit three pages, and you will be able to see the Displet Pop in action. Sign up for my Newsletter and you will receive valuable information in your email box courtesy of...me:)

- **Bublaa Embeddable Forums:** This is a forum on my website (http://jeffoakes.me/forum/) where visitors can discuss various topics, meet with authors I publish, and ask me questions. I also put notices here when I publish something I think members will like. Membership is free on my site, but can be restricted if you wish through the settings.

- **BuddyPress Group Tags:** Tags are a uniquely blogger kind of thing. Many who follow blogs like to choose from a tag cloud or tag group to find similar articles to the one they are reading. If you want to add a tag cloud to your site, just get this plugin then choose the tags when publishing. I will explain this more fully tomorrow when you write your first post.

- **CB Press:** If you plan on selling anything through ClickBank on your site, this plugin is a must. Easy to use, it creates a ClickBank marketplace right on any page you choose.

- **Custom Author Byline:** If you are going to have more people than you writing for your site and want to restrict them yet still ensure they receive their proper byline (recognition), just add this plugin.

- **Feedfabrik Blogbook Printing:** Once you have created considerable content on your site, you may decide you want to convert your blogs into a book or books. Using this plugin, you can easily convert these.

- **Form Maker:** If you would like to collect very specific information from commentators or anyone else on your site, you can add a form. Of course, getting them to enter their information requires some coaxing, but this allows you to build customized forms for whatever you are seeking to accomplish. There are many form-maker plugins, but this was the simplest one I found. If it will not do what you want, look around and you will find one to suit your needs.

- **PayPal Responder:** If you want to accept payments through PayPal directly on your website, use this plugin and you are set.

- **Readers From RSS 2 Blog:** For a simple RSS creator, this rocks. You can turn your feeds into a marketing tool for many uses.

- **Simple Share Buttons Adder:** This is another social media sharing plugin that I find useful on a couple of my sites. It is not necessarily better or worse than the one I recommended earlier, simply different.

- **Translate This Language Translation Plugin:** I searched far and wide and this is the best translation plugin I found. If you'd like to see how it works, go to http://jeffoakes.me and read any page or blog. In the upper right-hand corner of the content, you will see a blue button which reads "Translate." If you place your cursor over the button, a dropdown menu will provide you with language options. The translation is not perfect, but it is the best and simplest I have found yet.

- **Widgetize Pages Light:** This allows you to place widgets where ever you want. Normally, you cannot add a widget to a page or post. With this plugin, you can. This really makes building your website flexible. I strongly recommend this one.

- **WP Simple Galleries:** If you want to add a thumbnail gallery to a page, this is the plugin you need. Developed by WordPress, I have found no better for this task.

This list of plugins should suffice to keep you busy for a while. As I mentioned earlier, there are literally thousands of plugins you can get. If you have seen something on another website, you can rest assured you can find a plugin to do it for you. The biggest difficulty sometimes is figuring out how to find what you need. The way I do it is to see if I can find out the proper name for the function and enter that in the search box. When I am not able to do this, I either browse the Popular plugins or try to guess at what it is called, often again, and again, and again...until I eventually find what I seek.

Just play around, browse the plugins, and have fun.

Tomorrow you write your first post.

Day 14: Write First Post

If you are not a writer, you have likely been dreading this chapter. No worries. I am going to turn you into a writer. Before getting started writing your first post, I want to lay down a couple of ground rules which should help.

1. Remember, **first and foremost, You are the expert**. This is **Your** website and you are the one with the knowledge. If you don't get something exactly right when you write it, chances are few of your readers will catch it. You can always clarify later. Just know that you already know more than you know you know, you just have to loosen up and let it come out.

2. Next, just **write from the heart first**. Don't think too much about what you are writing for now, just get it down. Don't try to edit or including everything you think needs to be in here. Tomorrow we will edit using our full knowledge and powers of reason. We will not even publish this today, but merely save it for publishing tomorrow. So relax and just let the words flow, without judgment.

3. **Don't think you have to use big words**. One of the most successful American writers, Mark Twain, once said that his success was a result of only using four letter words, nothing greater. Of course, this was overstating it a bit, but he did use simple language. It is true in writing that less is more. Just be yourself and write as if talking to a friend.

4. **Draw pictures with words/describe what you need to explain**. If you are writing about a ball in your front yard and it is important that your reader know that the ball is a certain color, shape, texture, or size, include that information. If it will suffice to say it is a Soccer ball, just say that. And if you can't really put what you want to say into words or it would take too many to explain...

5. **Add images**. You can always take a picture with your phone and upload it to your website. I will teach you all about how to do this and believe me, using an image is far easier than trying to write some things. Just think about some of the images I have put in this book. Would it have not been much harder if I tried to describe everything I have shown in pictures? So just remember as you write, if you can add a photo, you will find yourself having an easier time writing what you want to say. Get the photo out and refer to it as you write. Then you can add it where it goes later.

I hope that helps. Are you ready to write?

There are two ways you can do this. The first is to write in a Word Document (or other such program) then copy and paste it to your site and the second is to write directly on your site. I am going to explain how to write directly on site for really, it is just as easy as writing in a word processor.

The first thing you need to do is log in to your site and go to the dashboard.

From the left menu of your dashboard, place your cursor over the option for "Posts." Normally, you would "Add New," but since this is your first post, there may already be one started for you by WP. So let's go to "All Posts" and find out. Click that.

I started a new blog on the free WordPress site just to show you what you should see. In some cases, there will already be an example blog. You can either delete it, or write over it. I suggest you simply choose "Trash," and get rid of it for sake of following along. This is a handy feature if you ever want to get rid of a blog post entirely, rather than simply unpublish, which we will discuss here soon. If there are no posts, this is what you will see. I created this site mainly for this example, though I am considering making it real. The site is http://votenoneoftheabove.wordpress.com. The purpose of the site is to draw national attention to the fact that voting either Democrat or Republican only results in the same corruption and nonsense we have been getting out of Washington for decades. I believe we need to pull a "Brewster" on the establishment and get rid of them all—start with a totally clean slate and send a message that we've had enough. But this is not a political book, so let's start building your site.

Another reason I created this is to show you what a Free WP site looks like, should you not choose to pay for hosting (go totally free). Notice that the "wordpress" in the address is the only difference. Now, after you add posts to your site, this will populate as a list for easy access. You notice below the word "Title" that there are "No posts found." This is because we have not written one yet. The other reason I started this blog is to show you how to write a blog. I told you the purpose of the site so that you will understand my writing process and hopefully be helped as you write your own.

Notice beside the word "Posts" just below the gray the button that reads "Add New." WP makes it easy to add a new post from many different places when in Admin mode. This is one such place. Click on Add New now. I will tell you more about this feature of the site later after you have created your first post.

This is what you should see.

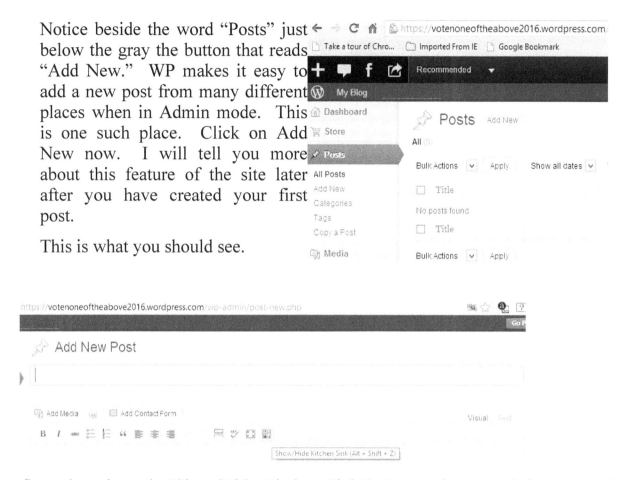

Notice first where it reads "Show/Hide Kitchen Sink." Just to the upper left corner of this text box is a funny little icon like this...

If you place your cursor over that icon, you will see "Show/Hide Kitchen Sink." Click on this to fully open the editing features and once you do, this is how it will look.

The reason I had you open this feature is so that you can see just how similar to your Word document this edit screen on WP really is. Also, there are functions you will use here as you write and I am going to explain the most important/basic features from the start.

Just below "Add New Post" is a title box. Put your title here. Notice in the example following how I put the title "Vote None of the Above: Why?"

As you can see, I write a brief introduction. I did this to show you a couple of things which will be helpful as you write.

1. Notice that I started the title with the name of the site and began both the intro paragraph with those exact words and then put a subheading in the middle with the same. This is for both SEO purposes and to draw reader attention to the fact

that this is what this site and this particular post is about. As I choose new posts, I will use the same basic concept, though with different subjects/keyword combinations. For this post, the keywords I will use are "Vote None of the Above." I should tell you that I have done NO research into these keywords. I only chose them for example purposes. Your first post should introduce your personal feelings about your website. There will be pages to do something similar, but not with the emotional feel that you want to place in a blog. A blog post is more personal, less professional. So write about how the subject of the site makes you feel, why you are excited, angry, saddened, whatever.

2. Notice the "Permalink" just below the Title line. If you put your title in right away, once you add content this will automatically place your keywords/title into the link. These setting can be adjusted, but that is for another course. For now, if you want to alter this, simply click "Edit" to the right of this link and you can change it to whatever you choose. But for SEO purposes, it is best to leave it as is. Of course, if you change your title/keywords, you will want to edit accordingly.

3. Now notice your editorial choices on the kitchen sink. From the left, you have "B" for Bold font, "*I*" for italics, the ability to strike through a word for effect, then bullet points, numbered lists, quotes, left align, centered, and right align. Just to the right of these are two faded icons that look like the links of a chain. These are light because no words are highlighted for linking or unlinking. We will discuss this later in this chapter. Just know where these are. Then you will see four additional icons. For now, the only one you need to concern yourself with is the ABC with the check mark. This is your proofreader. Once you have written your post, you can proofread it automatically simply by clicking this icon. Misspelled words show up in red, grammar issues in blue and green. You can even go into your settings menu (on the left on the dashboard) and choose what "Writing" settings to apply to this proofreader. For now, leave it be. And don't feel that you have to obey all the rules of writing. That last sentence would have been flagged for everyone knows you don't start a sentence with "And."

4. Below this is the secondary kitchen sink I had you open. From the left, you can adjust the TYPE of font used, but not the specific style of font. See in the area where I wrote the first paragraph how a box is obscuring a portion? The top word here is "Format." When you select this box that currently reads "Heading 2," this is the box that appears. "Paragraph" is the type I wrote the body of the material in and when I wanted to put the heading in the center, I clicked the "center" function from the top part, opened the Type, chose ">Heading 2" then typed the words "Vote None of the Above." To return to normal, I will now choose "Paragraph."

5. Next you will see U for underline, a justification tool, font color selection,

clipboards, format removal icon, special characters, indentation icons, undo, and a handy help button. These are all similar to what you will find when using Word, though in much simpler format with less clutter so many of you reading this will already be fairly familiar with these features. If not, help is a click away.

6. Now to the far right at the top of the kitchen sink, you will notice two tabs. The first reads "Visual" and the second reads "Text." The visual should be darker which means you are writing in Visual mode, or what was once called WYSIWYG (What you see is what you get). The second is for adding HTML and will be covered in an advanced course. Stay out of this mode unless you know what you are doing. Of course, as with all aspects of writing in WordPress, should you find that you have accidentally written in this mode, simply switch

and make any changes needed to make your document appear as you want. There is nothing done that cannot be simply undone in WP.

7. The last thing to note is at the bottom of this edit box. A list of suggested links will appear and I will tell you about these after you have finished writing. Just below these is the "Word count." As you will see, I have written 97 words. For a blog post, write at least 300 and for a page at least 500. This is a blog, so your goal is a minimum 300 word count, though more, even much more would not hurt. Less will hurt, so write at least 300—I cannot emphasize this enough. Too few words will cause the search engines to disregard this page completely and too many such pages will drag your site down in the search results. Finally, you will notice to the far right that this "Draft Saved at 5:58:58." This is the auto-save feature so that should something happen to your internet, you will not lose all your work. You can later return and choose a saved draft from your list under "All Posts." This saves every five minutes by default, which you can change in your Settings should you choose.

8. One last thing. I recommend a subheading every two to four paragraphs, both to break up the material easily for readers and for SEO purposes.

That is all you need to know for now about writing in WP so what I want you to do now is write. After you have written enough, return here and I will help you publish.

Are you ready to publish your post?

Here is mine, which I wrote just for this example.

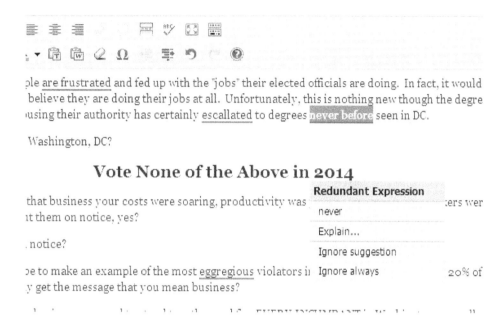

First, I ran the proofreader and have been informed that I misspelled two words and have some grammar issues. The green "are frustrated" I am not going to change—this is how most people speak and I believe in writing in common tongue. The second, "never before" is indeed redundant. To change it, all I need to do is click on the word "never" just below the explanation. To access this dropdown menu, I simply clicked on the underlined expression. To change the word "escallated" to the proper spelling, I click on the word and choose from a selection of possible options or, if the choice I want is not in the selections, I choose to ignore then look the word up and manually change it. Simple.

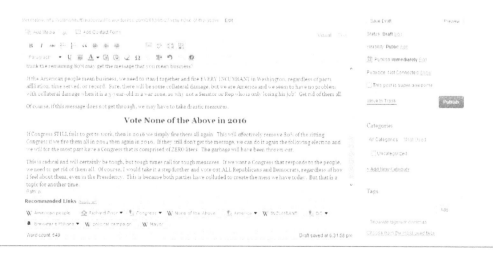

The first thing you may notice if you compare the three images proceeding this is that there are three slightly different, though nearly identical Subheadings. One without a date, one with 2014, and one with 2016. This I did primarily for SEO purposes, but really, there only need be a single subheading with the keywords used. As long as you used subheadings that are natural to the content, you will be fine. Don't worry much about SEO and keywords at this point, for on Day 18 we will edit for this purpose. On Day 17 (tomorrow) we are going to edit for clarity and readability. If you wrote in a simple way, this will likely be little more than an exercise in proofreading.

Notice at the bottom of the previous example (2016) that now the suggested keywords are well-populated. As you write, these appear and you will want to decide which to include and which to not. One goal of a good website is to provide value to readers and links to related, explanatory information is a great way to provide this value. So decide which links add to the content and which detract. In the case above, all of the links would make sense to include, so I will either click on each, or simply click on "Apply All" on the left, beside where it reads, "Recommended Links."

Now we are going to publish this, but refrain from making it public just yet. This will allow the search engines to pick it up, but without making it publicly seen just yet. Don't worry that it is not optimized...the search engines will further note this once we edit. For now, you simply want to announce your presence.

So on the right of the edit screen shown you will see "Visibility: Public Edit" and "Publish Immediately Edit." I should note that on your screen, you will have Zemanta recommendations as I have not yet added these to this blog. Tomorrow you will see the results of this addition. For now, these options will be just below the Zemanta Recommendations.

Look at the following example. I have opened both of these options so you can see what they look like.

The Publish immediately is set by default, but if you want to set a date and time to publish, this is how you would do so.

Above this, however, the visibility is set to public by default. If you want to put a password on a page, you can do so here. If you want to make the page private for some reason, simply click the round button to the left of "Private" and click "OK" just below. Do this. We are going to make this private for now as it is not ready for public consumption. We will make it public tomorrow, then optimize the next day. In a future book, I will explain more uses of this feature for as you progress, you will find this to be very useful. For now, we are going to make all pages and posts public, except for today.

Once you have done this, look below this to the blue "Publish" button. Once you click this, your post is published whether public, private, password protected, or delayed. Any time you want to edit this post, you can and tomorrow you will notice that when we return, this button will no longer read "Publish" but rather, "Edit." This is because you can only publish once, but you can (and should) edit often.

See you tomorrow.

Day 15: Fundamentals of Good Web Writing

Like it or not, Google has set the pace for what is considered "good" writing for the Internet. Of course, as I stated earlier in this book, the founders of Google built a search engine that could locate material that had value for readers and their goal has not changed. Google continues to seek ways to modify their algorithm so that the content searchers locate using their service is right on target and useful. As a result, some SEO managers love Google and others hate them. Generally speaking, those who hate Google are those who seek to bend or outright break the rules—seeking easy ways to do what takes time and attention.

The fact is, it takes time to write good content. Just as a great novel has yet to be written by a computer program, good web content must come from the mind and skills of humans. There are no shortcuts.

So just what is Google (and by way of extension, all search engines) looking for in content designated "good?"

We can get clues from the latest Panda and Penguin updates which were designed to do several things. In tandem, these two updates have turned the content marketing world upside down for they required first the constant flow of new or updated information; second, that human readers find the content to be valuable enough to link to it, return, and remain for a time; and third that the content not be plagiarized. In other words, the content must engage the readers, be fresh, and original.

So how do you do this if you are not a professional writer?

First, recall the rules I laid out in Chapter/Day 14. Here they are in brief as a reminder.

1. You are the expert.
2. Write from the heart...write as you speak.
3. Avoid a big vocabulary...use simple words.
4. Describe only what needs to be described, then do so in detail as needed.
5. If you can provide a photo to help describe, do so.

Now, here is how you are going to edit your blog.

Look for redundant sentences. If you have said something once, repeat it only if emphasis is needed. Read through what you have written and if you catch yourself repeating something that does not need to be repeated, get rid of it. Remember, you are the expert and you know if you need to simplify what you are explaining.

Read what you have written aloud to yourself or a friend. Listen to how it sounds. Does it sound natural? Does it sound like you speak? Look for places where you can use contractions if THAT'S, how you speak. Get it? If you normally use contractions in speaking, write it so. There's a tendency to write out all words when writing/typing, but on reading, you will catch yourself and say, "I don't talk like that." So change it. Make it sound natural.

Next, it has been said that repetition is the mother of learning. This is true. If you write for your website every day (and you will if you want traffic), before long, you will find that writing will become much easier and more fun. Like any skill, it takes practice and time to master, but in a short time, you will find writing for your site much easier.

Of course, if you simply don't want to write for your site, you can always contact me at cjeffoakes@365crazywebtraffic.com and contract me to do the writing for you, but I recommend trying to do it yourself for at least a month. Give yourself time and you will surprise yourself.

Check to see if what you've written is fresh, new, and something others would want to read. If something sounds outdated, try to find a fresh way to say it. This means avoid being cliché' and this can be done by adjusting the user writing style settings. To do this, go to "Users" on your dashboard, then choose "Personal Settings" as shown below.

You will then arrive at a screen as shown next.

Proofreading

Automatically proofread content when:

☑ a post or page is first published
☐ a post or page is updated

English Options

Enable proofreading for the following grammar and s̶

☐ Bias Language
☑ Clichés
☐ Complex Phrases
☐ Diacritical Marks
☐ Double Negatives
☐ Hidden Verbs
☐ Jargon
☑ Passive Voice
☐ Phrases to Avoid
☑ Redundant Phrases

Notice that I like to avoid Passive Voice, Redundant Phrases, and Clichés. I recommend that you stick with the last two for now. Many of us speak in passive voice and don't know it, so really, you need not concern yourself with this. But cliché and redundant phrases can cause readers to find what you have written to be cumbersome and boring, so you want to be made aware of these when proofing your work. After you have made your choices (and you should read over all within this option), click the blue "Save Changes" button located at the bottom and the top of the page on the left.

Next, check to see if you have included any irrelevant information in what you have written. If it does not need to be there, take it out. No matter how great a story or joke or whatever is, if it is out of place in what you have written, remove it. If it is so good and belongs on the website in some form, put it into a post where it fits or make it an entire post/page on its own.

Also, be clear and concise. Just as with avoiding redundancies and irrelevant information, you need to see that what remains clearly explains what you are trying to convey. Remember that you are the expert, but your audience is made up of differing levels of knowledge. Try to explain information in such a way that both novices and people of expertise such as you will both enjoy reading the material. This is best accomplished by the acronym KISS—Keep It Simple and Stupid. Your role in writing is to teach. To teach, you must understand what you are trying to say. If you understand it, you can simplify the concept. I find it helpful to try to explain things so that if a fifth grader were reading my material, he or she would understand it. Do this, and most people will enjoy what you've written.

Remember that people found your page/post because they were looking for information about a topic that you are writing about. They have questions and want answers. Try to think of what questions they may have and answer those. In other words, be informative.

Finally, think of places where you can add fresh images of your own creation. These are always best, but not always possible. We'll discuss images in greater detail on Day 25, but for now, I am going to teach you how to use Zemanta to insert images. I am also going to teach you how to insert your own so if you have these on your computer, get ready to put them to use.

What do images have to do with good web writing, you may be wondering? Everything.

Images help clarify information and the search engines look for images which not only break up the material so that it is more visually appealing, but also help better explain the material presented. Thus, good images only help your website, but be careful not to over do it. All you need for an average blog (300-500 words) are one to three images. For a Page between 500 and 1000 words, two to five will suffice.

So, let's add some images. For this, I am going to use Wallys Weird Stuff.

For now, we are going to add images from Zemanta. This is the tool I had you add as a plugin which appears directly beside your edit screen. You'll notice all the images of pizza and the references to pizza in the Related Articles to the bottom. This is because this is a page on Wallys devoted to providing Weird Pizza Recipes...and I do mean Weird. But notice at the top where it reads, "Current Recommendations." Just below that is a tab which reads "Zemanta" and beside this is another tab which reads, "My Sources." Both are important.

One of the last things to know about writing engaging content has nothing to do with your writing style nor images, but rather with linking related material. This gets people moving around on your site, which the new Google updates read as engaging your audience. We will discuss this further on Day 24. For now, I simply wanted to make you aware of this tool.

To add images from Zemanta is very simple. All you need to do is left-click on the image and a box like the one following appears.

I clicked on an image of "CiCi's Macaroni and Cheese Pizza." When I did, the image automatically transferred into my edit screen, exactly where my cursor was placed. If I don't like this placement, I have some options. If I wanted it placed somewhere else, I can simply click "Remove" in the lower right and re-position my cursor where I want the image to appear and click on it again.

If I prefer the image appear on the left or in the center, I simply click on the appropriate choice at the top of the box that opened. I can also decide how large or small I would like the image to appear by choosing from the "Size" portion or adjusting to a Custom width.

Finally, if I prefer another caption or would like to add to it, I can do so simply by editing it from here or removing the caption completely by unchecking the "Caption" box. I strongly recommend only that you add keywords from your article, ideally as the first words in the caption. This is for SEO purposes. I also suggest not removing the "Credit" information for to do so could cause copyright infringement. Once done, click "Done" and the image is in your blog.

However, again, nothing done in WP is ever without simple editing.

If, once the image is on my blog and I decide I do not want it there or on the page at all, it is a simple matter to undo the choice.

Look at the next image, which shows how to either remove or further edit this image.

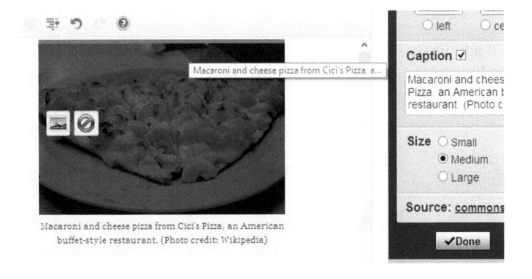

Macaroni and cheese pizza from Cici's Pizza, an American buffet-style restaurant. (Photo credit: Wikipedia)

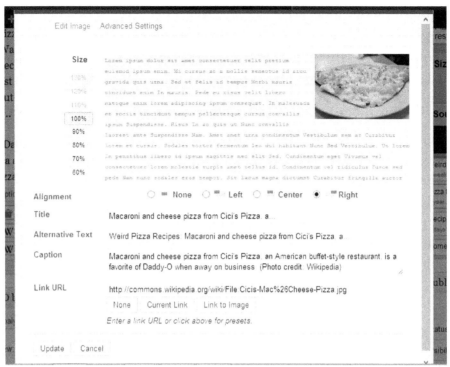

If you left-click on the image, the box reappears to the right, but notice now how the image has picture icon on the left along with an icon for "no" and is shaded? If you click on the "no" icon, the image is removed. If you want to do further editing of the image, click on the picture icon. Click on that icon now. This will open an entirely new screen as shown in the previous image.

This is your image edit screen. Notice that there are two tabs at the top, "Edit image" and "Advanced Settings."

Advanced settings allow you to alter the size of the image more precisely than in the Zemanta edit box as well as add borders and even alter the CSS if you know how. To change the size simply requires altering the numbers in the vertical and horizontal planes of the function, so I am not going to say much on this except that the simplest way to maintain good image results is to simply multiply the size figure in the two planes by the same number. For instance, if there is a 100 in the V and a 200 in the H and you want the image to be 50% larger, simply multiply both numbers by 1.5 and enter 150 in the V and 300 in the H. Simple.

On this main edit screen you can only decrease the size and then by increments of 10% from 90% - 60%. So if you want to shrink the image a great deal, choose 60%. Once you click on the update at the lower left, you will see the new size of the image. If you still want it smaller, click on the image again, then the picture icon again, and repeat the process. Repeat until the image is the size you want.

You can also alter the alignment just as with the Zemanta edit screen.

But most importantly here you will notice that you can alter not only the Caption here, but also the Title, the Alternative Text, and the Link URL. For Zemanta images, this will populate automatically. For your own images, you will need to add this information and I will be showing you this next.

The Title is what appears when a viewer places their cursor over the image.

The Alt Text is used for SEO purposes for this is what the Search Engines see when searching for the image. Notice in the example, that I've added the words "Weird Pizza Recipes" to the Alt Text. I added this so that the search engines will register that this is a weird pizza recipe. Anyone searching for weird pizza recipe images, will find this image in the results and potentially choose to visit my site. Always be sure to add the keywords for the article to the beginning of the alt tag.

Lastly is the link URL. If you leave it be, then when a visitor clicks on the image, they will be provided with a larger version. This is especially useful if you have a gallery of thumbnails or want them to be able to get a closer look at what you are describing. If, however, the image is for a book you are selling or another website you are promoting, you will want to change that link URL to the one which will take your visitor to where you want them to go. It could be the sales page on Amazon where your book is located, a Sales page on your site, another website, anywhere...you decide.

Once finished with any changes you are making, click update and this edit screen will close. On day 25, I'm going to teach you how to upload and use your own images.

The last thing you're going to do as far as editing your post is to simply take a last overview look at it.

Check that your word count is good. If so, go to the top and re-read the article. You will be viewing it pretty much as it will appear once on the site, so just scroll through, reading lightly and deciding if you want to tweak the article further.

Congratulations, you have created an article which will appeal to human readers.

Tomorrow, we are going to ensure that this post is optimized so that the search engines will find it appealing as well.

Day 16: Optimize From the Start

Website Optimization. Search Engine Optimization. SEO.

Whatever you choose to call it, this is perhaps the most confusing element of creating a website for newbies and the most controversial among veterans.

I fall somewhere in between. I entered the fray around the time that the White Hat SEO crowd and the Black Hat SEO folks were battling it out over who was "better." Of course, because the Black Hat SEO folks were doing things under the fray and Google was not amused, they fairly lost the war. This is not to say that the Black Hatters are no longer around, they are, but their techniques no longer work, though many people get suckered into buying their "services" still. Of course, who's to say that they won't find more shortcuts, but Google has developed an algorithm that "learns" and sniffs out cheats, so cheating the system is becoming increasingly difficult and costly.

Because I was just learning when all this was going on and could not afford the services of the Black Hatters anyway, I decided to simply find out what Google wanted and do it. Unwittingly, I was joining the ranks of the White Hat SEO crowd.

I would also like to inform you at this point, that only ONE of my websites is fully optimized. The others have been intentionally left not so because as mentioned earlier, they are all in one form or another, experiments in SEO. If I were to completely optimize the entire site, I could not determine exactly what was drawing traffic. I may not be the only person taking this approach, but I do so simply because I am a scientific person at my core. So I have applied the scientific approach to individual pages on my websites and in so doing, I've managed to learn exactly what works and what does not.

Ironically, I recently came across a plugin called SEO by Joost, which fairly teaches a person EVERYTHING I discovered. Awesome. I knew then, that what I had sorted through by experimentation had already been proven by others. This is the heart of the scientific method: duplication of results.

Also related to SEO, is ease of navigation. One of the best ways to get your website ranking is to have people actively moving about on you site and this is best accomplished by creating easy ways to navigate and find what they are seeking on your site, rather than searching for another. Thus, the more information you have on you website, the more useful it will be to visitors and the longer they will remain. The longer they remain, the better your site looks to the search engines and the more people find you site. This allows your site to grow and grow.

So I am going to teach you how to optimize your posts/pages from the start. Optimizing the site will be saved for the Navigation discussed on Day 27.

Access your post edit screen for the blog you just wrote the day before. Below the Word Count portion, you will notice "WordPress SEO by Yoast." "Yoast" is simply the pronunciation of the creator's name, Joost. This is short for Joost de Valk.

Joost de Valk has created one of the best plugins for optimizing a website AND learning how to optimize. Everything is simple, direct, and informative. If you fail to optimize the page, there are plenty of indicators and directions. The entire plugin is free.

I recently came across another plugin by Joost de Valk, which is out of the scope of this book. In fact, I came across it while doing some fact-checking for this book and put it aside until I could check it out—which I have not yet done. So I can neither endorse nor discourage this particular plugin, but given the creator, I am confident it will be great. You can read about it at http://www.stateofdigital.com/yoast-wordpress-video-seo/

Everything following this is part of this plugin, but I am going to present it in chunks.

The first thing you notice about this are the tabs along the top which read "General," "Page Analysis," "Advanced," and "Social."

This is part of what makes this particular SEO plugin so great...it is thorough.

Starting with the General tab, this is what you will see. For easy reference, I

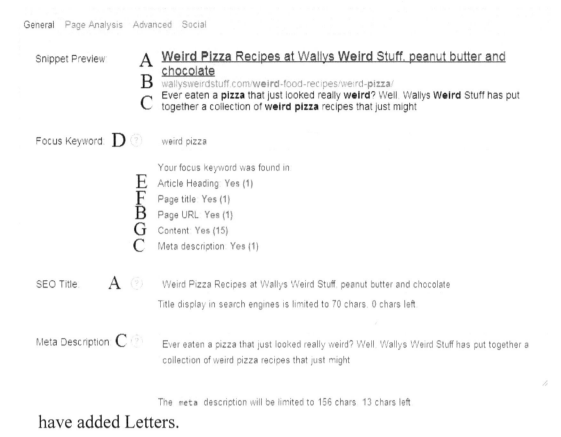

have added Letters.

Starting from the top, let's look at each element.

- **A** – This is the SEO Title. You will see near the middle of the page, a line, which will populate in light gray, the title of your article, whether a post or a page. If you want to change it, you simply type in this space and you will see the top "Snippet Preview" will change accordingly. This is what you see when you get your search results when looking for something in the search engines. If you don't control what is there, the search engines will by default simply choose the title you have chosen for the article. You want to control what appears. For instance, one element you want is the keywords you have chosen right at the start. Unless there is much competition for this keyword string, your material will appear at the top of the results when someone enters that exact search string. If you search right now for "weird pizza recipes," you will find WallysWeirdStuff.com on the first page—because there is considerable competition for these keywords. But that is not bad considering this site is only one month old as of this writing.

- **B** – The next element you see is the link URL for this page. This is the

URL that appears just below the Title line of your main edit screen. This can be edited and should include the keywords chosen. Note however, that this URL begins with "weird-food-recipes" followed by "weird-pizza." This is because this is a second tier page under the main page heading for Weird Food Recipes. If you look at the home page now (http://wallysweirdstuff.com), you will see a green navigational bar and at the lower right, is Weird Food Recipes with a tiny down arrow to the right. Place your cursor over this and you will see that Weird Pizza appears as a dropdown secondary page. I will teach you how to do this on Day 23.

- **C** – Next is the Meta Description. You can either choose this, or let the search engines simply provide the first 156 characters of your article as a snippet preview. You want to control this, especially adding your keywords, ideally at the start of the snippet. Near the bottom of the function, you will notice a box in which to do this.

- **D** – The focus keyword is here for two reasons. First, I should inform you that Google will not look at this, but other search engines will. Google WILL notice how often a keyword string is used in an article and the keyword string producing results for this is weird pizza recipes. My wife wrote this one and perhaps should have used all three in this page, for "weird pizza" in the search results has strong competition. Mojo's Weird Pizza in Australia dominates the entire first page of results. But this largely doesn't matter, for we are ranking well regardless and who knows, we could rise in the ranks for the double string in time. The main reason this is here is to help you focus on the keywords for this post or page. This allows this program to analyze how often and where you have used the keywords.

NOTE: When I had you write your post, I did not tell you to focus on keywords, but rather to simply write. This was so that you would not get encumbered by the SEO elements of writing. In the future, you may find it easier to write with certain keywords in mind from the start. What I want you to do now is decide what your post is about—what is the subject. Choose two or three words which will best describe the subject (ideally, three) and enter these into the Focus Keyword space.

If you wrote from the heart as I instructed, you will not likely have these keywords in the places in the article which will satisfy the search engines. That's ok, we are about to correct that. Once you have your keywords chosen, you can click on the "Update" button on the right of your screen and you will see that this program will inform you about whether your keywords are showing up correctly or not.

- **E** – Does the keyword combination appear in an Article Heading? If not, all you need to do is change it. These are the headings you entered as you broke up the information. Be sure the keyword combination appears in at least one, ideally the first. If you did it right and click "Update," you will see the program will tell you "Yes," along with a number in parentheses to indicate how many headings have the focus keywords contained within.

- **F** – Does the keyword combo show up in the Title? If not, then add it, ideally at the beginning. This is the both the title line at the top of your edit screen AND the SEO Title (**A**).

- **B** – Remember how to edit the link URL? Be sure the keywords appear in the URL, just below the Title line on your edit screen.

- **G** – Does the keyword combo appear in your content...the article? If not, now you can go back and edit from the head. You write first from the heart, just getting words on the page, then you edited from the head for human readers, now you need to edit from the head for the search engines. Just be sure that what you change makes sense to humans as well. It is best to place the keywords at the beginning of the article if possible (at least the first sentence or two) and at the end of the article (in the last paragraph), but you want these scattered throughout to some degree as well, for this is the subject of the content. Note too that once you get the hang of doing this, you will be able to write an article by first choosing the keywords to use, then writing an optimized article that will both satisfy the search engines and be pleasing for human readers as well. I simply broke the material down like this so that you could understand each element and how they fit together.

- **C** – Make sure that the keywords appear in the Meta Description. If you do a search for something, anything, now, you will find that the search results will return such snippets. Take a look at the descriptions and how many actually contain the keywords you chose. You will find that the most prominent results will have the keywords in bold somewhere in the description.

Ok, this explains the first part. Once you have all the elements under the Focus Keyword section reading "yes," we can move on to the finer aspects of optimizing your post. I know this seems like a lot and it is if it is all new to you. But it really is very simple and this tool will become your best friend as you build your website. Let's continue.

Notice the tab to the right of "General" titled, "Page Analysis." Click on that tab. You will see a screen like this...

General   Page Analysis   Advanced   Social

To update this page analysis, save as draft or update and check this tab again

- The copy scores 75.3 in the Flesch Reading Ease test, which is considered fairly easy to read.
- The keyword / phrase appears in the URL for this page.
- Keyword / keyphrase appears in 1 (out of 8) subheadings in the copy. While not a major ranking factor, this is beneficial.
- The images on this page contain alt tags with the target keyword / phrase.
- This page has 22 outbound link(s).
- The keyword appears in the first paragraph of the copy.
- The keyword density is 1.76%, which is great, the keyword was found 18 times.
- The page title contains keyword / phrase, at the beginning which is considered to improve rankings.
- The page title is more than 40 characters and less than the recommended 70 character limit.
- In the specified meta description, consider: How does it compare to the competition? Could it be made more appealing?
- The meta description contains the primary keyword / phrase.
- There are 1025 words contained in the body copy, this is greater than the 300 word recommended minimum.
- You've never used this focus keyword before, very good.

Note first that along the left side, you will have a series of dots. These will either be green (which is good), yellow (needs attention), orange (really needs attention), or red (must be fixed).

This will tell you such things as "The keyword does not appear on the page" or "The page does not have outbound links." All you need to do to get your post or page optimized is correct anything that shows up with a red or orange dot. The yellow dots indicate that you could make it better, but these are not absolutes. If changing something that has a yellow dot beside it does not make sense, leave it.

Notice that one thing this does is tell you how easy your content is to read. One of the key elements of this is simplicity. Short sentences work best, but remember, if you are writing for a highly educated reader, you may want to write to their level and include longer sentences. This will lower your score, but you need to write according to your readers. In general, most people prefer short sentences. Most people prefer simple words. We surf the web mostly for leisure and entertainment, so simply is almost always better.

One of the most common alerts this will present has to do with Alt Tags for images not containing the keywords. If you change the keywords used, these will need to be fixed. If you have forgotten how to edit the alt tags for images, simply look back at yesterday, or look ahead to Day 25 or the Appendix.

Another thing you will notice near the center of this example is Keyword Density. Don't get too hung up on this for while it is important, it is not the be all and end all of Optimization. Some SEO "experts" will strongly state otherwise, but I can tell your from experimental evidence, this is not as important as it once was. I will teach you more about this tomorrow.

Much of what you will find in the page analysis is pretty direct and simply to figure out. This is mostly a simple guide to help you correct any elements which are not ideal for SEO. Of the greatest importance here, however, is what you will see to the right of this.

Beside the "Update/Publish" button, you will see...

If the dot beside "SEO:" is green, your post or page is good, regardless of what appears in the Page Analysis tab. This is because if you have enough elements in place to have an optimized page, you will have no difficulties ranking with the search engines. However, if there is stiff competition for the keywords you have chosen, you will want to get the post or page as good as possible. Just don't get too hung up on perfecting the page.

The next tab is "Advanced." No need to get too involved here for now, though as you learn more, you can really use this to good effect. For now, all you need to be aware of is the following...

If you have a page that you don't want to appear in the search engine results, choose to have the search engines do a "Nofollow." By default, all pages are followed by the search engines, but sometimes, such as with a page which simply does not need a great deal of content (like you Contact page, which we will discuss on Day 22), you may choose to have the search engines ignore that page. Thus, this page will not appear in any search results and you will not be penalized for not having enough content on the page. You would also use this for hidden (private) pages (such as a Thank You for Subscribing page – discussed in a future Month), or for members only (password protected) pages. The choice is yours. Leave it alone and any page you create can appear in search results.

Finally, the "Social" tab simply allows you to alter the Meta Description for either Facebook or Google+ sharing. This is an element of Publicizing which is reserved for next month, but for now, you only need to know it is here. If you do nothing with this page, whatever description you entered in the General tab is what will appear when sharing this post/page to these social media groups.

That is all for today. Tomorrow, I will discuss Keyword Density and proper use and selection of keywords for posts and pages. We have touched on this throughout this book, but to advance we need to make sure you understand some of the finer aspects of this feature of building a website. See you tomorrow.

Day 17: Good Keyword Use/Density

Keywords are how the search engines find content. The content of a website can be articles, blogs, sales descriptions, contact information, legal matters, Q & A's, FAQ's, or whatever information is put onto a website in written form. Even the images and videos must have words if they are to get the attention of the search engines, because the search engines cannot see—they can only read. Hence, keywords, or keyword phrases, are vital to getting information noticed by these algorithms.

Must has been studied and written about keywords in the decade and a half since Google first launched. All SEO experts know that Google and the other search engines use keywords to locate content, and all know that Google has the best algorithm for returning accurate results. But Google does not say if there is a specific density, or quantity of use for keywords.

Still, most who have researched and studied this element of getting pages/websites found have determined that a good density of keywords on a page seems to fall somewhere between 1 and 3%. In other words, if you were to take all the words on a page, then the keywords used, and divide the total by the times the keyword is used, you would get ideally, between 1% and 3% keyword density. Here is the formula…

Number of keywords on page / total words on page = Keyword density

Also understood is that the keywords used must accurately reflect the subject of the page so that the search engines do not become confused. If the search engine cannot determine the subject, it will reject the page. Too many rejections and the site will be rejected. Hence, it is important to use keywords.

But here is a funny caveat.

The search engines do not entirely rely on the keywords you use to determine whether to send someone to your page/site or not. Sometimes people enter such obscure search terms that your page, even if not directly about something as revealed in your keywords, will be provided as a result. This is because the search engines today look for more than only the keywords you have chosen. In fact, Google no longer uses the Meta Tags for keywords—their algorithm records all important subject and descriptive words and catalogs these. So when someone searches for something you may only touch on briefly, perhaps as an example, the page may result if it matches the search terms used.

To illustrate: Recall how in the last chapter I used "Weird Pizza Recipes" as an example for explaining how to optimize your post. The subject of the chapter was SEO and if it was a page on my website that would be a likely keyword. The chapter was in no way about weird pizza recipes. But if someone were to search for something like "Pizza recipes in SEO," it is possible that this article would appear in the search results (if it was a web page). The reason is because the web crawlers which record and document the locations of all descriptive and subject words, will connect the two completely different subjects and return the results that someone was seeking.

Back to density of keywords.

Now, for those using WordPress and the SEO plugin I recommended, you need only refer to the Page Analysis tab of the Yoast Plugin to determine if you are using a good keyword density.

For anyone not using this, no worries. There is a tool on the web that can be used to determine whatever keyword density you believe is best. Go to http://live-keyword-analysis.com. For copyright reasons I cannot show an image of the screen but it is very simple to use. All you need to do is write in a word processor, then copy and paste the content into the space provided, type the keywords you want to check, and in live-time, the tool will tell you precisely what the keyword density is for each keyword. Now, a drawback of this is that only single words can be entered so but if used right, this is a very useful tool.

If it seems like I am giving you a bit of a break today, rest assured I am not.

Today, I want you to write another post. This time, I want you to choose the keywords before you write. You are going to enter these keywords into the "Focus Keyword," space of the General Tab on Yoast, then start writing. But there is one more thing to do first.

Remember the Google Keyword Tool? Go there now.

Think of a subject related to your website and enter two to four keywords to describe what you are considering writing. See what results you get.

If you are satisfied with the results, namely, that the keyword string has either low or medium competition along enough monthly searches to satisfy you, then write about this set of keywords. If not, then check the suggested keywords provided by Google. The same process you used to decide on a name for your site, you can use to decide what to write about. Remember, a page (or post) is a part of a site and can have different keywords from the site. Still, it would be good if you can incorporate your website name /keywords into all pages and posts, but if not, you need not worry too much. The search engines are going to find your material anyway if you write according to a clear topic (keywords).

The only difference not putting your site keywords into an article makes is that the site overall will lost some SEO juice. Still, if the material is related to your overall theme and is useful to your readers, use it.

So spend some time deciding what to write about. Make notes. In fact, go on an make a list of keyword combinations you will want to use for your website/articles and you need only do this research every week or so.

Once you have the keywords you are going to use, write your post. To get started, I am going to show you one more way to begin. Go to your homepage. If you are in the admin screen of the homepage, you will see a

gray bar running horizontal across the top.

See where it reads, "New?" Place your cursor over that and a dropdown menu will appear. From this menu, you have the choice of a Post, Page, Media, or User. Choose Post or Page and you will be brought to the edit screen. Because you are now going to write another blog, select Post.

You are ready to write your next post. Once you have done so (or during, if you feel confident enough), check your writing for style and SEO elements. Once optimized and ready to publish, click Publish. Tomorrow, we are going to build your Home Page and discuss the elements that you will need to have a credible website.

Day 18: Creating Pages

By now you know the difference between posts and pages. You have written a couple of posts and may even be getting some traffic from them already. If not, don't worry too much, you will.

One very important page is your Home page. This is the page that will typically get the most traffic. This is in part because this is the most prominently displayed link people will come across (as this is simply your domain name) and in part because people tend to check out the home page after landing elsewhere IF they like your site. So this is the page which gets the greatest traffic in most cases. There are surely websites where this is not the case, but these are likely such well-known, established websites, that people have no need to go to the home page. Some of these which come to mind are Craigslist and Wikipedia.

But for most of us, the home page is the most important page, so we need to make it a good one.

Another term you will often hear is Landing Page and while in many cases the Home and Landing Pages may be the same, this is not necessarily the case. In fact, use of the term "Landing Page" is fairly misleading, because in reality, all pages on your website are potential "landing" pages unless you protect the entire site with a membership. This is because for most websites, visitors can enter via any page on the site (or any which is public). So most of us need to be sure that every page is just as good as the Home page and/or the Landing Page.

Of course, to be clear, a Landing Page in the strictest sense is a copy directed page which is used for the purpose of extending advertising in such a way as to increase conversions of a product or service. Specifically, a Landing Page will usually be entered via a link in Social Media or invitation and the visitor often has some indication prior to "landing" there, what is in store. The goal of this page is to get people to buy.

That said, some still use the term "landing page" so loosely that you will sometimes hear the home page referred to as such. If you are planning on having a landing page for selling something, we will discuss that next Month. For now, I want to be clear about what is important and how you should build your most important page, you Home page.

To be clear, pages are different from blogs in the sense that working with pages is finite to some extent. In most cases, website owners will decide on a basic structure of their website and the main pages will be static for the most part. To understand this better, think of a website as you would a newspaper.

When you pick up a newspaper, the first thing you notice is that it is divided into sections: A, B, C, and so on. Each Section is generally a specific form of pages. A is often General and World News. B is often Local News. C is often Sports. D is often Classified Ads. You get the idea. If you pick up the paper every week, you will notice that these sections remain the same typically (I did know of one Newspaper owner who liked to change it up, but he had a VERY small newspaper and understandably, never grew. This is because humans are creatures of habit...we like some degree of routine in our lives and newspapers fit nicely into this routine.)

Thus, a website should have certain "static," or set sections. Of course, the information within these sections will grow over time as more pages are added, but the basic structure should remain the same unless it needs to be changed for some very important reason.

Part of the reason you should not change the structure is because people will be linking to you. When you alter a page location, you lose the links to any pages nestled within because the links don't know to change. Think if this like a trip to Wal-Mart. At one time, Wal-Mart had the habit of constantly moving the location of products on their shelves. So last week you went to Wal-Mart and bought a certain item. You return this week to get another, but it has been moved and the department clerk has no clue to where it was moved. Unless you REALLY needed that item, chances are you just decided to get it elsewhere or not at all. Links are like that. If lost, people will just go to some other site unless they really want to visit yours. Blow your links and you blow tons of potential traffic. Do this enough and you blow your site.

So you want to determine a basic structure and leave your site as such. You can always add categories of pages, just as you could build an addition to a store, but if you move things around too much, you will turn off visitors.

So, what is the best way to determine structure for pages and why are we discussing this here?

A Home page often acts as a sort of Index. When people visit a home page, they often want it to be clear about where they should go to find what they want. Think of a Home Page as a Store Greeter or an Information Desk. On entering a business for the first time, it's nice to be greeted by someone asking how they can direct you. You say, "I want to find a tennis racquet," and they direct you to "sporting goods." Or you say, "I'm here to get an x-ray" and they send you to the second floor. You get the idea.

But to know what to put on your home page for directing visitors, you must know what sections to direct them to and where these are going to be located. So let's break down your site into sections.

To divide your website into sections, you must first know what your goal is and what you can offer to readers. Of course, certain pages are must-haves. These are: Legal Pages, Sitemap, Privacy Policy, About, Contact, and Home.

In addition, you may want to divide your site such that anyone entering in any location can quickly locate what will be useful to them. For instance, if you have are building an eCommerce website, you will want to have pages for prospective clients, affiliates, and partners. If you are selling a particular type of product or service, you may want to break that into sections under a single main page called "Our Products." If your site is all about teaching something, you may want to divide the content according to subject. But as a general rule, less is more. In other words, try not to clutter your navigation tools too much, but strive to be clear.

One of the best methods I have ever heard for determining the layout of a website is to get a stack of index cards (or sticky notes) and write on each card a page you would like to have on your website. Then stick these on a wall and try to categorize them all under as few categories as possible. For instance, if you take a look at http://criminaljusticelaw.us, you will see that I have

| Home | About | Issues | Corrections | Crime | Philosophy | Enforcement | Law | Free Books |

CRIMINAL JUSTICE LAW
EXPLORING ISSUES, DEVELOPING SOLUTIONS

broken the information there as...

This is a "non-commercial" site in the sense that I do not sell anything here. This site is for entertainment and educational purposes only, so I only include information in this navigational bar which pertains to what my readers will find useful. As this is still a new (and experimental site) you will notice that this site does not have a legal info, privacy policy, contact, nor sitemap page. As I am not currently collecting email information, a Privacy Policy is really unnecessary at this point and since I am not selling anything a legal (terms and conditions) would be silly. Still, these pages will be needed for future ranking and when I add them, these will be in the footer and only for SEO purposes. Likewise with the sitemap, which is often looked for when someone wants it (and usually looked for in the footer—more on this later). But you can see from this example how I have broken this site up so that readers can quickly navigate to the type of Criminal Justice information they may be seeking. If you place your cursor over any of these navigational tools, you will see a dropdown menu of article choices (pages) embedded within.

Now take a look at http://collapseconsultants.com.

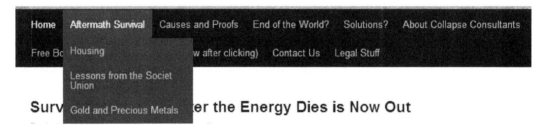

Notice that I have placed my cursor over the navigation for "Aftermath Survival" and a dropdown menu has appeared. Notice too that the segments for this site are such that if someone is new to the idea that the dollar can collapse, they can go to "Causes and Proofs" to learn more. If someone already believes the dollar is going to collapse, they may want to check out "Aftermath Survival." And for the skeptics, there is a section for "End of the World?" Also, I provide a section related to possible "solutions" for anyone who wants to believe such a possibility can be averted. And naturally, I have the "Legal Stuff" which contains my Terms and Conditions and Privacy Policy. There are a couple of other sections, but these are the basics.

Are you starting to get an idea about how to section up your website?

Good, let's continue by discussing what kind of elements you will want to include on your home page. The following items are pretty much musts for your home page if you want to provide either the best experience possible for visitors or convert as many as possible into customers. Thus, regardless of whether you have a commercial website or not, these elements will only make your website home page better. We'll consider each, then you will be ready to start your home page. I say start, because we are not going to complete the home page until the last day of this month. Before we can put the finishing touches on your home page, we need to add some additional pages.

Must-haves for the Home Page

Here are the must-haves for your home page...

- **Headline** – You have already added your headline earlier when working in the Themes section of your WP site. See how WP really simplifies things?

- **Tagline** – A tagline is sort of a secondary headline that further clarifies what visitors to your site can expect. You did this as well earlier, but you may have a clearer vision of what you are planning with this website, so if you want to change it, simply go to your website in admin mode, place your cursor over your site name at the top left of the gray bar, and from the dropdown menu, choose "customize." This will open a menu that allows you to alter this Tagline.

- **Benefits** – You want visitors to your website to discover quickly just why your site has value. Just as you may walk into a department store or restaurant, look around briefly, then decide whether to remain or not, you need to provide some clues and stated benefits of visiting your website. It you cannot think of why people should come here, they certainly will be clueless. The way you do this is by telling them why your site is either different or what they can expect. One good way is by using bullet points. Simply welcome visitors and tell them that they can expect (three to five good bullet points are fine).

- **Action above the fold** – If you are running an ecommerce site of any sort, you should have action buttons. You've seen these. There will be some sort of offer that virtually anyone coming to that particular site will like along with a "Register Now" in a large orange or red button or the words "no thanks" usually small beside it. Place this "above the fold" which is a newspaper term which means literally, above the fold of the paper—the part you see first before you flip it over. You can even use this technique to gather emails for your newsletter campaign, though I prefer a slightly different approach as I have touched on earlier and shall teach in another book.

- **Features** – You are going to want to perhaps guide your visitors to some of the more popular areas of the site. This can be done by adding images with captions to take them to specific pages, written commentary with links, video, or guidance boxes (a box with brief info and thumbnail with a "read more" button or link).

- **Credibility features** – If you are a member of the BBB, Chamber of Commerce, have received special awards or recognition, whatever, put it on your home page. Blow your own horn, though gently, here. There is nothing wrong with this and everything right. Consider, if you walk into a store and there is a sign in front of the cash register that reads BBB, would you consider that business more or less credible? Certainly more, but they were blowing their own horn, were they not? Yes, but gently. Do the same on your home page. Let people know about anything that shows you are credible. I had two such elements on my site http://jeffoakes.me. My phone number was prominent and yes, this adds credibility, so if your business website is promoting a land-based business, be sure it is easy to find. The other is my certification from oDesk as shown below...(I have since shut down this site and will be revamping it with a new domain name.)

- **Navigational elements** – Next, you want to be sure that the navigational elements are easy to find. If people cannot figure out how to navigate your site, they will leave. Think of it like going to a store and on entering, you cannot figure out how to find what you need. You likely will not stay long, especially if there is a similar store close by. Competing websites are even closer—just a click away. Help people find their way around and they will stay. We've already discussed this in depth earlier so let's move on.

- **Supporting media** – Images are great. Video is even better. People like media, perhaps more than words...or maybe equally so. Hard to say and much depends on the visitor. But one thing is certain, if you can add images and especially video to your home page, your visitors will likely stay longer and visit more—especially if the video changes or has channels.

- **An offer** – People love an incentive. Give them a reason to like you by giving them something they can use and they will come back. On Oakes Writing Consultants, I used to offer anyone a Free Web Analysis. Once you have built your website, contact me and I will do the same for you. The free web analysis will let you know what elements are in place, which need to be added, how optimized your site is, and provide you with a roadmap to growing your traffic.

- **Resources** – If you know of other resources that will be helpful or useful to your visitors, provide an easy way to show them. One old method was to create a links page, but today, these are less used. Instead, create a "useful resources" or "recommendations" page or section on your home page. It is the same thing, but with a more tailored feel. Of course, in doing so, you are fairly sending your visitors away from your site, so you may think this counter-productive. Not so, if done right. If you provide an in-depth resource, people will index or bookmark your site and return because you are providing a valuable service. At times, they will stay and view other pages on your site and even buy from you at some point.

- **Action below the fold/last** – Just as you put an action button or choice above the fold, if you are an ecommerce site, you should add the same below the fold, especially near the bottom of the page. This will give visitors one last chance to take the action you desire before moving on to either another page or another site.

- **Testimonials** – You have gently blown your own horn, now let a few of your best clients blow the horn for you. Some quotes, along with photos or videos is never a bad idea. Just don't overdo it. One or two will suffice. Too many and people will think you are trying too hard—which you are. Remember, less really is more in many things and this is one of them. If you have a lot of really good testimonials, create a separate Testimonials Page and label is such. That way, if anyone does want to go through more than a couple, they can.

Finally, just to be clear. Pages on you website are longer and more informative than posts. Also, pages tend to be more static, unchanging than blogs. Blogs are good for keeping your visitors informed of the latest changes, updates to services, information, or products, general information, press releases, and anything else that need not be considered core to the business, but is good for promotional use. Think of pages as you would books in a library, but blog posts are more like magazines and you will be able to decide whether something on your site should be a page or a post.

So now you need to get started on your homepage. If you are still using the Twenty Ten theme in WP (and you should, I told you we were going to work on the "same" page), go to your site now.

I want to show you one more thing about themes in WordPress. Open a second tab with your website.

In some cases, you can edit the home page from the gray bar along the top by using the "Edit" button. In some cases, you must edit the home page by accessing the template itself through the dropdown menu when you place your cursor over the site name on the gray bar. And in other cases, you cannot edit your home page at all IF you set it up the way I told you earlier. In one of the tabs, go to Themes and when these appear, choose the "Customize" Feature. On the menu that appears to the left, click on "Static Front Page." I am now going to show you the difference between the two types of pages.

Look at the home page in the first tab. If your page is set like we agreed earlier, your home page will show the two posts that you wrote previously. Now in the second tab, change the home page to "static" and you will see two more options open. The first will read "Front page" and the second will read "Posts page." Under "Front Page" (by clicking the dropdown feature) there may be an option for "About" which was pre-populated. This is because you have yet to create a dedicated Home page. For now, set this back to "Your Latest Posts" and we are going to create your Home page. On the last day, you will have several pages populated and we are going to put this all together. I simply wanted you to note the difference for now for most of the themes in WP operate with this feature. The exceptions are those themes which come with pre-loaded templates and for these, you will need to enter theme options to modify the page.

Your home page

From either your dashboard or from the gray bar along the top, add a page. For the title put "Home."

After this, you are going to write this page as an introduction to your website. Don't tell about yourself or why you started this site, for that can wait until you write your about page. For now, just write about what visitors can expect on arrival here. Tell about the purpose of the website, explain any pages you have planned as if these already exist, and tell your readers how they will benefit from visiting often. If you have plans to give them something by way of a special, if you have awards and honors to show or testimonials from former clients or whatever, present them as well. Also, be sure to tell them about any other websites or resources which will be helpful to them (but don't send them to your competition if you are going to have an eCommerce site. For instance, if you are an A/C repairman, you may recommend Trane A/C units, but not the local Trane repair company, unless that is you.). Finally, be sure to separate each of these subjects by headings and present the material in as logical a way possible, ideally with a view to how your visitors may perceive the information.

At this point, don't concern yourself with getting fancy, though adding images from Zemanta would be good. A couple should suffice. Also, optimize the page. Your keywords here will be "Yourwebsite Home page" or "Home page of Yourwebsite."

After you have finished writing your BASIC homepage, look at the right side of the edit screen. There are a couple more things to show you now. Look at the following image...

Just below the "Publish" button you will see "page Attributes." Here you can choose tiers for your pages (Parent), the templates to be used, and the order in which you want the pages to appear across your navigation bar.

First, notice the "Template" function. In this particular theme, there are only two choices but some have many. The best way to decide which you want is to simply change it, see how it looks, and if you don't like it, change it again. In this Theme, the choices are "Default" which provides a single sidebar to the right of the main text body or "One column, no sidebar," which will provide a full page with no sidebar. For your home page, it is usually best to go with the second option, the full page.

Below this you will see a "0" and obscured by the dropdown menu in the illustration is the word "Order." Simply put, this is the numerical order you want the pages to appear across your navigation bar. In the following illustration, the "Home" page is "0," the "Aftermath Survival" page is "1," "Causes and Proofs – 3" and so on. That is all there is to it.

Next, consider the Parent section. There will be "no parent" at this point and your home page will not have one anyway, but as you add pages, if you want to add subpages (as you saw in the earlier example from Collapse Consultants), you can add tiers of pages simply by choosing the parent page you want this, the new page, to appear under. I will show you what this looks like once you have these pages in place. Remember this example provided earlier?

This is how it looks in the Parent edit choice screen...

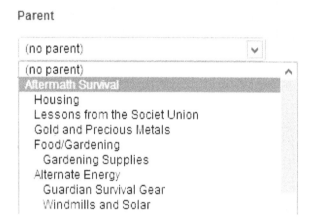

When I wrote the "Housing" Page, I simply opened this menu then selected "Aftermath Survival" from the choices. This placed it as a subpage within the main page as shown previously.

After you have finished with your settings, Publish, and tomorrow we will create your About Page.

Day 19: About Page

Your About page is the second most important page on your website. This is a page to inform your readers about WHY they should visit by letting them know what you provide and who you are. But be sure not to make it some bland list of you or some rambling bio on your life.

As pages go, the About page is typically the second-most visited page on a website. This is because people want to know who they are dealing with and why they should bother. What makes YOU so special that they should spend their valuable time with YOU?

Let visitors know what you look like.

As for what you should include, be sure to put a photo of yourself on the About page if that is important. If you have a traditional brick-and-mortar business, put images of your business there and anyone important to your clients. For instance, if most of your clients come to your business because of your parts department, post images of the parts people here along with very brief bios and how they can help.

If you run a family business, a good photo of you and the family is a nice touch. Just don't go overboard. Remember, that the About page is really more about your visitors, namely, what they will get from coming you your site.

Some things to remember when writing this page are...

Let the readers know why you care.

Be sure to convey your own passion for your subject. You had a reason for setting up this site and that reason should become clear once they read about you. Of course, if you are building this website just to make money, you may not want to say that...though you could. Honesty never hurts. On WallysWeirdStuff.com, I openly state that the site is there to help people find (and naturally buy) weird stuff. But Wally is a character, developed to bring a sense of different to the site. We are building an entire life for this guy and from that life, we are attempting to make searching for and buying weird stuff fun. Time will tell if you succeed in this goal.

If your website is there to support your traditional brick-and-mortar business, teach your readers about what you do through the website and tell them that is what the site is about. For instance, if you run a body shop, you may plan to provide tips on repairs, touching up scratches, windshield repair, or any other aspect of your business. Naturally, most of your readers will not attempt to do repairs at home, but you will grow your name as an expert. Clearly, you have a passion for body work or you wouldn't have gone into that field. Share that passion on your About page.

If you can create a video for your about page, put it there (I will teach you about this on Day 26).

Don't forget to include your name.

You'd be surprised how many people have websites and don't tell people their name. On the About page, you should include your name. This does a couple of things.

First, a name establishes instant credibility. It tells people that the website was built by a real person, not a computer, not a corporation. Facebook has Mark Zuckerberg. Google has Larry Page and Sergey Brin. Apple had Steve Jobs. You ARE your business and your business IS you. Your About page should tell people who you are and why you are important in their life.

Get Visitors active on your site

Just as you engage the readers immediately on your Home page, you should use the About page to get them visiting other pages on your website. Be sure to include natural conversation about what they will find and include links so they can find it. On Day 24, I am going to teach you how to include links on your pages/posts.

Of course, after you have written your About page today, there will not be much to include in the way of links other than the first two blog posts you wrote...include them (I will show you how in a moment). Later, as your website grows in content, you will want to update your About page so that it reflects any changes and additions. Just as you will add to your Home page over time, you are going to be adding, changing, and tweaking your About page through time. These two pages should be the most edited and altered pages on your website.

Open a new page and once on the Edit screen, you are going to type simply "About" in the title line. Below, when you do the SEO part of the work, you will alter the SEO title to read "About (your website) and add "about (what you do briefly) about (why) about (whatever else you think should be there until you reach the 70 character limit). The goal in writing an SEO title is to put in words which people will likely search and use all of the characters permitted if possible.

Get writing and once finished, return here for some additional instructions. Remember to write at least 500 words (300 for a blog post, 500 for a page).

Back so soon? Good Job.

Remember the Zemanta feature found at the right of your edit screen?

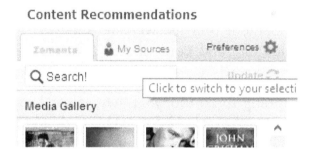

By default, the screen will show the first tab at the top labeled, "Zemanta." Click on the tab just to the right of this and it will bring up "My Sources." This will populate a list of your content. As You have added no image content to this feature, there will be none to show but below this, you should see the two blogs your wrote earlier.

Now notice at the very bottom right corner of what you have written, you will see the word "Zemanta" in orange. Place your cursor just beside this and then click on one of the two blogs you wrote as shown in the list. Note, however, if these do not appear this is because there were not enough subject or keywords written in common with this page. Generally, however, you should have them appear because when starting out, we all tend to write very similar information. When you click on this blog, it will appear at the bottom of your About page in the edit screen and after you have published, it will appear at the bottom of the page. Add both.

To see an example of my About page, go to http://criminaljusticelaw.us

One of the first things you will notice is that when you land on my Home page, you are also on my About page. I did this because I determined that in this case, to create both at this point in time would be extraneous. So I blended the two. Some websites today don't even call their About page that. Instead, they simply tell about the site and what visitors can expect on the Home page, while providing useful navigation tips and such. In this way, the two pages have been merged.

Just keep that in mind. With the changes continually taking place within the Google algorithm, the old "rules" are being modified daily. The rules of writing remain the same at this point it seems, but the company appears to be doing away with some of the "required" pages.

As I have already stated in this book, some of the former required pages MAY no longer be necessary, but to be safe, it doesn't hurt to include them. In the end, the only "wrong" is in not getting traffic to your website. And the reality is that traffic comes from a variety of sources, but in the end, content is the key. Add good content to your website and you will get traffic. This book teaches the basics of good content and a future month will go into greater detail for those who really want to get volumes of traffic.

That's all we're going to do today. Later, when I teach you how to add links, you should return to your About page and add any links you think are necessary. See you tomorrow and we'll work on your Contact page.

Day 20: Contact Page

Your contact page is one of the most important pages on your WP website if you plan on using this site as a marketing tool for a primary business or are selling something online. Of course, if you are only providing a website which is designed to teach or entertain, you may decide to limit the information on this page to an email, but whatever your goals with the site, you need this page.

The contact page does more than simply provide a way for visitors to contact you.

The contact page identifies your website as credible and worthy of visiting. Both to the search engines, which look for this page when deciding credibility, and to visitors, this page tells them that you are real and you are serious (even about having fun as the case may be).

So be sure to have a contact page. What do you include?

If you are only offering an entertaining website, you can simply include an email address. If you chose to build through BlueHost or HostMonster as I recommend, you can go into your BlueHost Control Panel and you will find a dedicated page for setting up as many email accounts as you like. You will see it easily along the top blue navigation bar. Click on email and follow their simple instructions.

(NOTE: In the Appendix I provide a more extensive list of hosts in case you want to shop around a bit.)

You will set up your email by choosing a name, which will be attached to @yourwebsite.com. Most people, especially if this is a business website, will choose either their first initial and last name or first and last name. For instance, my email for criminaljusticelaw.us is cjeffoakes@criminaljusticelaw.us. Creative, huh? Of course, the email address for the website accompanying this book is cjeffoakes@365crazywebtraffic.com. Again, you can see my incredible creativity in setting these up.

Your contact email doesn't need to be creative unless the website is something unusual and you want to convey some unique image. Keep it simple and you will be fine.

Once you have this, you can create a Contact page just as you would any other. Choose the location for this page, put your new email into it (or you could even use the gmail you set up or any other you desire—there is no wrong way of doing this), then publish.

Now, if you don't want your contact page to appear on the main navigation bar along the top, but prefer it either in a side navigation or the footer, simply make it a Private page and add it later.

If you are planning on using this website as a support (marketing arm) site for an existing business, be sure to include any other information that clients will use when doing business with you. If you generally advertise your phone number, fax, or any other information, be sure to include it here (you will also want this information in your header and footer—we will discuss doing this on Day 27). If your address is important, include it. You want to make it as easy for your clients to do business with you as possible.

Many local businesses also like to use this space to include contact information for key officers, sales personnel, parts departments, service, or any other departments in their business whereby clients may want to contact someone directly. One of the nicest things about a website is that you can include information at a much lower cost, in a more visually appealing, and extensive manner than can be done with virtually any other advertising medium.

So don't be afraid to include images of sales reps, photos of your shop, or a video from your CEO. In other words, not only do you want to make it easy for clients to find you, but you also want to encourage them to do so. This is especially important if they are prospective new clients.

I have seen many websites which do not provide these elements (which are free), yet will spend hundreds of dollars on full-page ads in the Yellow Pages. I am not knocking the Yellow Pages, but why not do the same thing here when the cost is so much lower?

Remember, if your website is a marketing tool of your business, make it so. Market your business to your clients.

In addition, you can even use this page as a means of collecting emails. If someone wants to contact you, why not have them provide certain information up front?

On the standard WP Edit screen kitchen sink, there is a simple form builder and you could use this. However, if you check plugins, you will find some really great form builders that will collect the email from comments, forward the email to your main email box, and at the same time add the email to your email list.

In the previous image, you can see how I have built a simple contact page. I then clicked on "Add Contact Form" above the kitchen sink and a window appeared. I chose some simple parameters and the program added the two last lines you see above (which start with "[contact-form][contact-field]". If you go to http://criminaljusticelaw.us/contact-2/ you can see the final result and leave a message if you'd like.

One final word on this.

Remember the word count and keywords even when setting up/writing this page. For this page, your keywords should relate directly to your business, perhaps even be the same as your business name. Another prominent keyword to use is "contact," many forget this, but you should include the word "contact." At least a few times. For instance, perhaps you have a local business. Add "Contact Information" or "Contact" to every individual and phone number listed. For example, if you have a Parts Department, put "Contact ABC Company Parts Department" and the number. Then, for sales, "Contact John Jones – ABC Company at" and "Contact Sue Smith ABC Company" and "Contact ABC Company Service Department at…" You get the idea. Just use Contact and the name of your company and even including the exact location frequently is a good idea as well. This will help the search engines zero in on your business, especially your CONTACT page

If your word count falls below the 500 word threshold, you can simply have the search engines ignore the page as follows. However, it would be much better to get the word count up there by telling about various persons in the company and how to reach them. After all, if the search engines cannot find your contact page and someone is searching for contact information about services you provide, you may not appear.

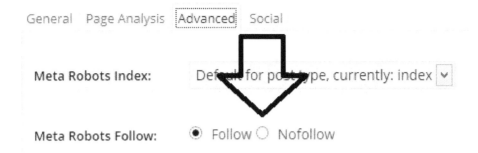

General   Page Analysis   Advanced   Social

Meta Robots Index: Default for post type, currently: index ⌄

Meta Robots Follow: ⦿ Follow ○ Nofollow

On the Yoast SEO options, choose the "Advanced" tab. The "Meta Robots Follow" option will by default choose to "Follow" this page/post. By selecting the "Nofollow" option, you can shut this off and prevent the search engines from including this page in the search results. Below this are some additional choices, but we will save these for a later book. All you need for now is to either let the search engines find this page (ideal) or not.

As previously said, it would be far better to add more content to the page and be found, especially if this is a marketing arm of your business.

The way to do this is to add bios of persons your clients may encounter when doing business with you, information related to parts and service, such as hours of operation, locations, services offered, brand partners, or any other relevant information which will make it easier for prospective customers to decide to do business with you. You can even put a couple of testimonials on this page (one at the top, one at the bottom), any awards you hold, business memberships—anything to get the word count up and encourage others to do business with you.

In addition to the contact page, you are going to need legal pages if your site is to be viewed as credible by the search engines and visitors. These will be discussed tomorrow.

Day 21: Additional Pages

Legal pages are those pages which you must have on your website to be both credible in the eyes of the search engines and your visitors. Think of these pages like you would the small legal notifications you see when entering a traditional brick and mortal business. In front of the checkout, there will be a notice of fees for returned (NSF) checks. You may see a notice informing you of cameras in place. Or there could be a sign posted at the front door, "No shirt, no shoes, no service." These are all examples of legal notifications. Another is often placed by the checkout in the form of a small leaflet covering in detail the return policies if you are using a credit card.

A website is no different and when Larry Page and Sergey Brin created the algorithm that became the Google search engine, they included a search for certain legal pages within their code. The crawlers would look for these pages as identifying marks of a credible website and if a site did not have these, the site would be excluded from natural search results…at least on the first several pages anyway.

The algorithm was changed often since the beginning and most notably in 2011, 2012 with the Panda and Penguin updates, but there is no indication that these credibility elements were eliminated. About the only real change as far as these elements were concerned is that they no longer carried the degree of weight they once did. In other words, a website without these would no longer be excluded from results, only penalized. Thus, if a website has great content and does everything else right, but does not have these legal pages, it could still get reasonably good traffic from the search engines.

That said, it is your choice whether to include these or not, but why omit something that is so easy to include?

"Easy?" you ask? "I'm not a lawyer," you retort.

Easy.

To include these pages does not require being an attorney and writing with complicated legalese. Indeed, for most websites, including this information can be as simple as you wish. The average website, especially if it is a blog site, will not be engaging in the kind of practices that get websites into trouble. Hence, although these policy pages are necessary for helping your SEO, they are not really needed by your visitors—few will ever read them anyway, facing facts.

Another concern may be that these pages will consume some of your navigation bar and indeed, who wants several pages which never/seldom get read to clutter up the main navigation? No one. So here is what you do. You can either create tiers of pages or include links to these legal pages in your footer.

Tiers of pages

One of the easiest ways to avoid clutter on your navigation toolbar is to organize it. You have seen websites where when you place your cursor over a page heading in the main nav a series of additional pages popout therefrom. Here is an example from Oakes Writing Consultants which will show you what is meant (http://jeffoakes.me). although this site is shut down, I show it for a couple of reasons. First, it provides some key contact information. I really don't mind hearing from my readers, especially if you would like to hire me for writing or consulting. Of course, if I am unable to answer my phone, please leave a BRIEF message. I am VERY busy these days, but I will return your call as soon as I can.

The other reason I show this is because the tiers of pages on this site was very clean and easier to see in print than some of the other sites I currently run. I wanted you to see the point I make very clearly.

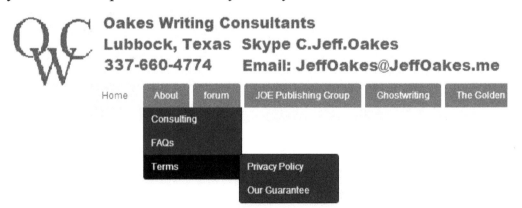

Notice that the "About" page has three tiers of pages beneath: Consulting, FAQ's, and Terms. The terms has further tiers, namely, the Privacy Policy and Guarantee page. In this way, this website provides the legal necessities without cluttering the main navigation toolbar. This is because in most cases, if a person wants to read the terms or privacy policy, they will look for them. Another reason is because really, the terms and Privacy Policy are so simple in the case of this website, they are not needed so much.

We will go into more detail about why shortly, but for now, you need to know how to create these tiers of pages. Doing so in WordPress is very simple. If you want to start a page titled "Terms and Conditions" now, feel free. Further in this chapter you will learn what to include, but for now, you can get the set-up in place.

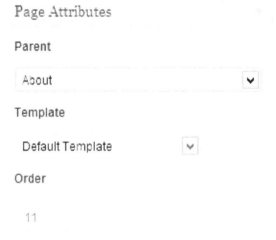

Go to "New Page" from your dashboard and type Terms and Conditions or simply, "Terms" into the title line. Then scroll down until you see "Page Attributes" on the right side of your screen.

Notice in the example that the Parent page reads "About." On yours, it should read "no parent." Using the dropdown menu (the tiny down arrow on the right), you should get a list of every page on your website to this point. To choose a parent page, simply click on the page you with to assign as parent (in this case, I choose the About page). Then you can decide which template to use for the page (which depends on the theme you chose as each theme has differing template choices). After this, you can choose the order in which the page will appear under the parent. Notice that in this example, the order is "11." Since there are only three pages under this parent, I could have numbered them 1, 2, and 3, but I was feeling rather ambitious the day I assigned the number and knew only that I wanted the terms page to appear last.

I did the same with the Privacy Policy and Guarantee pages. In the Page Attributes function, I simply choose the Terms page as the parent, then assigned the Privacy policy with a lower Order number than the Guarantee page, which placed them as you see in the earlier illustration. Simple.

Footer

Another way you could place the legal pages into your website is to put them in the footer area. Indeed, many websites today put these into the footer because they recognize the need for the pages, but that few of their visitors really care to read these pages. Of course, some site owners make these pages fun and flippant, to encourage people to actually read them, but the choice of how to write these generally boring, but necessary pages is entirely up to you.

On Day 25, you will learn more about how to actually create a Footer area and include various elements therein. For now, just know that this is an option. You can go ahead and create your legal pages and later place the link into your footer. Simply make the page "Private" for now and when you are ready to include it in the Footer region, just add a link to it.

Popup Window

Some websites use a popup window to inform you of T&C, Privacy, and related legal information. In the case of some of these, you must check a box to indicate that you have read them. Sites that use these are generally websites with large legal departments telling them that they better ensure that people are either reading the terms or that they at least claim to have read them.

This is because the website is likely offering something free, but taking something in return. Google is famous for this. Google gives so much, but what do they get? Simple. Your information. Information they have used to become one of the best advertising companies the world has ever seen.

The information that Google gets is not so much about you as it is your computer. Everyone who uses your computer after you have accepted Google's Terms and Conditions and Privacy Policy has their usage tracked. Google has very sophisticated programs that aggregate all this data and draws conclusions upon it. Then when someone places an ad with Google for something these programs have ascertained would be of interest to you, the system automatically puts these ads in various locations as you surf. Thus, you are provided with targeted advertising, which is proving to be the most effective ever designed. This is why you rarely see ads for stuff you have zero interest in. Genius.

But this collection of data could not be made possible without you agreeing to the terms of the use of the Google tools the site gives away. And before you decide you are going to stop using Google out of fear they are spying on you (which, in effect, they are, though with your permission), Yahoo, Bing, Ask, and all the others do the same. The only difference is that Google has mastered the concept.

Indeed, if you at some point grow your website to the point that you can do the same, such a popup window is advisable. And even if you don't get to that point and you simply want to cover your you-know-what better than with a static T/C page, then there are plugins you can get to create these pages and popups. Just go to your plugins search function and type in "Terms and conditions" or "privacy policy." The resulting list will include numerous free plugins which are simple to install and use. Many of these provide both generic and customizable templates along with various popup features.

So, what should you include in these legal pages?

Terms/Conditions

A Terms and Conditions page, or TOC for short, is generally used for two primary purposes.

1. A Disclaimer

2. Actual Conditions of Use for a site

Consider the first. Most TOC pages are simply nothing more than legal disclaimers such as "we are not responsible for the reliability of the information contained on this site." In other words, what sounds like the site owner does not stand behind his/her claims is in reality their way of saying that if you do something to bring about harm as a result if the information they are providing, they refuse to take responsibility. We are all familiar with such disclaimers—we see them on Carnival rides, drink containers, at the end of instructional videos.

Essentially, unless your website requires the second kind of TOC, yours will be some kind of disclaimer. To what extent you want to feign responsibility for what you write depends on you. I, for one, take full responsibility for what I write. I do my best to provide accurate information to my readers at all times, but naturally, should anyone misconstrue what I write, I cannot control that. To give you some idea about what you may want to include in a Terms & Conditions page, the following is taken from my own.

Oakes Writing Consultants Terms and Conditions of Use

1. Terms

By accessing this web site, you are agreeing to be bound by Oakes Writing Consultants of Lubbock, Texas Terms and Conditions of Use, all applicable laws and regulations, and agree that you are responsible for compliance with any applicable local laws. If you do not agree with any of these terms, you are prohibited from using or accessing this site. The materials contained in this web site are protected by applicable copyright and trade mark law.

2. Use License

1.   Permission is granted to temporarily download one copy of the materials (information or software) on Oakes Writing Consultants web site for personal, non-commercial transitory viewing only. This is the grant of a license, not a transfer of title, and under this license you may not:

1.   modify or copy the materials;

2.   use the materials for any commercial purpose, or for any public display (commercial or non-commercial);

3.   attempt to decompile or reverse engineer any software contained on Oakes Writing Consultant's web site;

4.   remove any copyright or other proprietary notations from the materials; or

5.   transfer the materials to another person or "mirror" the materials on any other server.

2.   This license shall automatically terminate if you violate any of these restrictions and may be terminated by Oakes Writing Consultants at any time. Upon terminating your viewing of these materials or upon the termination of

this license, you must destroy any downloaded materials in your possession whether in electronic or printed format.

3. Disclaimer

The materials on Oakes Writing Consultant's web site are provided "as is". Oakes Writing Consultants makes no warranties, expressed or implied, and hereby disclaims and negates all other warranties, including without limitation, implied warranties or conditions of merchantability, fitness for a particular purpose, or non-infringement of intellectual property or other violation of rights. Further, Oakes Writing Consultants does not warrant or make any representations concerning the accuracy, likely results, or reliability of the use of the materials on its Internet web site or otherwise relating to such materials or on any sites linked to this site. The only exception to this policy is in regard to content created for and purchased by customers of Oakes Writing Consultants; such materials are warranted completely as expressed in **Our Guarantee**.

4. Limitations

In no event shall Oakes Writing Consultants or its suppliers be liable for any damages (including, without limitation, damages for loss of data or profit, or due to business interruption,) arising out of the use or inability to use the materials on Oakes Writing Consultant's Internet site, even if Oakes Writing Consultants or a Oakes Writing Consultants authorized representative has been notified orally or in writing of the possibility of such damage. Because some jurisdictions do not allow limitations on implied warranties, or limitations of liability for consequential or incidental damages, these limitations may not apply to you.

5. Package Guidelines

With the writing packages we offer, although we provide the content, link-building, and social media interaction with your customers, we do need you to do your part. It is very important that every article is posted within 3 days of receipt by you, for regularity is important to developing traffic. In addition, during your initial consultation, we will discuss keywords to be used on your web site and select 3 primary and 7 secondary.

Before we can provide any packages, we will first ensure that your web site is optimized and seen as "credible" by the search engines. Without this foundation, we will not allow you to waste your money. However, should you opt for one of our packages, we will evaluate your site and provide you with what is needed to get it in shape for your content marketing campaign. For further information on this, see The Golden Triangle. Whereas we will provide the links, tags, titles, and descriptions for you to apply to the pages, it is your responsibility to implement these exactly as we provide.

6. Revisions and Errata

The materials appearing on Oakes Writing Consultant's web site could include technical, typographical, or photographic errors. Oakes Writing Consultants does not warrant that any of the materials on its web site are accurate, complete, or current although every effort will be made to ensure correct and current information. Oakes Writing Consultants may make changes to the materials contained on its web site at any time without notice. Oakes Writing Consultants will, however, make every effort to update the materials as new information becomes available.

7. Links

Oakes Writing Consultants has not reviewed all of the sites linked to its Internet web site and is not responsible for the contents of any such linked site. The inclusion of any link does not imply endorsement by Oakes Writing Consultants of the site. Use of any such linked web site is at the user's own risk.

8. Site Terms of Use Modifications

Oakes Writing Consultants may revise these terms of use for its web site at any time without notice. By using this web site you are agreeing to be bound by the then current version of these Terms and Conditions of Use.

9. Governing Law

Any claim relating to Oakes Writing Consultant's web site shall be governed by the laws of the State of Texas without regard to its conflict of law provisions.

As you can see, my Terms and Conditions page is nothing fancy and to tell the truth, I got it from a site that provides free T/C provided certain elements are altered. The site that provided it is no longer on the web, but another that does pretty much the same thing is called SeqLegal. Their links is http://www.seqlegal.com/free-legal-documents/website-terms-and-conditions. SeqLegal includes the following restriction.

"That express licence contains certain limitations. If you use this document, you must retain our   credit; and if you publish terms and conditions based on this document on a website, you must   link to this website. If you want to be free from these restrictions, you can buy a full licence."

That is pretty reasonable if you ask me. To use the terms and conditions provided by SeqLegal, they just want a link. Sounds like they are link-building and kudos to them. You will learn more about link-building tomorrow.

In addition, if you search the plugins on WordPress, you can also locate numerous Terms and Conditions plugins for various purposes.

For instance, the second purpose of a T/C is to ensure that anyone using your site or something you provide on the site are fully informed of the terms you impose on their use as well as the conditions under which the site or materials may be used. The restriction by SeqLegal is a very good example of such conditions.

Another is Google, Yahoo, and Bing. When you sign on to use these services, especially the email services, the terms page will popup and force you to acknowledge that you have read these. This is because there are certain restrictions with which you must comply or you can have your account suspended. In addition, the company is likely going to send cookies to your computer and for this, they must disclose to you that they are doing so.

In short, the T/C is nothing more than either a disclaimer or a disclosure…or both. You need a T/C page.

Privacy Policy

A privacy policy is nothing more than a page informing visitors to your website about how you will use (or not use) information gathered from them when they visit. This is another page whereby many websites such as Google and Yahoo go on to inform users that they will use cookies to track their Internet usage so that they can use that information for marketing purposes. And that is what they do.

The big websites that give you something free always use the cookies they send to your computer for some purpose, usually marketing. Sometimes it is simply for research related to their business and sometimes it is research so they can sell to you better. Regardless of the reason, the privacy policy is just a legal way to let you know what you can expect in the way of privacy (or lack thereof) when agreeing to their terms and conditions.

You need a privacy policy as this is one of the parameters used by Google to determine whether your website is credible or not. In the past, not having a T/C page or Privacy Policy would have meant that your website would not have ranked at all for search results. That fairly changed in 2011/12 when Google developed their Panda/Penguin updates and eliminated the Page Rank system.

That said, the need for these pages did not entirely disappear. Having them is still better than not and surely at some point in the future, the Page Rank system will return in some form. So have a page for your Privacy Policy.

Building one need not be difficult nor complicated. Following is the Privacy Policy from my website, jeffoakes.me.

Your privacy is very important to Oakes Writing Consultants of Lubbock, Texas. Accordingly, we have developed this Policy in order for you to understand how we collect, use, communicate and disclose and make use of personal information. The following outlines our privacy policy.

- Before or at the time of collecting personal information, we will identify the purposes for which information is being collected.

- We will collect and use of personal information solely with the objective of fulfilling those purposes specified by us and for other compatible purposes, unless we obtain the consent of the individual concerned or as required by law.

- We will only retain personal information as long as necessary for the fulfillment of those purposes.

- We will collect personal information by lawful and fair means and, where appropriate, with the knowledge or consent of the individual concerned.

- Personal data should be relevant to the purposes for which it is to be used, and, to the extent necessary for those purposes, should be accurate, complete, and up-to-date.

- We will protect personal information by reasonable security safeguards against loss or theft, as well as unauthorized access, disclosure, copying, use or modification.

- We will make readily available to customers information about our policies and practices relating to the management of personal information.

- We never sell your email or other personal information to 3rd parties.

At Oakes Writing Consultants, we are committed to conducting our business in accordance with these principles in order to ensure that the confidentiality of personal information is protected and maintained.

C. Jeff Oakes

Oakes Writing Consultants, Lubbock, Texas

The first thing you may notice about my Privacy Policy is that it is devoid of legalese. I did this for a reason. I do not have a complicated website nor do I collect cookies of visitors. The only information I collect comes from subscribers and only for the purpose of providing them with updates to my blogs and sending newsletters. Simple.

But if I were to build something more complex and wanted a Privacy Policy written in such a way as to cover all my bases, as it were, I would simply get a plugin. Once again, if you are not sure about writing a privacy policy, just get a plugin and follow the directions. Nothing to it.

Day 22: The Importance of Links

Aside from content, links are the most important elements of any website. Without links, there would be no Internet and without an Internet, there would be no websites. Thus, links are vital. Today, you are going to learn how to build links. More than this, you are going to learn how to build links properly.

There are 4 steps to building a link.

1. Determine the page to be linked
2. Copy the address of the page to be linked
3. Determine the text in which to embed the link
4. Embed the address into the text

Fortunately, WordPress makes building links very simple and along with some of the plugins you can add to your website, these can be made even simpler.

There are only three kinds of links. These are:

> ➢ Internal
>
> ➢ Outbound
>
> ➢ Inbound

Today, you are going to learn about each along with how to add them to your WordPress website and why. You are going to learn them in the above order, but understand that no single kind of link is more important than another, simply different. Indeed, each kind of link is important for reasons explained in a moment, but for the sake of the way the search engines view your website, you need to understand that there needs to be a balance of the three. Indeed, the search engines, Google especially, quantifies your website in part based on your use of links. So knowing how to add links, what kind, and where is important.

Internal Links

Internal links are simply links that connect pages across your own website. Your site navigation bar is a set of internal links because they help visitors move from whatever page they land at your website in to any other page they want to visit. These links are on your website to help visitors move around your website better.

Thus, you want to make finding appropriate links to other pages as convenient as possible. Having these links placed into your website does a couple of important things.

First, the search engines rate your website based on how many internal links you have. More than this, however, Google search engines are getting very good at seeing your links and judging how well visitors can move about within your site. If the search algorithms determine your site is easy to navigate, your ratings are higher.

One of the key parameters in the Google updates is how engaging your website is to visitors. The more engaged they are, the higher your site will rank and the better position your pages will rise in the natural search results. I don't have to tell you, but the higher your pages appear in natural search results, the more people will find you. Thus, you want to get your visitors moving around in your website and the best way to do this is will easy navigation tools, such as well-placed links.

Indeed, in a later book you will learn about such things as bounce rate and time on site. These are two parameters that the search algorithms rate and which either benefits your search results standing or harms it. No need to concern yourself with these things for now—just know that you need to make it easy for people to move around on your site and stay awhile.

So now let's look at some ways to make your website more engaging via internal links.

One of the best ways to get readers more engaged is to suggest additional articles at the end of one they have already read. Related to this is to add such suggestions throughout the body of an article. Do both. How do you do this?

First, let's discuss adding at the bottom of the page as this is far simpler than you can imagine.

Recall earlier when I had you put the Zemanta Editorial Assistant plugin into your website? I also had you add Related Posts by Zemanta. It is time to put these to work.

You've already used the Zemanta Editorial Assistant when putting some images into your website. Just below the images, you will see "Related Articles."

Notice that these are articles related to what you have written and some will be your own posts, but most will be from other websites. There are two ways to use this to gain advantage.

First, to insert any of these articles to your post/page, you simply need to click on it. Notice too that in the upper right corner, you have the option to either add it with a thumbnail image or as a link. This is useful if you want to include just some related articles in the middle of your current article, but you could add thumbnails—there is no right or wrong, just do what looks right. If after viewing the post live it does not look right to you, undo it. Simple.

In addition, you must understand that the links you now create by adding these into your site are internal if the articles are your own, but are outgoing if they lead someone to another website. In the segment on outgoing links, you will learn how this can be used to your advantage. For now, just understand that these are links, but are made very simple to add thanks to this plugin and these links are great for engaging readers.

However, the real juice rests in the Related Posts plugin. If you have not done so yet, go to your plugin library (from your dashboard, click on plugins>installed plugins). Scroll down until you locate the Related Posts by Zemanta and under it will be the Settings link (unless you have not activated the plugin, in which case, activate it, then go to settings).

There is really not much to the settings screen. You can choose how you want the thumbnails to appear, what size, and what style. The thing I want you to see is near the very bottom, so scroll down.

☑ Auto Insert Related Posts (or add `<?php zemanta_related_posts() ?>` to your single post template)
☑ Support us (show our logo)
☑ Display Related Posts in Feed

Save changes

Just above the "Save Changes" button, which you must click every time you make changes to the settings, you will see three check boxes. The most important one is the "Auto Insert," the top check box. If this is checked, the plugin will automatically select the most relevant posts written by you (on your site) and add them at the bottom. A little further up in the settings, you can control how many posts appear. If you don't want any to automatically appear (which would be counter-productive), uncheck the box. It should be checked automatically, but you want to be sure.

This simply adds thumbnails/links to posts at the bottom to encourage visitors to move around on your website. In the past, each link and thumbnail had to be added manually. In fact, you need to know how to do this so let's add some manual links now.

First, go to your edit screen of an article you want to add links to. It helps to open a couple of browser tabs with your website. Locate the article you want to link to. In the following example, I am editing an article called "Juvenile or Adult" in my Criminal Justice Law website. I want to link a sentence in this article to another article titled, "Criminal Justice Trends: Juveniles in Jail." To do this, I highlight the words to be linked (shown by the arrows) then click on the link button on the dashboard (4th icon from the top left in the example).

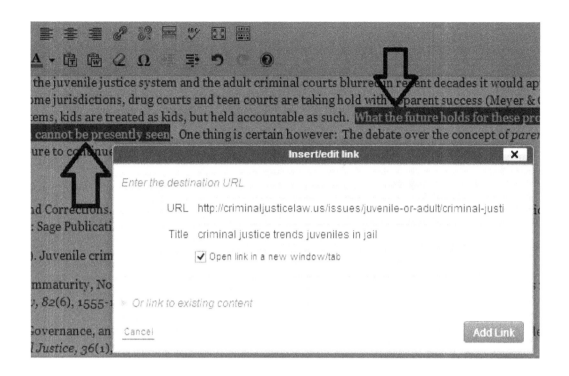

This will cause a box to open as shown. I opened the article to be linked in a separate browser tab and then copied the address; I then pasted the address into the URL line in this link edit box. Then I put in the title and clicked on "Open link in a new window/tab" so that if someone clicks this link, it opens another window. This is both a convenience to them so they can bounce between articles and a benefit to me because the longer both windows are open, the longer the time shown on my site in the eyes of the search engines.

Once I have completed these steps, I click on the blue button at the lower right corner of this box which reads, "Add Link." The box closes and the link is set.

Notice too that just above the link for "Cancel" at the lower left of this link edit screen is seen ">Or link to existing content." I could have just as easily looked up the article I wanted and just clicked on it. I can search using this feature or scroll through all my pages/posts. Once I locate the one I want, I click on it and the link and title are auto-populated.

So you can see from this, there are many ways to add links, some easier than others. There is no wrong way to do so, just different. So add links any way you like…just add links. Of course, don't go overboard.

Other things you can do to add internal links is to add widgets with archives and such. These will help readers navigate your site as well. On Day 27, you will learn more about using widgets to aid navigation.

NOTE: If you have both Related Posts by Zemanta and the Zemanta Editorial Assistant (as I do), you may want to use one or the other, but not both. Or you may want to use both. It is up to you. All that will happen is that you will have two sections at the bottom of your pages/posts for related articles. The first will contain outbound links to other websites and the second will contain your own. This is the order these appear when using both. There is no wrong, just a personal preference and that is your call.

For now, recall that Zemanta can provide related posts on other websites. These are called outbound links. Consider these now.

Outbound Links

Many new website owners neglect outbound links, reasoning that they would rather not direct people away from their website once they have them there. Others don't know what to include or why.

To clarify, outbound links are necessary for a few reasons...

1. The search engines rate your site based on how well you link to other websites/pages. This is because by so doing, you add value for your readers. No website can provide ALL the answers to questions a reader may have, nor can a single website provide exactly what someone is seeking every time. By adding appropriate links to outside material, you create a better experience for your visitors and they will thank you by returning to your site.

2. You have likely visited a site or two and found such links. One of the concepts in the early stages of web-building was to provide a "Links" page, though these are rapidly disappearing. Part of the reason is that it is more natural to provide useful links in the content of pages on your site and generally, more useful. This is not to say you should not create a Links page, but it is not as important as it once was.

3. Links which are related to content on your site are useful and appreciated by visitors; links which add no related value, are not—even the search engines will penalize you for these. So be sure that outbound links add value. In other words, if your best friend asks for a link to his cooking website and you have a real estate site, be sure that the link makes sense, such as in an article about kitchens. If the link does not fit naturally, the search engines will notice as will your readers—both will

react negatively.

So in this section, you are going to learn about creating good outbound links. You already know more than you think for when you added the articles on other websites in Zemanta, you were adding outbound links. Go to the edit screen of one of your blog posts or pages now. I am going to show you a couple more shortcuts to adding relevant links.

What follows is an example from a website I do some blog work for. The website is CharterFlightGroup.com and the article used for this example is titled, Top 10 Reasons to Choose Charter Flight. I chose this example because I have to be careful when adding links to their website. When adding to my own site, I can make a mistake or two, but with my client sites, I never link to competitors. I am showing you this example so that you will understand a few key points about adding outbound links. (And BTW, if you ever need to charter an aircraft, you cannot go wrong with CFG. I highly recommend them.)

At the bottom of your edit screen, there are a list of suggested "In-Text Links." Generally, these are all fairly safe to include because they will relate to words in your blog post/page. However, watch them because once in a while something really obscure will appear here that you may not want to link to. To add these links, you can either click "Apply ALL" in the lower left corner, or click on each individually. In addition, you will note that some will have a tiny down arrow to the right of the link suggestion. This indicates that there are more sources than the one displayed. For instance, under "TSA" there will be a link to their home page, as shown by the home icon in the image, but there is also a Wikipedia article I could link to as well. This I can add by clicking the down arrow button and choosing that particular link. You can only link to one using the automatic method.

However, should you want to add the other to a particular word in your text, you can simply click on the link as suggested which will open the website in a separate browser tab/window. Then find the text to which you want to link, remove any link added automatically, then copy the address from the open webpage and paste it into the link adding edit screen as described in the earlier segment.

Now, on the right of this example, you will see where I have placed my cursor over an article suggestion in Zamanta. This is an article for a competitor of Charter Flight Group. I can tell this by clicking on the article, which will take me to the website. Once there, I can see it is an article about another charter company—this is not a link I want to include on my client's website, so I do not.

You need to know about this because although you do want to add external links using Zemanta, the plugin does not discriminate—you must check out any web page suggestion that seems as if it is in some way conflicting with your own.

This is not to say you never want to link to a competitor, you may, but you should at least have the ability to make a conscious decision on the matter and this is how you do.

Another way to add outbound links is through the locating of articles on your own, then clicking the link icon on your kitchen sink to open the link edit screen, and adding the link manually (or copy and paste).

Just remember that you want your outbound links to be in harmony with the spirit of your website and you want to decide which to use. Don't just accept all suggestions. Consider whether your readers will be benefited by the added link or not.

Inbound Links

Inbound links are not only the most important, but also the most difficult for new website owners to develop. In this section, you are going to learn some simple ways to get great inbound links. However, an entire book could be devoted to this topic (and will soon), so for now, you are only going to learn some basic tricks to get you started in the right direction.

First, understand that inbound links are links that are posted elsewhere so that people may locate your website and/or particular pages on your site. Many new website owners make the mistake of only creating links that point to their home page. However, the best way to build links is to link to specific pages on your website. Put these links anywhere they would be applicable.

For instance, my website JeffOakes.me had a page specifically about Common Link-building Strategies. This page will be added to 365CrazyWebTraffic.com very soon. I mention this example because the link for the strategies page appeared in a broader scope article about building links in general-------------.

Do this with any links you add on the Internet. If you find a website about dogs and you have a blog article that is appropriate to that site, even though your website is about real estate, try to get a link on the site pointing to your blog about dogs. If you point the link to your home page, anyone going to that link is not going to search for the article, but simply leave. This will have a negative impact on both your bounce rate and user engagement...dropping you lower in the search rankings.

In the course of my writing for clients, I subscribe to a great many newsletters. One, which is a prominent online real estate magazine in Australia, is noteworthy for this discussion. The magazine had a subscriber list and regularly posted fresh content (some of which was ghost-written by me for a client to contribute—for good reason, I will not name the magazine). However, something I noted on receiving my weekly newsletter was that although the newsletter recommended the latest blogs, each blog link took me to the home page. From there, it was up to me to locate the article. It did not matter which article I clicked on in the newsletter, I went to the home page. Needless to say, I let my client know this so that he could let the editors of the magazine know—that was six months ago and they have yet to correct the problem.

To be clear, the reasons this is a problem are several...

- Few people will search the site for the article mentioned in the newsletter unless they REALLY want to read it

- I tried a couple of times to search for the posts and they were often buried in the archives. This grew frustrating and eventually I left off trying. The newsletter would just get deleted from my inbox on receipt.

- If a newsletter sent contains a single link back to the site, that is a single landing page. If that landing page is the home page, you cannot tell which articles are getting the visitors to go to the site. But if each blog post mentioned in the newsletter has its own link, you can check your stats and know at a glance which are most effective. Then, to get even more traffic, you can boost promotions of those posts. The site was missing a great tool for marketing and continues to miss it today.

To be clear, when you add links anywhere, whether in a newsletter, in a comment on someone else's website, or wherever, be sure to make the link point to the page you want people to go to. Doing so is very easy. Let me show you how.

Let's say I want to find a place to put a link from a page on my CriminalJusticeLaw.us website. The first thing I will do is choose the page to be linked. Now, I do not have to be logged in as an administrator to do this, but if I am it won't make a difference. The first thing is to choose the article. Notice in the following image that I have placed my cursor over the main navigation toolbar and am about to choose an article.

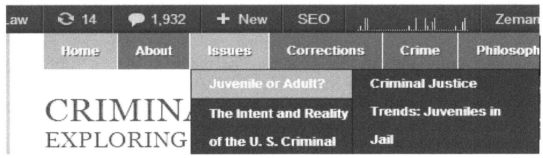

I am going to choose the article "Juvenile or Adult." When I click on this navigation link, it will take me to the article desired the same as it would if I were a visitor to the website.

The only thing that has changed is the page. I am now on the article I want to link to somewhere on the web. Notice the address at the very top (right above the grey bar). All I will need to do to add this link somewhere is to highlight it, copy, then paste it where I want.

That is the easy part.

The hard part these days is finding a place where the link can be included. Most websites today have spam filters to prevent links from being added without some form of moderation. In fact, if you try to add a link through Yahoo, CNN, or any of the major websites, it will fail. So adding links is tricky, which is why there will be an entire book devoted to that topic—coming soon.

For now, just look for places where links can be added, whether these are top websites or not. For instance, you may be reading something you've come across and decided that you have an article that would fit well for readers here. See if there is a comments section (usually at the bottom of the page), then attempt to add a comment with a link. If the comment sounds spammy, it will usually fail. But if your comment is on target and adds value to the conversation thread, the administrator will likely allow it, along with your link. In some cases, they may even add your link more prominently to their website if they like what you wrote.

A good way to locate sites for these links is to go to WordPress.com.

Log in.

Then scroll down until you see a "Topic" search window on the right. Enter a topic. In this case, I entered "juvenile justice."

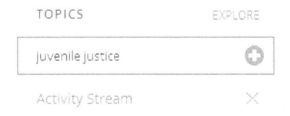

This provided me with a listing of six articles on various websites. The first one was…

Public Welfare Foundation Grants

The Foundation's Juvenile Justice Program supports groups working to end the criminalization and over-incarceration of youth in the United States. Specifically the program makes grants to groups that are working to advance systems reforms that will:

205 more words

3 days, 21 hours ago on AYSPS Research & Grant News

Comment (0)   Like (0)   Reblog   Follow

This blog certainly appears to fit with the topic I wish to create a back-link to so I am going to go to the page by clicking on the title "Public Welfare Foundation Grants." Once there, I will scroll down and comment. When I comment, I will do so in such a way that adding the link to my post will make sense.

Leave a Reply

I took a look around your site and like what I saw. I run a website called criminaljusticelaw.us and am very interested in keeping in touch respecting your research, particularly into juvenile justice and incarceration rates. I shall link to your site via my own and would welcome guest bloggers should any wish. You may wish to check out http://criminaljusticelaw.us/issues/juvenile-or-adult/

C. Jeff Oakes: You are commenting using your WordPress.com account. (Log Out / Change)

Notice that in my comment I add information that connects both sites, add a link to the page which helped me find them, and let them know I will be linking to them as well.

They will likely allow the link, but to be honest, at this point the link will not carry much link-juice with the search engines. This is because the site is very new, with few backlinks to it, little standing in the search rankings, and virtually zero traffic. So why did I link to it?

Some would say to not bother with these sites, but I hold a different philosophy. I am here, so why not add a link? Also, the site may grow. Indeed, this is a joint project with students and faculty at a major University, so it is very likely to grow. This could bring traffic my way. Even if it does not, it is a link and it only took a couple seconds to add it. The other option would have been to leave and search for "better." I still can, but may as well leave my mark while I am here. Besides, I like the site.

But I did like this website and meant what I said about linking to them. Thus, we can have a symbiotic relationship. I can help them grow and in time they can help me. At the moment, my website gets far more traffic than theirs, but they may not know this. Doesn't matter. I would like to help them and if they return the favor, both of us benefit.

Thus, at the end of the article I added as a link in the comment of their website, I added my own plug for their website and a link to them…

To be clear, this may not be a great link at the moment from or to them, but one never knows where these go. I have added obscure links in the past and found that I get a couple of visits a day from them. Then, these were linked by others and the result was far more traffic than I would have received otherwise.

Now, in addition to adding links in comments, you can and should add links in Social Media where appropriate, in social bookmarking websites, in directories, vertical portals, and anywhere you can add one which is appropriate. By appropriate, remember this simply means that the added link makes sense and fits with the theme of the pages linked.

This will be enough information to get you started. Because link-building is such an important element of growing a website—because links are the life of the Internet—Month Two will focus entirely on link-building.

Leaving Links Where They Are

One final word on links. Once you add a permalink location in your website, that is, once you have created the page and location for that page, LEAVE IT WHERE IT IS…unless there is a VERY good reason to change it.

The reason is that when you move your pages around on your website, you change the link, the address for the page. If people have linked to you, you LOSE those links. Moving webpages is a great way to KILL your website, so don't do it.

Day 23: The Use of Images

Images, pictures, photos…call them what you will, have a special and unique place in websites. Images can be the reason for the website, such as in photography (and admittedly, pornographic) sites or images can be used to illustrate a point. In the case of most websites, images support the site content by illustrating a concept, showing people involved in the story, teaching how to do something, or any multitude of reasons. Images also have the power to draw traffic to a website, provided they are properly used.

For instance, if you were looking for an image of a homemade volcano for your son's science fair project, you could type "homemade volcano images" into a Google search and you would get more images than you would know what to do with. Go on, give it a try.

Here is one I found to illustrate a point. When you click on an image found in the search results pages (SERP's), to the right of the image will be the name of the image along with a link to the website where the image is located. Google does this automatically for all images in the database. Now, if you are reading this in Kindle, you can click on the image to the right and just as you could in the Google search, you will be taken to the website where this image is located. For those reading this in print, the site link is http://www.homeschoolwithwinnie.com. I have no idea who Winnie is nor can I tell you whether this is a great site or not. I simply used it as an example to illustrate how you never know what an image will do for your website.

I am sure that some of my readers are going to visit the website for whatever reason and the site owner is likely going to wonder why suddenly traffic has increased. If they know how to use their analytics tools, they will discover the link is originating from Amazon in some cases and in others, people are simply typing it in. Regardless, the site will surely gain traffic from this addition in my book. And good for them. I chose the image simply because it reminded me of one I built when I was 10.

(Note: A later book will cover analytics in complete detail)

That is the power of images...in particular, original images. You put them on your site, you make the alt tags read as a good description of the image, and the search engines often return results whereas sometimes, people link to you and provide further results.

So, before moving into where to locate images, how to add these to your site, and optimize them so that the search engines can better locate them, I would first like to make one point clear.

Original images are always better than images from other sources. I will show you a few places to find suitable images, but your original images will ALWAYS be better. Case in point: The image shown above is an original. I know, because out of curiosity I checked out the website and it turns out that the volcano was made with pumpkin spice Play-doh®. Cool.

Anyway, you get the point. If at all possible, create your own images for your website.

Where to Find Images

There are literally hundreds of places where you can find images for use on your website. Some of these will charge you and some only want credit. In most cases, persons with images on the web simply want credit, usually in the form of a link. This is called attribution. Of course, it is certainly a courteous thing to contact the owner of the site from which the image originates to request the use of the image. Offer to include a link back and most will write back and say sure. If not, you would be wise to avoid using the image.

If you live in the United States, there is what is called the "Fair Use Act" whereby you can generally use images which have no stand-alone value if only using them for illustrative purposes AND you name the source of the image. This is why you can often see the same image appear across several newspapers after a big story. But if an image is a stand-alone work, that is, the image is art and was created as such, it cannot be used without the creators express permission. If you are unsure of whether to use an image or not, you have a couple of choices: Use it and possibly suffer consequences later, confer with your attorney, just ask the owner, or simply not use the image.

As I state repeatedly, it is always best to use your own images you created. Today, with smart phones and cameras everywhere, creating images is not difficult.

So where can you get images for the cost of attribution or cash? Here are some of the top image websites…

If reading in Kindle, simply click on the image. If in print, simply type the name into a search engine and the first result will be the site. Each of these sites get copious amounts of traffic and are well-ranked. You will have no difficulty locating them.

The nice thing about using these sites is that each provides information on the use of images. You will get details about how the author of the image would like to be listed for attribution along with costs for purchasing the rights. Also, you should note that if you create your own images, you can add them to these sites and either get paid, or get links. Hint, hint.

Finally, there is a VERY simple way to get quality images in a snap using WordPress. In fact, you already have the plugin on your site.

Adding Featured Images

Adding featured images simply means using Zemanta to add images to your pages and blogs. This is very simple to do as will be explained in this step-by-step tutorial. However, understand that once the images are added, you only boost traffic for other sites with these. Why?

Because Zemanta is a sharing plugin. It is an excellent sharing plugin and used correctly, it can help you boost traffic as well, but when you use an image from Zemanta, you will be leaving the link to the origin site and often, must leave the attribute information in the caption. You can alter the alt tags, which may help bring some traffic to your site, but this does not happen often.

That said, there is a way to add your image to Zemanta as well so that whenever someone uses one of your images, you get both credit and traffic. This will be covered in the last segment of this chapter. For now, let's add some images to your site.

Choose a page and go to the edit screen.

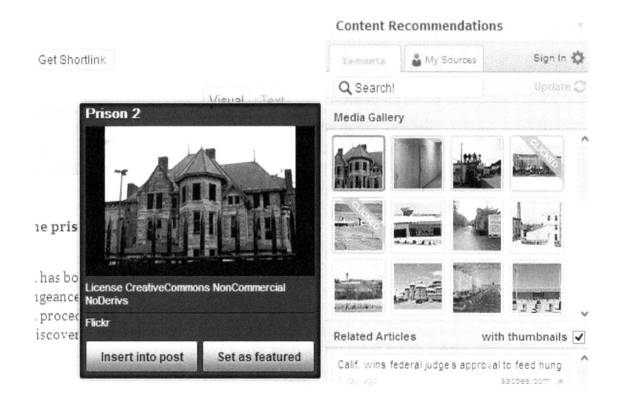

For this example, I chose an article from my criminaljusticelaw.us website. The article is one of my more popular, titled *State and Federal Prisons: A History of Growth*. I chose it because I already know that Zemanta will have plenty of images from which to choose and because of the nature of the material, I am often not able to create my own images. In the above example, I wanted to show one of the prisons built in the early years located in Pennsylvania, far from where I live.

This is the "Content Recommendations" section of Zemanta—you've already seen this and used the lower portion. To add an image to a post/page, simply…

1. In the edit box, place your cursor where you want the image to appear.

2. Then move your mouse so that your cursor appears over the image you want to use. A window will popout to the left of the Content Recommendations screen as shown (the large image which reads in the upper left, "Prison 2").

3. You have two options here.

   - Insert into Post

   - Set a Featured

4. To set as featured means that when this article appears in recommendations, this is the image which will accompany it. Also, if you have the Zemanta Related Posts plugin, when the plugin automatically choses related posts to put at the bottom of your page, this is the image which will appear. To do this, simply click on "Set as Featured."

5. To insert into your post, you can either click on that button or left-click on the image. The image will then be added to your post/page.

6. Next, as shown in the image following, a box will appear which allows you to choose whether to add the image on the left, center, or right of where you placed your cursor. You can also add or not a caption (if you do nothing, it will by default add the information in the box below "caption." I recommend you do not change the credit). Also, you can choose a size. There are customizations which you can perform and these will be discussed next.

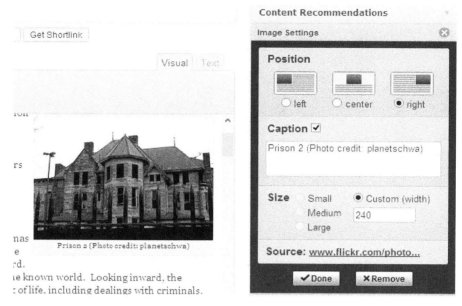

7. For now, you need only click "Done" and the image will appear as desired in the post/page.

Editing Images

Editing images added is simple.

From your edit screen, just click on the image you wish to edit. It does not matter if the image was added from Zemanta or from your media files (to be discussed next). The technique is the same.

So we are going to use the image from above of the prison. I would like to change a few things about it to make it more search engine friendly in accord with my content along with making it a custom size as I did not like the size choices. There may be some other changes I will make along the way.

Take a look at the next image. When you left-click on the image in your edit screen, you will see two icons appear in the upper left corner...

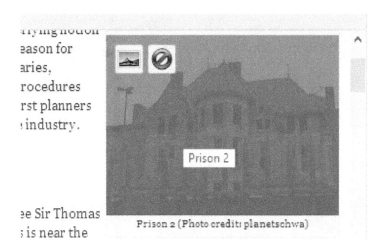

Prison 2

Prison 2 (Photo credit: planetschwa)

The picture icon allows the editing and the "No" symbol is used to delete the image from the post/page. Click on the icon in the far left corner, the picture icon. You will then be taken to a screen which looks like this...

Notice first that at the top, there are two tabs: Edit image and Advanced Settings. For now, stay in edit image. You can see below this a sizer then to the right, some text in Latin, and then your image. The Latin is just there to show you how the image will appear nestled in the body of the text. But you can scale down the size of the image in increments of 10% using this function on the left. In fact, if you place an image into your page which is far too big, you can keep returning to this edit screen and keep scaling it down until it is the right size. In other words, you can scale it down 60% of the original size, take a look, still too large? Edit again by scaling it down and if still too large, edit it again. But what if you want it larger? I will discuss that momentarily.

First, look at the rest of the changes you can make from this screen.

Again, you can change the alignment and if you choose, alter the title. The title is only there for your use and does not appear anywhere other than in your media library (discussed in the next segment).

Below this is the Alternative (Alt) Text. This is the text that tells the search engines what appears in the image. For my SEO purposes, I am going to add "Early State and Federal Prisons." Because this is only read by the search engines, I do not need to add anything fancy, just a good description which both ties to my page content and still accurately described the image.

Below this, I can again alter the caption should I wish.

Last is the Link URL. This is a touchy area. If you alter the link URL for an image which requires attribution or credit of any kind, the image will disappear from your site after a few days. If attribution of any kind is required, you must leave the link as is. However, if you are editing one of your own images, there are a few things you can do.

- Leave the link which appears by default: if this is your own image, the default link will allow someone to click on the image to get the full-size version. Great if you are adding thumbnails to a page.

- Change the link to another page on your site which expands on the information herein.

- Change the link to another website completely, such as a landing page for a sales site (or as I do in many cases, an image link will take a visitor to the Amazon page where they can buy whatever book I am promoting).

In other words, if the image is yours, you can make the URL anything you want.

Now go to http://365crazywebtraffic.com/demo-page/

You will see an image of traffic entering a laptop against an orange background, kind of like the cover for this book. In fact, this is the beginning of the artwork I designed for the book cover. It is on the site to show you how to edit images. The first image you will see on the demo page is the unedited version of the basic image I created for the book. The next image shows what I am about to do.

On my Dashboard edit screen, the same edit screen I use to work on articles and blogs, I can edit images as well. Here is the same image, but from the perspective of my editorial screen.

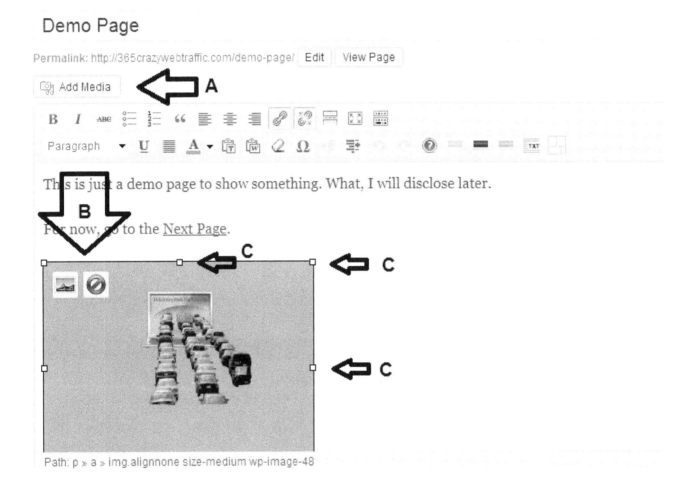

You can see the kitchen sink running across the top and the text that I put on the page earlier. Notice the letter "A" arrow. You already know about the selections made using what is shown by the "B" arrow. Now check out the three arrows marked with a letter "C."

Just like adjusting images on your MS Word program, you can alter the size and scope of images using these square points on the image when in the edit screen. Go on, play around with this. When you are ready, we will continue.

Now, on to the Advanced tab and the fun stuff. Click on the "Advanced Settings" tab.

Advanced Image Settings

Source	* http://farm1.static.flickr.com/36/110982694_388062be0f_m.jpg		
Size	Width 240	Height 180	Original Size
CSS Class	zemanta-img-inserted zemanta-img-configured alignright		
Styles	border: 2px solid black; margin-top: 2px; margin-bottom: 2px;		
Image properties	Border 2	Vertical space 2	Horizontal space 2

Advanced Link Settings

The upper portion of this screen looks just like the previous tab but below will appear as shown in the above image. We are not going to get into some of these settings as they are for more advanced courses, but there are two portions here which you need to know about now.

The first is the size.

You can adjust the size of an image to literally anything you want, but be aware that some changes, especially if making them larger, will cause blurring to occur because of resolution issues. So when expanding the size of a smaller image, you may have to play with this a bit.

See where it reads, "Size?" Then you have the width and height. To make properly scaled images, simply take what is in each box and multiply it by the same number. For instance, suppose I wanted to make the image almost 2 times the original size. I can multiply the Width (240) and the Height (180) by something near to 2. So I will choose to make it 1.75. All I do is multiply both by that amount and add the result into the appropriate boxes. Like this…

240 x 1.75 = 420   and   180 x 1.75 = 315 So…

Source	* http://farm1.static.flickr.com/36/110982694_388062be0f_m.jpg
Size	Width 420 Height 315 Original Size
CSS Class	zemanta-img-inserted zemanta-img-configured alignright
Styles	border: 2px solid black; margin: 2px;
Image properties	Border 2 Vertical space 2 Horizontal space 2

With the changes made, my image will appear 1.75 times larger and will be properly scaled.

Next, notice the "Image properties" at the bottom. This allows you to add a border and spacing around your image. By default, these are zero, but I wanted some slight border so I added 2's across them all. This populated the "Styles" portion just above it automatically—this is normal. This will add a border and some spacing around my image. If I don't like the exact sizes after checking out my page, I can simply come in here and make changes.

Anything else in this section just leave alone for now. If you want to learn more, just go into WordPress.com and get into the members forum. These are truly advanced items. The two I have given you though are musts—in my opinion, they are (or should be) considered basics.

Upload Your Images to Your Media Library

When you create your own image, whether using your MS Paint program, Photoshop, or a digital camera/smart phone, you can upload these to your WP website very easily and use them in your posts and pages. In this segment, I am going to show you one way to add these to your media library and in the next segment, you will learn another. The steps in both cases are essentially the same and doing so is very easy.

The first thing to know is that once you have created or added an image to your computer, you need to know the file location.

Now go to your dashboard.

Along the left side, just below where it reads "Posts" you will see "Media." Place your cursor over this and a window will pop out for you to either access your Media Library or Add New media to it.

Click on "Add New."

After this, another window will open which looks like this...

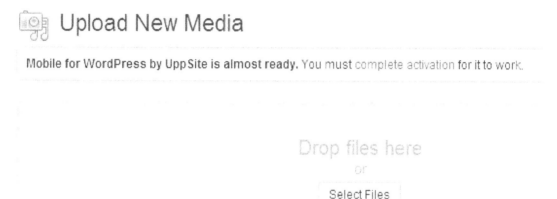

Choose the "Select Files" button from the center and you will then be taken to your PC file selection window. Locate the image to be added and either double-left click on the image or highlight it and click Open. Then you will see the image you chose appear below the uploader screen. To the far right will be a link to edit the image. Editing the image will take you to the same editing screen you used in the previous segment. If you are not ready to edit now, no need. It is now in your library. You can edit the image at any time simply by going to your dashboard, placing your cursor over the Media tab, then selecting "Library." Simple.

You are using the multi-file uploader. Problems? Try the browser uploader instead.

Maximum upload file size: 10MB.

 criminaljusticecollage2water   Edit

Note, you can also add video and sound files to this library, but in order to add these to your site, you will need plugins for adding them to your pages in this way. We will discuss adding video/sound files on Day 26.

This is really all you need to know about this so let's move on to adding images from your library to your blog.

Add Images from Your Media Library

Adding images to your blog/page is very simple using WordPress. In fact, you can not only add images from your library using the function you are about to learn, but also add images into your Media Library as well using this feature.

To access this, simply go to the edit screen of a post or page.

Once there, notice just below the title line and above the kitchen sink of the edit screen the "Add Media" button.

Click on "Add Media" and you will be taken to a screen similar to the previous segment which allowed you to Select files from your PC. Note, wherever your cursor is in the article to have the media added is where the image will appear, just as when adding with Zemanta.

The nice thing about adding in this way, you not only will add the image into your post/page, but simultaneously to your library as well. This effectively saves a step, but is only useful if you add the media at the time you write the post or page. If you want to add media for future pages and posts, it is generally best to use the media function from the dashboard.

When you click on Add Media now, you will see your library along with two tabs at the top. Choose the tab which reads, "Upload Files."

Insert Media

Upload Files   Media Library

All media items   ⌄

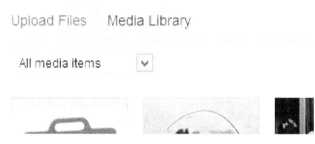

When you choose to "upload files" you will then be taken to a screen exactly like the one in the previous segment. Simply choose "Select Files."

Now, a nice thing about this feature is that if you have multiple images you want to upload for use, you can do so. Simply click on each file you want to add and open them all (up to 10MB). They will all upload to your library and you can them add them into your post/page as desired.

In the case of this example, I used the website WallysWeirdStuff.com because I had 5 "baby dragon skeleton" images I wanted to add an article about. Don't ask me what they are—I don't know. A friend found them and decided to let us write about the things.

Notice first though, that when I select the image to be added to the site, I need to add the Caption, Alt text, and Description. This is where adding unique images can be beneficial. You can see what I added and the alt text is the text you will recall that is read by the search engines. I simply entered the same as for the description, though I could add much more in the description. In fact, the description is best used by adding more descriptive words about an image. For the most part, however, the alt tags are the most important.

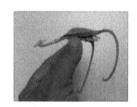

IMG_0647.jpg
August 21, 2013
2048 × 1536
Edit Image
Delete Permanently

Title   IMG_0647

Caption   Baby Dragon Skeleton?

Alt Text   baby dragon skeleton foun

Description   baby dragon skeleton found near lubbock texas usa

In any case, I can then repeat the same process to add the remaining images, but with one exception. I do not need to upload because I did all five images at once. Now to add the remaining images to the post, I simply need to add them one at a time by placing my cursor where I want the image to appear in the post, then clicking on Add Media, choosing the image I want from the Library, and adding the needed tags and captions. Below the text options are the size options, which you already know about. If I want to do further editing to the images, I can do so by clicking on the image and editing as described earlier.

Simple…like everything in WordPress.

Oh, and if you'd like to see all of the images just go to Weird Baby Dragon Skeleton at WallysWeirdStuff.com.

Add Images to Zemanta

Adding your images to Zemanta is very simple. You want to authorize Zemanta to add images so that when someone looks at the recommendations, your unique images may come up. Then, if they add the image to their site, the link back to your site is embedded, same as when you do so.

This helps you in two ways.

First, you get links and possibly traffic therefrom.

Second, you get links and if these come from a site with ranking and traffic, the search engines reward you with better ranking. Thus, the more people use your images, the better your site will become.

To add images, simply open the post/page edit screen and at the top of Zemanta you will see two tabs. The right tab reads, "My Sources."

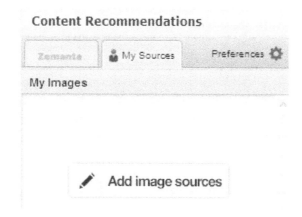

Just click on the "Add Image Sources" in the center and you will be taken to your Zemanta dashboard via another window/tab in your browser.

You should see your blog/website listed but if not, simply add it where it reads "Blogs I Write."

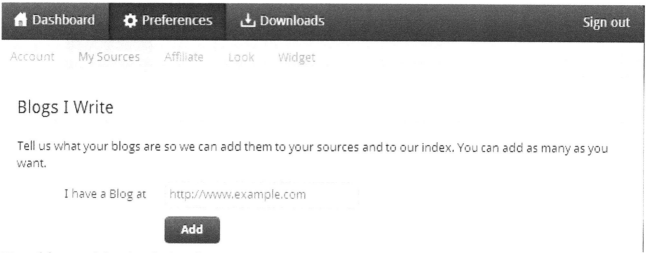

To add your blog/website, just enter the complete URL and click "Add."

Done, Zemanta will now automatically include any blogs and images included on your site in their listing of recommendations. Then, if someone writes something similar to your content, they may choose to include your post/page. This gives you a link and added traffic.

This is all for today. By now you should have a good idea about how to add images, what to do with the images you add, and how to make sure the search engines locate your images. Tomorrow, we add video and/or sound to your site.

Day 24: The Use of Video/Sound Players

When it comes to using video and sound on websites, one must be careful. You must remember that search engines cannot see or hear, so when adding video or sound, good descriptions need to be added to the alt tags and the meta descriptions.

As a general rule, I am lazy when it comes to video and I don't use audio at all. I could, I suppose, but I have yet to see where audio alone makes much of an impact unless someone is promoting music. The reason I am lazy with video is largely because I am camera shy and partly because I also have a channel on YouTube. I would rather put my videos there, then transfer them to my website.

But you can do this any way you want. Here are the pros and cons.

If you add a video to your website only, the video supposedly has a much better chance of getting seen and found by the search engines. Because it is unique, you should get listings alongside the major video players, namely, YouTube, Vimeo, and Daily Motion. However, in testing the situation using Google as the basis (as this is the largest search engine), I have found that YouTube Videos tend to get more notice than the others (Google owns YouTube). This should not be the case, but it is from the tests I have conducted.

What I have found is that if a video is placed onto YouTube first, then embedded into a website using the embedded html, the search engines have a tendency to show the website as results over the actual site. Thus, whereas conventional wisdom would dictate that a video originating on the creator's website would get more traffic, just the opposite occurs when the video is added to YouTube first.

And the best part of this is that if you sign up for an Adsense account along with your YouTube channel, you can derive ad revenue from the video, even when placed into your website after. And in YouTube, adding the tags and other cool stuff is made easy.

So, you can either use a plugin for video and audio or start with YouTube (video) or iTunes (audio—the iTunes player can likewise be embedded into your site the same as the video. So from here on out, I will only discuss the video aspect for it is the most relevant and adding audio is the same technique).

Let's begin.

Plugins

Plugins, as you have guessed by now, are great. Today, you can get a plugin for your WordPress website which will do virtually anything you find on any professionally designed website. This includes audio and video players.

In order to find a plugin which will work for you, simply type in what you seek.

In the case of an audio player, simply go to the plugin search and type in "audio player." You will get a list of over sixty plugins which are available for addition on your site. But not all are created equal.

In the case of the one I have included in the following image, I recommend this one or one like it for a couple of good reasons.

First, the plugin has been rated five stars, which means that other users have found it to be great. Between four and five stars is good.

Second, this plugin is simple to use. Notice that you can use "a shortcode" to implement this player. All this means is that once you have installed and activated the player, you simply locate the settings or similar information. In this will be a code that will be enclosed in brackets [xxx]. All you need to do to add this to any page on your site is add that shortcode (brackets included) wherever you want the player to appear. To learn how to add files, simply go to the plugin homepage, which is easily found via a link either at the end of the description after installation or in the settings menu.

Generally speaking, for a plugin to get five stars means that it is simple to learn and use.

Compact WP Audio Player   1.5   ☆ ☆ ☆ ☆ ☆   Compact WordPress Audio Player plugin is an HTML5 + Flash hybrid t
Details | Install Now   an mp3 audio file on your WordPress post or page using a shortcode.
                                                     all major browsers.
                                                     This audio player plugin Supports .mp3 and .ogg file formats
                                                     Features
                                                     The audio player is compact so it does not take a lot of real estate ... B

Video plugins are the same. To locate a good video plugin, simply type "video player" into the search and look for the good ones (4-5 stars). Again, once installed you just look for the link to the home page if you have any problems, but generally, the higher rated plugins make using the plugin simple.

As I mentioned, however, I don't use these because I have found it far better to simply add videos via YouTube, then transfer them to my site.

YouTube, Etc

One of the easiest ways to add video to your website is to add it first to YouTube. You can start your own YouTube channel free and creating/uploading videos is simple.

You can create videos using either the cam that comes on most computers today, but this is not the best method as these usually have very poor resolution and sound quality. Smart phones are much better and once the video is created, it is simple to upload these to YouTube.

Just create short videos, less than three minutes works best if using a Smart phone. If you have an actual video camera, you still only want to create videos that are no more than five minutes as these seem to do best for YouTube audiences. And once you add these to your website, five minutes usually loads better than longer videos too.

A note on creating your YouTube channel and adding videos: Create a channel name that will dovetail nicely with your website. Try to incorporate the exact name of your website into your channel. This will add to recognition and credibility. In addition, even if you do not learn how to make your website information easily known on your YouTube channel, people will find often find you using your channel name.

For purposes of this book I am not going to go into great detail on YouTube. A future book will deal with the specifics as there is much to know. For now, you simply need to know that adding videos to your website in this way greatly simplifies the process and benefits you by giving added exposure.

Once the video is loaded to your YouTube channel, it is very easy to transfer it to your website. This is explained in the next segment.

Embedding HTML

Once you have a video on YouTube, all you need to do to add it to your website is right click on the video and copy the embedded html.

The way to do this is as shown next.

This is the first video I ever created for YouTube. I was playing around with my Smart phone and an idea for demonstrating the difference between a website without traffic and one with. The title is "Bushes" and it plays for less than a minute.

In creating this example, I right-clicked on the video and the box you see opened. Notice the highlighted portion which reads, "Copy embed code." If you click on this, you will have just captured the html for this video. Now you need to transfer this to a webpage.

To do this, go to the page you want to add the video to.

For this example, we will go to http://365crazywebtraffic.com.

I am going to create a new page just for this example titled "Videos." It can easily be found from the main navigation bar. In the edit screen for the page, I will click on "Text" as shown in the following image.

Next, I will ensure that my cursor is in the edit box.

Then, go to the desired video on YouTube (or really, whatever video file sharing site you use—the terms may be different when right-clicking, but the concept is the same). Right click and copy the embedded html code from the video.

Now in the edit screen of the page where you are placing the video you simply need to right-click again. This will open a box as follows.

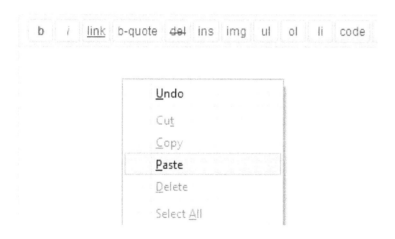

Simply click "Paste" and you will then see something like this...

This is the html code for the video. I pasted it into the "Text" section of your edit screen because this is where code is placed. Had I accidentally pasted it into the "Visual" screen, when I viewed my page, I would have seen the following INSTEAD of my video.

Fixing this mistake is a simple matter of returning to the edit screen by clicking on "Edit Page" at the top navigation as shown in the previous image (just above "Site Building"). This will bring me to my edit screen and all I do is highlight the code, cut it, then click on the "Text" tab in the upper right corner of my kitchen sink, and paste the code into that field.

Click on update to the right...

And now when I click "view page,"

I see that the video has been added to my website.

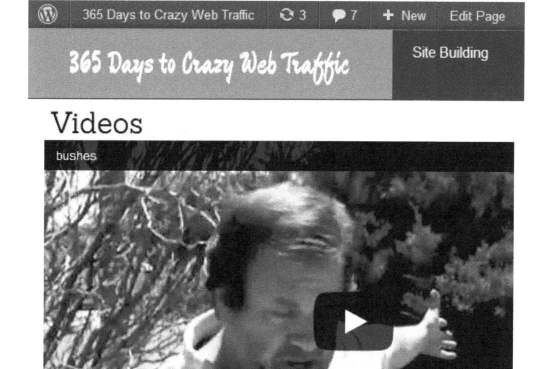

Now, a couple of things you need to know about adding videos.

The first is that just as with adding written material, videos are copyrighted material. You can add other peoples videos if you'd like, but you must credit the video properly and provide links to the channel from which the video came. In addition, if the copyright holder ever asks you to remove the video, do so immediately. This rarely happens, for most like the added exposure you give with the credit and link, but at times it does. This usually occurs when someone is using the video in a way that was not intended by the copyright holder or is in some way harming their website or business. Just remember that if someone asks you to take it down and you have every reason to believe they have the authority to do so, remove it. It is a simple matter of cutting the embedded code and not re-pasting. Or just highlight it and hit your backspace key on your PC. Either method wipes it from your page once you click on "Update."

The next thing to know is that wherever you place your cursor in the "text" field, this is where the video is going to appear. So say you wanted to provide an introduction to the video, as shown in the next image. All you would need to do is go to the Text field, locate the end of the sentence, hit "enter" on your keyboard so as to add a space, then right-click and add the code. Once you return to Visual mode, you will see a pink box in the edit screen. This is your video.

If you pasted the video into the Text field without adding some space or words prior to adding the video code, simply go back to Text mode, add your cursor to the start and type a couple of words. Now return to Visual mode and continue typing.

As you will notice, the words separate from the pink box (the placeholder for your video). You can also add your cursor in this mode to the lower right of this placeholder and begin typing or hit enter to begin typing on the line below the video. Either way, the words will appear below the video when you view it on your website.

Play around with videos. Find some you like on YouTube or wherever and try adding them. You can easily take them out when finished playing around just by highlighting the code and erasing it.

For instance, perhaps you find a video on Yahoo, try adding it. Or maybe there is one on the website for your local news channel, try copying the code and placing it.

One of the things you will notice when you start to do this is that not all videos can be added in this way. Part of this is because of the type of video creator in use by the site. Flash videos, java script, and many others cannot be easily (or at all) copied and added. Some use these simply because this is all they ever used and other sites use these because they don't want other websites promoting their content.

But you will see that often, you will be able to do copy videos and add them to your website.

Now the cool part.

Other people will be able to do the same with your videos. So if you get good at creating videos that other people would like to share, be sure to learn also how to add text and/or links to your videos. This is advertising for your website and the more people add your videos to their website, the better. This will add to your exposure and over time, add to your traffic.

This is why I fail to understand why anyone would want to create videos in such a way that they cannot be embedded into another website, especially if the originating website derives their revenue from advertising. Even the advertising added to the video follows, so if someone clicks an ad on my video, even if it is on someone else's website, I get paid.

So what I am saying is…

Please…feel free to add my videos to your website. I like getting paid.

That's all for today. In the next couple of days we will wrap up this book and you will be well on your way to website guru-dom. Tomorrow, we will discuss navigation, for traffic must be guided if it is to properly flow.

Day 25: Navigation

Navigation is perhaps one of the most important element of any website. In the Page Rank days, navigation was even one of the parameters upon which Page Rank was either granted or denied. Although Google no longer uses the system and likely does not demote a website based on navigation, they don't need to.

A website with great navigation and all other elements in place will be a website that people enter, stay a while on, and move around. Thus, the traffic patterns will be registered by the search engines and the site will achieve better positioning in the SERPs (Search Engine Results Pages).

A website that has great content but poor navigation will penalize itself. People will enter, read the page on which they arrived, then leave if there is nothing to keep them there. The site will develop a high "Bounce Rate" and the search engines will decide that the site is less worth promoting than some other. Thus, the site with poor navigation will kill itself—it does not need Google to penalize it further for having poor navigation. The market will do that.

That said, how can you ensure that your website is easily navigable and that people stay and move around on it?

Today, you are going to learn the five key areas whereby you can make your website more navigable, more friendly to your visitors. You are going to learn some basics of how to manipulate traffic patterns to your advantage, but a future book will get into greater detail. In this one, you are going to learn what you need to know to have the traffic come to your site and stay awhile.

The five key areas of concern for navigation are

> Header

> Footer

> Sidebars

> Widgets

> Body

You are also going to learn a basic method of optimizing the site for navigation. The better your navigation for your readers and the better the search engines can navigate your site, the more traffic you will get. It is that simple and that important.

So let's begin.

Header (address if local search required)

Your Header is the area of your website that covers the top of the web pages. This is the main navigation area of all websites and this is where you are going to put the most important elements of your website. This is where you will put a link for…

> ➢ Your Home page
>
> ➢ Your About page (if different from the Home page)
>
> ➢ Contact information (if important to the purpose of your site)
>
> ➢ Privacy policy and Terms/Conditions (especially if selling something or collecting information from your visitors)
>
> ➢ Your Blog (if separate from the Home page—some websites simply allow the home page to carry a running collection of the most recent blogs)
>
> ➢ Any other pages you deem important to visitors to your site

In addition, if you have a local business, you will want to place your business address and contact information in the header. Include city and state and do so in text, not an image. Remember that the search engines cannot read images so when you add your contact information to the Header, it need to be in a form that the search engines can read. Thus, if the theme you choose for your website does not support adding text to the header in this way, you will want to go back and search themes which do support text entries. By adding your local contact information the search engines can send local traffic to your site.

You have likely done this. You search for "movies" using your PC or mobile phone. The cookies which have been previously picked up by your browser identifies you as living in Dallas, Texas. So when you search for "movies," you get results for your area only. The same holds true for "plumbers," "apartments," "pizza," or whatever. The search engine will send results as found in the data base for your locality.

Thus, if you have a local business, you need this information in the header so that the search engines can send local searchers to your site.

Note too that when you enter this information in the header, it appears on every page of your website. Thus, no matter which landing page someone enters your site on, they will see your local contact information. Some will go to you, some will phone. In all cases, this expands your advertising/marketing reach so why leave it out?

Don't. Make sure that this information is there for if you are building a support site for your local business, this information is vital. Failing to add it makes the purpose of such a site fail and you will be wasting your time building.

Footer (sitemap, navigation, legal stuff)

The Footer is the bottom portion of your website and this is where you can add many of the same pages and links as in the Header. If you have a local business, be sure to clearly add your contact information, city, state, and phone number here as well.

Again, the Footer is carried over to all pages, so anyone navigating to the footer will have your local contact information at the ready. In addition, this provides more clear guidelines to the search engines that your location is_____. The easier you make it for both human and non-human readers to know vital information, the better it is for you. Your site will get better search results and more traffic. You business will get more traffic. You will make more money.

There are a number of ways to create the footer and what most people do is to create a custom menu. This is easily done in most themes on WordPress. (Note: if you happen to decide on a theme which does not easily provide for custom menus, simply go to the website which developed the theme. These always have FAQ's or other resources for understanding the finer points of that particular theme. If unable to get information in this way, head over to the Forums on WP.com and ask other users. Out of the roughly 60 million users in the forums, you are almost always certain to find someone who can help you through this part. I would love to be able to provide detailed information on every theme in WordPress, but for purposes of this book, that would be impossible.)

To add the custom menu for use in the footer, go to your site. If you have not logged in as Admin, be sure to do so. Once you do, you will see the Gray line along the top of your site. On the left, where your site name appears, place your cursor over this and a dropdown menu appears. On this menu, you will see "Menus." If not, then custom menus may not be possible in the chosen theme. However, you can alternatively go to "Dashboard" and once there, scan the left navigation for "Menus." Sometimes, that is how you locate these.

In any case, as you can see in the image, choose "Menus" and you will be taken to an editorial screen whereby you can modify/create custom menus as you see fit. There is no limit to how many you can create, though most people only make a couple for that is all that is needed, depending on how you add these to your website.

The following images show how to use this feature in the WP FlatThirteen theme, which is the theme I am currently using for 365crazywebtraffic.com.

Notice at the top where it reads, "edit your menu below, or create a new menu."

This lets you know naturally that you can edit the menu you choose from this screen or create a new one. By default, the main menu, which is the menu which appears below your header, is shown. As you add pages, some will default to this menu. For instance, most websites today place the privacy policy and Term pages in the footer. However, by default, these will appear in the main navigation/main menu. So when you are building your pages and want to move these to the footer, you will have to edit the main menu as well. For now, click on the link to create a new menu and you will then see...

Edit Menus

Edit your menu below, or create a new menu.

Pages   Menu Name [   ]

                                       Give your menu a name above, then click Create Menu.

Most Recent   Search

Notice that you are prompted to name your menu in the field to the right. I am going to call this one "Footer Menu."

Menu Name   [Footer Menu]   [Create Menu]

Give your menu a name above, then click Create Menu.

Then, to the far right I am going to click on the blue button which reads, "Create Menu." From here, I will be taken to a screen which now offers up some choices. I can choose from a list of "Most Recent" pages created, "View All" pages on the website, add special links, or even add categories to the menu. For now, let us simply choose the pages we want to include in the Footer menu.

Pages

Most Recent View All Search

☑ Terms of Use
☑ Privacy Policy
☐ Videos
☐ Resources
☐ Site Building

Select All   Add to Menu

Links

Menu Name   Footer Menu   Save Menu

Menu Structure

Add menu items from the column on the left.

Menu Settings

Auto add pages

☐ Automatically add new top-level pages to this menu

Theme locations

☐ Navigation Menu

Delete Menu   Save Menu

Notice that I have clicked on "Terms of Use" and "Privacy Policy." This is because I want to place these in my Footer menu. They will by default appear in my master/main menu and I will remove them later, but for now my focus is on this menu.

Notice too that there are some new options here. I can have the system automatically add top-level pages to this menu or not. Top-level simply means the top-tier page or parent page. Pages added below each will not be included in the menu. Note too that the Theme locations lists a Navigation Menu. This is something that lets me know I may have a problem (more on this in a moment).

I can also either "Save Menu" or to the left of this I can click the link to "Delete Menu." I would only use this if I decided that A) I no longer want this menu or B) I goofed and want to start over. Like I keep saying, there is nothing in WordPress that can be done which cannot be undone with ease.

Now, with the thought in mind that nothing done in WordPress cannot be undone with ease, I am now going to demonstrate this in action. I just mentioned to you that I may have uncovered a slight problem. Now I am going to go to the tab at the top and find out if this is really the case. The two tabs along the top are "Edit Menu" and "Manage Locations."

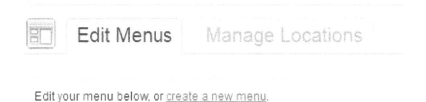

Edit Menus   Manage Locations

Edit your menu below, or create a new menu.

The Manage Locations is the tab I will use to move my menus around on my website, so if I have a problem, going here will show it up for sure. Let's see if this is the case.

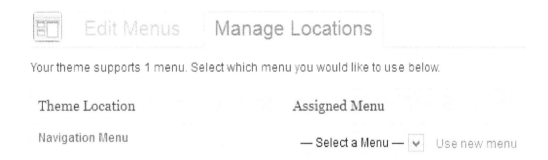

Can you see my problem?

This tab tells me that my "theme supports 1 menu." Uh, oh. I want more than one. I want two menus, one for the header and one for the footer. In fact, I may well want a third later in the side navigation. So what do I do?

Any thoughts?

Recall earlier when I mentioned that if needed, you can easily change themes? We are going to do that now. Waaaaaaay back on Day 11, I taught you how to choose a theme. You can review that chapter now if you'd like by clicking here if reading electronically. If reading in print, you will have to navigate the old fashioned way, using your fingers. However, if you retain information well, you may want to just follow along for I am now going to very quickly search for a suitable theme and change it. I may change it again later (for changing themes is so easy and I like to keep my websites fresh) but for now I want you to learn how to locate the elements you need and make course corrections. Building a website is somewhat planned and somewhat trial-and-error. This is part of the beauty of WordPress—changing virtually anything at any time is simple. So that said, let's find a new, more suitable theme. For now, I just want to find something that can support at least three menus.

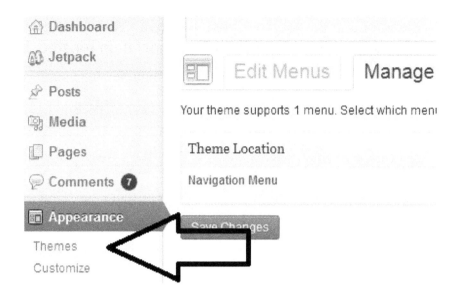

So, on the left navigation I am going to choose "Themes" as shown in the previous image. This brings me to…

Now I want to choose the right side tab which reads, "Install Themes" and I get a page which allows me to search by terms, filter according to a slew of options, or upload one I have on my PC.

For sake of this chapter, I am only interested in locating themes which allow me to modify menu options. You will notice that there are many other choices and once again, if I were to go into all of them, this book would be far too unwieldy and would likely scare you away. You are free to explore these other options of course at any time, for remember, if you don't like what you get, you can always revert easily. In the Appendix is an entire section devoted to playing around with Themes.

For now, we want to locate a suitable theme. In the following image I have shrunk the options for sake of space. Just notice that I have clicked on the "Custom Menu" option. This will filter my choices according to those themes which support additional menu choices. Notice that I am not making any other choices at this time. I will later, but for now and sake of instruction, I don't want to muddy the issue. Once I have chosen my option, I click on "Find Themes" at the lower left corner.

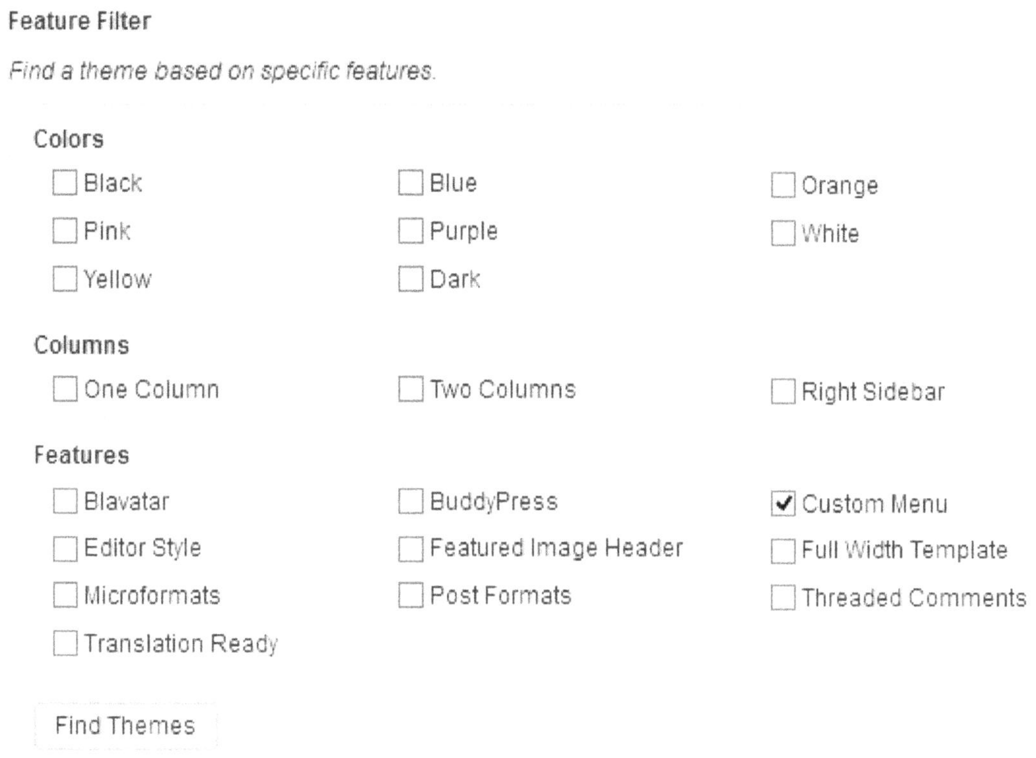

Feature Filter

Find a theme based on specific features.

Colors

☐ Black	☐ Blue	☐ Orange
☐ Pink	☐ Purple	☐ White
☐ Yellow	☐ Dark	

Columns

| ☐ One Column | ☐ Two Columns | ☐ Right Sidebar |

Features

☐ Blavatar	☐ BuddyPress	☑ Custom Menu
☐ Editor Style	☐ Featured Image Header	☐ Full Width Template
☐ Microformats	☐ Post Formats	☐ Threaded Comments
☐ Translation Ready		

Find Themes

I looked at the selections and found one called "ClassRoom Blog."

ClassRoom Blog
By apepperdesigns

Install Now   Preview   Details

Version: 1.08   ☆ ☆ ☆ ☆ ☆

ClassRoom Blog is a free wordpress theme for
Teachers and Educators to use for a class blog.
Elementary, Middle, Highschool and College
Professors have the ability to customize an easy to
work with education related theme. This theme is
released under GPL, GNU.

In checking the "Details" I am not really told much. Often, the theme designer will include information related specifically to what was requested in the search. In this case, nothing is included. But these should all provide for modifications, so I am going to take a chance. After all, if I don't like it, it is easy to revert to another. Check out the Appendix later to learn how to switch from theme to theme on a whim.

So I am going to click on "Install Now."

Installing Theme: ClassRoom Blog 1.08

Downloading install package from http://wordpress.org/themes/download/classroom-blog.

Unpacking the package...

Installing the theme...

Successfully installed the theme **ClassRoom Blog 1.08**.

Live Preview | Activate | Return to Theme Installer

Once the new theme is installed, I will get the screen you see above. Now click on "Activate."

I will return to the manage themes screen from which I can return to my site and see what it looks like.

The first thing I notice is that it has altered my header a bit so I will have to address that issue later. For now, I want to know if I can get the menus I need. So I go to the dropdown menu and choose Menus. Note too, that from the manage themes screen, there is also a link to the menu options.

Once at menus, I again head to "Manage Locations." Once again, I learn that the theme only supports one menu. It IS customizable, but there can be only one.

Bummer.

Back to the search function. This time, I am going to try something different. I am going to use the search feature.

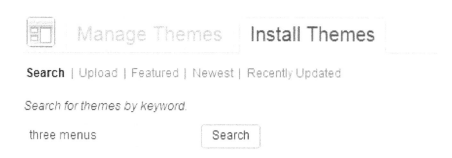

Notice that this time, I enter "three menus" into the search box on the theme installation screen. On clicking on "Find Themes," I am brought to a large selection.

Note. I wanted you to see the trial-and-error part of making these adjustments. When building your website, you will make many such efforts at fine-tuning so as to get exactly what you want. This is normal, though at times it can be frustrating. I hope though that this little exercise has shown you how to skin a cat in different ways.

In checking out the options, I eventually settled on installing a theme called Mantra. In reading the details of many, I found that they supported "3.0 menu versions" not "3 menus" as I wanted. This is why we read the details. However, Mantra stated that the entire site, menus and all, are fully customizable and seemed to indicate unlimited menus. So let's find out.

After activating the theme, I head over to the menu screen. I choose Manage Locations and find…

Success. Though the menu choices are NOT unlimited, I do have three options, which is what I was seeking. You can see these are a Primary, Top, and yes, Footer Navigation. Now all I have to do is create my menus.

To do this, I just choose the "Edit Menus" tab. I name my menus, edit as I see fit, then come back here to manage which goes where.

Excellent.

Sidebars

At this point, I am not sure if I can add a menu to my sidebar or not. I do know that the theme I have chosen provides for the Footer and Top navigation, but I am not sure what "Primary" means. With some exploring, I will find out.

The way to explore is to simply add a test page, then add this to the unknown menu, and see where it appears on the site.

However, even without this, sidebars can be used for navigation in most WordPress themes. We will discuss the use of Widgets in the next segment as these are the main way of adding navigation to the sidebars.

In addition, some sidebars have built-in navigation tools which can either be turned on or off.

For instance, in most themes, there will be a widget already in place to list in a table of contents style, your blogs. Often, there will be one in place to list blogs according to date. In either case, altering these to your preferences is simple.

Also, there will be a widget for text and if you know how to create your own html (which, I am sure you don't at this stage), you can add your own block ads for other pages in your site should you wish.

Too, different theme come with different sidebar options. With some, you cannot have any sidebars whereas with others you can have a left and right. In still others, the sidebars are fairly eliminated in favor of having four or five columns on your site. In other words, the options with WordPress themes, plugins, and widget permits you to use (or not) sidebars in virtually any configuration or for any purpose you can imagine.

Just remember that the key goal of the sidebar is to get people's attention and get them clicking on what you want them to click on. If it is an ad, careful placement will provide you with optimal revenue. If it is a navigation tool for other parts of your site, you want to make sure they can clearly use the feature. If it is a search box, again, you want it to be clearly seen.

The only other thing that needs to be said for sidebars is how to actually place them on your site if these are not already there by default.

Go to your edit screen for any page on your site. To the far right of the edit window, you will see the blue "Update" button and just below this...

…the "Page Attributes" function. This is where you choose page parents/tiers of pages. This is also where you will find page template options for whatever theme you are using. Once again, because each theme provides different options, it will not be possible to explain exactly what you have unless you are using the same theme as I. Still, from the above image you can see the options for this theme.

Notice that there is a default. This is always the case. But this theme comes with many different options such as sidebars to one side (either) or both. I can had no sidebar, or a specific type of page for my blogs (with this theme, these will default when building a blog page).

Thus, when building individual pages, I can choose to make them all the same or determine what sidebars appear on what pages.

This can be useful especially if I have a site that offers a variety of page styles. For instance, on my criminaljusticelaw.us website, I provide a store of items for anyone interested in criminal justice. Because I use an Amazon Store for this site (I will teach more on this in a future book), I am not able to include a sidebar. This is because of the way the store is designed by Amazon. Thus, in choosing the theme for that site, I had to ensure that I had the ability to eliminate sidebars entirely.

In addition, I may want a certain feel for groups of pages and another for others. Or, I may want certain ads and features to appear on blocks of pages and not others. Thus, I can create ads on one sidebar and something different on the other. Since the sidebars are uniform throughout the site, if I add a left sidebar, what I have included there will appear on all pages with that sidebar. Whatever is on the right sidebar will only appear on pages I have allocated a right sidebar to. Or, I can have both.

Again, this is just something you will want to play around with as your site grows and you begin adding more content and ads. But the thing that makes it all possible is the widget, which we will briefly discuss next.

Widgets

Widgets allow for a variety of options. You can add calendars, search boxes, quotes of the day, calculators, ads, menus, or virtually anything else you can think of. If you have ever visited a website and found something cool in the sidebar or within the body of the text which stood out, you have just seen a widget of sorts.

This is a text box placed here to demonstrate a Widget. If this had been a real Widget, something really useful would have appeared in this box.

A widget is simply a special form of code that allows for a box to be placed somewhere on the site so that you can add some stand-alone, complimentary material. For instance, look at the box to the right.

This is simply a text box added by the word processing program I use. However, on a website, this will be a box wherein you can add text or html so as to customize the space. Links can be added, video, audio, really, anything you want. Some websites add useful calculators that people can access without having to leave the page they are on and others add menus to help navigation. There are tons of plugins which use widgets as the foundation for what is provided.

Most themes on WordPress limit Widgets to the sidebar and footer, though some offer more options. There is even some special widget plugins which allows you to put widgets into the body of your content.

For now, all you need to know is that you can add Widgets to your sidebars to help make navigation much easier, among other things.

From the dropdown menu at the upper left corner (when you place your cursor over the site title), notice "Widgets." Choose this and we arrive at a screen that displays all your widgets. Without going into great detail as this will be covered in depth tomorrow, notice the options to the far right. You will see something like "Primary Widget Area," then the widgets which are currently in that area. Scrolling down a bit, you will likely see a "Secondary Widget Area," possibly a third, fourth, and so on. It may even read "Sidebar 1," "Sidebar 2," or "Left Sidebar," "Right Sidebar," or a number of other such monikers. The outcome of all these is the same, regardless of what the theme designer chose to call the area. These are the various locations for placing widgets around your website.

A simple way to determine where each appears is to click and drag a "Text Widget" into the field and type in something like, "This is a test to determine the location of the Second Widget Area." Then check your website. If you scout your site and do not find the test text, it could be because it appears somewhere not supported in the page template you are currently using for that page. Alter the template and the widget should appear somewhere. Give it a try if you'd like for there is nothing you may do that cannot be undone with ease. Tomorrow, you will become a Widget Master.

Generally, Widgets are pretty easy to figure out, but once in a while you may find one that is elusive. This is why Day 26 is set up exclusively for learning about widgets.

Adding Links within the Body and Elsewhere

Adding pages and links within the body of your pages is a great way to help people find additional useful information. This is known as in site navigation.

Recall on Day 22 we discussed the different kinds of links. Links can either point to your website from somewhere else on the web, point away from your website to some other site, or point within your site to other useful information. These are a form of navigation and the search engines do rate your site based on how much you balance these elements.

The way to use links within your website as navigation tools is simple: If you have written a page or added content somewhere that ties in to something you are currently adding, add a link to your own content. If you wrote something a month ago which will further clarify what you are now writing, add a link and let readers know why it is there. Also, be sure to check the box to open in a new window so that your readers do not have to jump back and forth. They can compare pages both at a glance by tabbing between them. This will help your readers, they will stay longer, and come back more often.

The search engines in turn will notice this and give you better marks, meaning they will be more apt to recommend your site as worthy in the SERP's.

Also, you can add widgets to the body of your copy if you have a special plugin or the theme supports it. There are many of both and the way to add widgets is to use the "Text" mode when editing. In some cases, a "short code" or "shortcode" may be used.

Short codes simplify the process of adding large bits of code to a page. Just copy the short code, often something like [pq] to the page in either Text or Visual mode, where you want it (where the cursor is), and voila, the item is added to the page.

In this way, you can add widgets to pages, then add whatever you want to the widget. Just always be thinking in terms of how you can make navigating your website easier for your visitors and you will be rewarded with more traffic.

Optimizing the Site for Navigation

Optimization involves not only getting the site in shape so that the search engines can find and index your site, but also so that your visitors can easily find the information they seek. Remember when I spoke of the Black Hat SEO folks versus the White Hatters?

The key difference between the two groups is that the White Hats concerned themselves with building websites that had value, were of use to readers. The Black Hat group was simply interested in traffic for the sake of traffic. There was no concern to whether anyone would return to the site or not or even whether the visitors found the information on the site useful or not. This is why Google did not like them. Google has been from the start, all about sorting out the good from the bad and only recommending, via their SERP's, the good.

If you get into the habit of constantly looking at ways to make the experience of visiting your website better for your visitors, traffic will come…and return…and often bring still more traffic with it. You want your visitors to have the best possible experience with your website and if you give them this, the search engines will notice.

The Panda and Penguin updates were feared by all when they first were announced. Not only did the Black Hat crowd shudder with fear, but even the White Hat crowd became nervous. Why?

The big changes brought by the updates were that,

1) Websites had to provide fresh material consistently

2) Websites had to become more interactive and engaging

3) Websites had to provide clearly written content

4) Websites has to provide original content

The Black Hatters feared the changes because of numbers 1 and 4. They mostly had the habit of providing clear content and the sites were often very interactive, but the page you would be rerouted to would often be simply a rehash of the same material.

The White Hatters feared the changes because they were unsure of how to make their sites interactive. Also, they knew that the programs were designed to learn. Too, many had even gotten into the habit of spinning some content so as to make redundant pages appear fresh. (Spinning material involves putting content into a special program which alters words by using synonyms and such so that the same article can be used several times yet seem fairly different.)

However, most have come to embrace the changes for in making websites more interactive and engaging to visitors, traffic rates have boomed on many websites whereas others have tanked. For a website to be interactive and engaging, the search engines look at how long visitors stay on a site, how often they view a single page then leave (bounce rate), and how many sites (popular or otherwise) link in. In other words, the search engines now study traffic patterns.

Think of it like this. If you were to stand in front of a row of store shops sometime and watch people come and go, eventually you would notice that some people enter and stay a long time. Some enter then leave. You would also see how many leave with bags of stuff and you would see how many go in and out of each store. It would not take you long to know which stores were the most popular and likely the best at which to shop. If someone were to ask you later where to go to get such and such, you would likely draw on your knowledge of these traffic patterns to provide a recommendation, saying something like, "Well, I did notice a lot of people going to shop B and leaving with a lot of stuff." The search engines do the same thing.

So what I am saying is this: Give the search engines a good reason to recommend your site and they will.

When the updates hit, even the White Hatters had fears because some had even developed habits which were not exactly in the best interests of their visitors. They hung to certain elements as if these were the Holy Grail. As you recall, earlier in this book we discussed these elements but I let you know that they are not necessarily necessary. What IS necessary is to give your visitors the best experience you can.

Give your visitors information. Give them accurate information. Give them original information and give them entertaining, education, engaging information. Provide references, preferably by way of links. And even if you just give references, the search engines will like your site and your visitors will be benefited. Everyone wins.

If you take some time to look at my CriminalJusticeLaw.us website, you are going to notice a good many essays which provide traditional references at the end of the articles but without links. The key reason I do not add links is because I would have to send people to academic websites to which, unless they subscribe, they will not gain access to the linked material. For students, they can simply add the reference into their school library website and gain the information as part of their program. For anyone else, if they do a search of these references, they will be taken to an academic site whereby they may subscribe if they wish. I just did not feel like providing the average reader with a link they cannot readily access. It just didn't seem like the right thing to do.

The way you optimize your site for navigation is to pay attention to navigation. In an advanced book you will learn how to use Google Webmaster Tools to further analyze your website, including internal links and such. This is useful for ensuring that all is functioning as it should. But for the novice starting out, just have a friend access your site from time to time and play around, moving from page to page. Ask another to perhaps locate certain bits of information, sort of like a scavenger hunt. In fact, send your kids on a scavenger hunt of your site.

Ask your visitors for comments and suggestions. Later, when you build mailing lists, you could even send them surveys asking direct questions about navigation.

To end, just remember to be mindful of navigation and the impact it has on visitors. Tomorrow, we explore Widgets and the next day, we build something vital for the search engines and the health of your website. We are approaching the end of this book and Month One, which means we are also approaching the beginning of an awesome journey. I hope you're enjoying the drive.

Day 26: Widgets

Widgets are one of the best tools ever developed for building websites. One of the best things about WordPress is that it is open-source software, which simply means that the company created the basic platform then made it available to computer geeks the world over…free of charge, as long as they do not alter the underlying programming and provide their goods free of charge as well.

This is why there are so many plugins and widgets available today. Millions of users who understand the relatively simple languages in which WordPress was developed have developed their own tools. These are offered in both free and paid versions, in accord with the rules established by the makers of WordPress. In most cases, the free versions are just fine, though sometimes getting the paid upgrade is well worth the small fees charged. In addition, most of the free versions stay totally free but rely on donations to help them continue improving their tools. If you can afford to donate, please do.

As a result of this, more plugins and widgets have been developed than could cover a volume of books.

In this segment, you are going to learn all you need to know to effectively use widgets on your WP website. Of course, you will not learn all there is to know, but simply all you need to know. That said, let's take a ride through widgetland.

To get to your widgets, simply go to your website (any page) when logged in as administrator. In the upper left corner where you see your site title on the gray bar, hover over the title and the dropdown menu will have "Widgets" as shown in the following image…

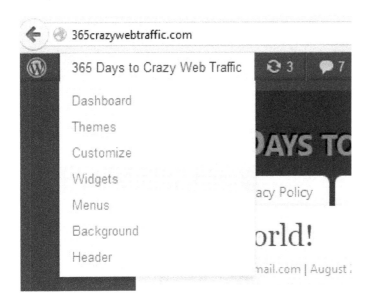

Click on Widgets and you will be taken to a screen which will show you all of your widgets included with your chosen theme. Some of the more common you will see are…

- ➢ Featured Posts
- ➢ Archives
- ➢ Calendar
- ➢ Categories
- ➢ Blog Subscriptions
- ➢ Askimet
- ➢ Tags, or Group Tags
- ➢ RSS Feed or Links
- ➢ Tag Cloud
- ➢ Recent Posts
- ➢ Recent Comments
- ➢ Related Posts
- ➢ Text

Of these, perhaps the most used is the "Text" Widget. This is because it is the most versatile. It can be either something you type into the widget that you want to appear where the widget is placed or it can be html as in the case of ads. First, I am going to show you how to add a widget to a sidebar or wherever, then we will discuss what each does.

You should know too that each theme has its own basic widgets and many plugins which you add will put a widget into your widget library. The basics you learn here should be enough to build your confidence towards exploring various widgets on your own.

Look first to the right when on the Widgets page.

There you will see something similar to...

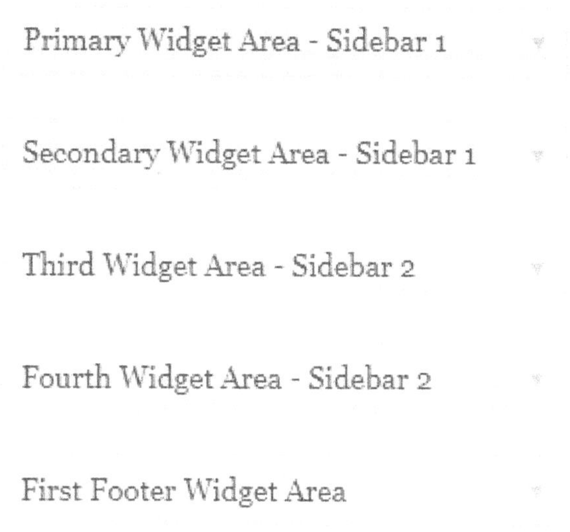

Primary Widget Area - Sidebar 1

Secondary Widget Area - Sidebar 1

Third Widget Area - Sidebar 2

Fourth Widget Area - Sidebar 2

First Footer Widget Area

As you can see, this theme has several widget areas including a primary and secondary area on sidebar 1 as well as the same on sidebar 2. There are even widget areas in the footer. Notice too that on the right of each there is a tiny inverted triangle, actually a down arrow. This opens the widget area so that I can edit it. If there is something in there I don't want to be there, I can take it out. If I want to add something, I can put it in. While open, I can move widgets into the order I want as well.

How do I move these around you ask?

Good question. Simple. Just left click hold on the desired widget and drag it to where you want it. In the following image, you will see that I have opened the Primary Widget Area – Sidebar 1. I found that it already contained a Search widget, Recent Posts, Recent Comments, Archives, and Categories. I want to add a Text Widget just below the search, so I grabbed the Text widget and dragged it to the space just below the Search Widget. As I entered the location, a dotted box appeared to let me know where the widget would be placed. Right where I want it. See?

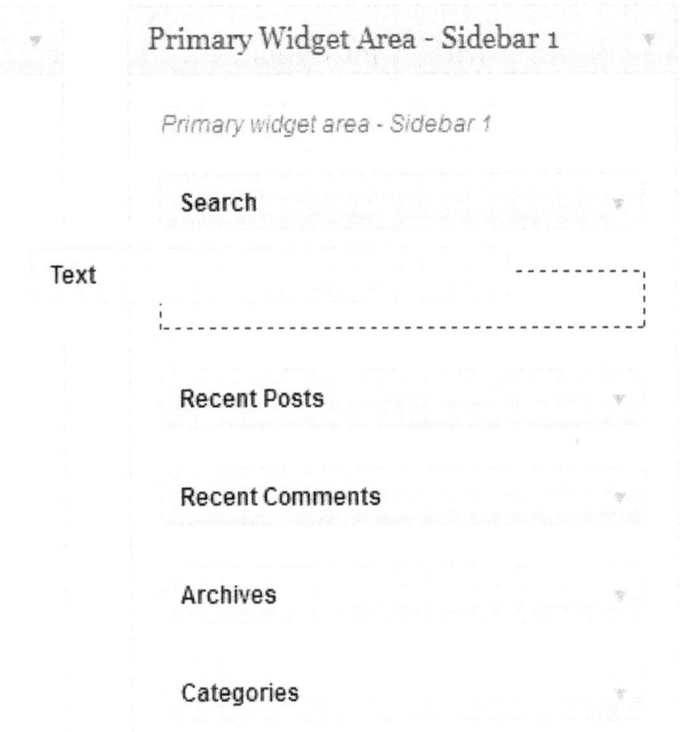

Primary Widget Area - Sidebar 1

Primary widget area - Sidebar 1

Search

Text

Recent Posts

Recent Comments

Archives

Categories

Now I want to add some text to the widget so I click on the inverted triangle and it opens.

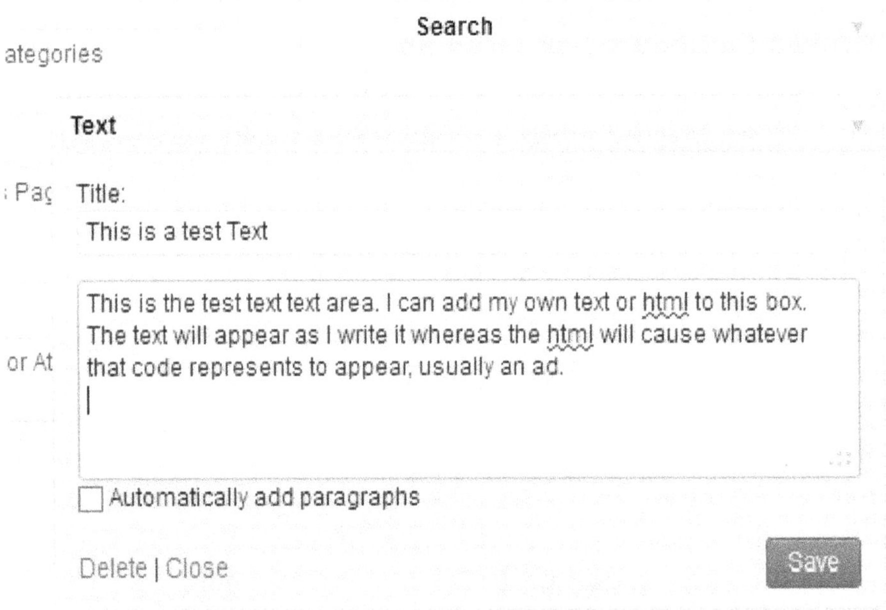

Search

ategories

Text

Pag   Title:

This is a test Text

or At   This is the test text text area. I can add my own text or html to this box. The text will appear as I write it whereas the html will cause whatever that code represents to appear, usually an ad.

☐ Automatically add paragraphs

Delete | Close   Save

Once you have added what you want to the text widget, you need to click on Save at the lower right. You can then close it and continue with moving widgets within the widget area in which you are working. Ok, that was a mouthful.

Something else to note about widgets. In the case of some, you can only have one and when you move it from the library to the widget area, that is it. In the case of others, such as the Text widget, you can have unlimited widgets. So when you move it from the library to a widget field area, another miraculously appears where you took the other from.

Now. Once we have added the widget, we want to see how it looks on the website. In addition, if I do not already know where Primary Widget Area 1 is located, it is time to find out. Note that with most themes, the widget areas are pretty direct—left sidebar, right sidebar, footer, and so on. This theme just wants to be different so I have to look for it.

So we are going to go back to the website. In the upper left corner again, I am going to hover over the site title again and a dropdown will read, "Visit Site." I click on this and I am on my home page.

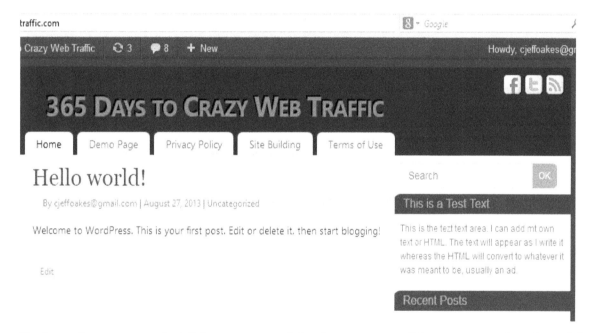

So here I can see what I have entered in the test text. You may notice that this is not the same wording as in the previous example. This is because after reminding you to click "save," I continued without saving. Then, when I was adding the information back, I decided to make it different so as to demonstrate another point.

Notice that there are misspellings. Text is Tezt and my is mt. There is NO SPELL CHECKER in the text widget. So whatever you put here, be sure it is what you want. This is a simple, WYSIWYG program. (For those who don't remember this old acronym, it simply means What You See Is What You Get.) This is the text widget. It is WYSIWYG.

Note too that the Search box is there where it should be and the Recent Posts widget appears below the text widget as it did when setting it up. This also tells me that my Primary Widget Area is the right sidebar. So I can assume the Secondary Widget Area is the left sidebar, right?

Not necessarily. To test it, I will need to open it up and place something into it. A test text widget is the simplest way. And recall when saving the text widget, there was also a "delete" link on the lower left. This will...hang on now...delete the widget.

Moving Widgets

Look at the following image...

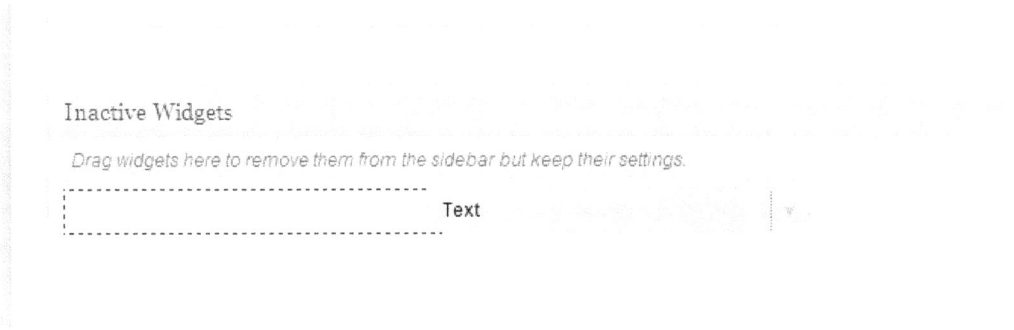

Inactive Widgets

Drag widgets here to remove them from the sidebar but keep their settings.

Text

At the bottom of the widgets area is this "Inactive Widgets" area. To move any widget into this area and thus deactivate it for a time, simply grab it by left-clicking on the widget and dragging it to this area. The same applies for moving the widget to the particular sidebar or footer area you want. Each such area has a tiny arrow to the right to open the full window and once open, you can move widgets in or out as well as see what is already there. Once you have the widget positioned such that it will go where you want it, you will notice a dotted block to indicate that is where it will drop when you release it (unclick your mouse button). That is all there is to moving widgets.

Go on an move some in and out of your sidebar and footer areas. With your website open in another tab, refresh the page and see what each one does. Play around with these until you've had your fill. Remember, if you don't want one in place, simply remove it. Deleting it from the sidebar area will not delete it permanently in most cases. Only the text widgets and form widgets you may create later (or will, in Chapter/Day 15) will delete when you do this. The other widgets will delete only from the sidebar or footer area, but not from the primary list of widgets.

This primary widget area is static, that is, you can only add to it if you upload a plugin and you cannot delete widgets from it. Of course, you need not use all the widgets in the area for that is your choice, but there is really nothing you can do here that cannot be undone with ease.

What else can I tell you about widgets?

Plenty, but the best way for you to learn about them is to explore. Play around with them. If you find one you are unsure of, add it to a known location in a sidebar or footer and see what it does. You can even search for widgets in the Plugins screen. Just go to the "Add New Plugin" screen and type "widgets" into the search box. As of this writing, there are 211 pages or over 2000 widgets available. And these are only the ones which use the term Widget in their title. There are actually far more than this.

I did, however, promise to fill you in on what the most common widgets do. So here is that list again, this time with brief explanations.

> **Featured Posts**: These are your blogs which are fairly recent or tagged as Featured. If you go to your settings menu on the left of your dashboard, you can adjust the setting for what is considered "Featured" or just let the system default. For now, leave the default until you know more. Then you will gain a better idea of how to make adjustments.

> **Archives:** Over time, you will accumulate a good many blogs. After several months, depending again on your settings, these will automatically "Archive." This simply means that they will drop off of most menus, especially the Calendar.

> **Calendar:** Your calendar will allow readers to look up blogs according to year, month, and/or date.

> **Categories:** As you create blogs, you can also create specific categories and subcategories. You can even add the same blog to multiple categories. If you use this widget, your readers can look within categories for those blogs which interest them most.

> **Blog Subscriptions:** This is a must. You want subscribers. Though

this book did not get into building subscription lists (emailing lists) and creating newsletters, a future book will and by the time you get to it, it would be nice to have a nice list built up. Don't worry if you cannot begin sending emails yet (though you can if you learn how to do so). You can always begin your campaign whenever you desire.

- **Akismet:** This is primarily at stats widget and I recommend against using it until you begin to get reasonable traffic, comments, and such. Personally, I never use it because it just seems ostentatious to me, but many like it. It is a personal choice.

- **Tags, or Group Tags:** One of the features of blogging is that word tags are used to help people located items of interest. In most themes, tagging is done automatically and in others, you have to manually determine the tags. This widget will create a listing of tags so that readers can locate blogs according to interest, much as the categories widget, but based more on exact words used in your blog.

- **Tag Cloud:** Rather than a list of tags, a tag cloud just sort of scatters the tags in a form of a, well, cloud.

- **RSS Feed or Links**: Many people with smart phones like to subscribe to RSS Feeds for these take the clutter out of the picture. In addition, RSS feeds provide them with all their favorite updates. RSS Feeds will be covered in another book, but these are not hard to set up with a plugin should you want to go it on your own.

- **Recent Posts:** This will display your most current posts according to the number set in your settings.

- **Recent Comments:** When people comment on your posts and pages, the recent ones can appear in your sidebar.

- **Related Posts:** When someone is reading a blog about horses on your site and there are other blogs you have written with the same word tagged, this widget will display these posts as "Related."

- **Text:** You know about this one. Use it, love it. This widget is a very good friend.

By now you should have a good handle on what widgets are and how to use them. As mentioned earlier in this book, you can get a widget for virtually anything you can imagine, for there is almost certainly someone else who not only imagined it, but created it. Seek and you will find.

That's all for today. Tomorrow, we explore a most necessary element to building a website that gets Crazy Web Traffic.

Day 27: Your Sitemap

The Sitemap is perhaps one of the most ignored and misunderstood of all website elements. It is also one of the most important. What is a sitemap, why is it so important, and how can you build one?

A sitemap is simply a navigation tool used primarily by the search engines to index your site. Think of it as a table of contents of the entire website. The search engine reads this index and uses it to place the information into order. Just as you earlier learned that you have files on your computer which lead to other files and still to other files deeper in, this is how a sitemap allows a search engine to read your site and send people to the pages contained within. It simplifies the process.

Today's search engines can read your site without a sitemap just fine, but if you provide one to them regularly, it makes the job of processing the information quicker and easier. Thus, the search crawlers will scan your site more frequently if your sitemap is regularly updated. Too, according to most experts, Google has built into their algorithm a way to read how fresh a website is. If it is not updated regularly, then the material must be old. If it is old, it gets relegated to lower SERP's. Thus, even if you update your pages regularly (and you should), if your sitemap is not, then it will take longer for the search engines to notice the changes. This could affect SERP's listings and traffic.

So how do you build a good sitemap?

Google XML Sitemap Creator

One of the plugins I recommended earlier in this book is the XML Sitemap Creator. The proper name of it is Google XML Sitemap and do not mistake it for the many others that use similar names. This is but one of many sitemap creators available with WordPress and certainly use whichever one you find easiest. I just happen to like this one and will teach you how to use it here. The only other recommendation I can make here is that until you are more versed in working on your website, try to find one that updates to Google and/or other search engines automatically.

But even with that, it is usually best to send the sitemap to the search engines yourself. Here is what you do.

Create Your Sitemap: Each plugin has a way to create the sitemap. Stay away from those which state they will create it automatically, send automatically, and clean your toilet bowl in the process. Few actually perform. Some do, I am told, but I have yet to find them. Of course, it never hurts to try, so if you want to, go on. If, after installing the miracle sitemap builder, you see no traffic results, you may decide to uninstall this one and find another. In any case, you will generally need to "build" your sitemap, which is really nothing more than clicking a few buttons.

Build a Sitemap page (or not): At one time, the search engines demanded a sitemap page but today it is optional. To be sure, some visitors like these for if they are lost, a sitemap is a great way to get your bearings. Perhaps you are looking for a specific article you recall reading on the site…a sitemap page helps. The pros and cons of building such a page, if you choose to do so is that as mentioned already somewhat, if you have a very complex website, as tends to happen over time, some visitors will find having a sitemap page useful. But building one is very time-consuming, especially for new people. Also, when new, your website will not have much content so such a page is fairly wasted and will need to be updated each time you add new material. The way to build it is to create a page of links to every other page, putting the exact titles and listing the information just as you would a table of contents, with subheadings for subpages, and so on. Most people just build the sitemap in the background using a plugin then submit it to the search engines.

> NOTE: At this time, you are going to learn how to build the sitemap, but hold off a bit. This is something basic you need to know, but if you send your sitemap to the search engines before you actually have content, your traffic possibilities could be harmed, not helped. I always recommend at least thirty pages of good content on your site before creating and submitting. But this is something you need to know so here is what you do.

To "build" a sitemap using Google XML Sitemap Creator (the one to send to the search engines), simply go to your dashboard. Along the left side near the bottom you will see "Settings."

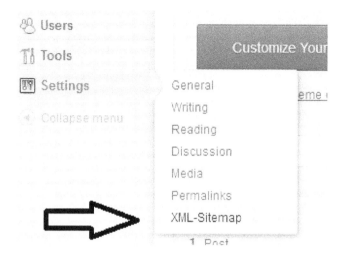

Then on the popout menu you will see XML-Sitemap at the bottom. Click on this. You will then go to…

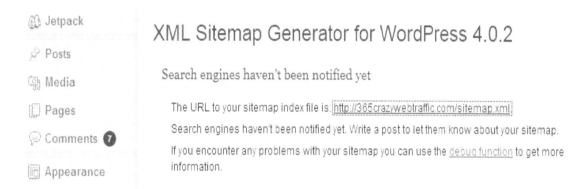

On this page, you can see that your sitemap already has a URL. Click on this and you will be taken to the sitemap for the site. As you can tell, creating the sitemap using this plugin is automatic. But to get it to the search engines, you have to submit it. In this case, it tells you to write a post to let the search engines know about the sitemap. This is a new feature and one I do not recommend. There is additional information on this page which will be addressed shortly.

The reason for not recommending using this approach is because your human readers will then likely go to your sitemap and find a page which is useless for them, as you will see shortly. Remember, you want your site to be as user-friendly as possible. Look at the following image, which shows what my sitemap for 365crazywebtraffic.com looks like at the time of this writing. As I have not yet populated the site with much information, the sitemap is brief.

XML Sitemap

This is a XML Sitemap which is supposed to be processed by search engines which follow the XML Sitemap standard like Ask
It was generated using the Blogging-Software WordPress and the Google Sitemap Generator Plugin by Arne Brachhold.
You can find more information about XML sitemaps on sitemaps.org and Google's list of sitemap programs.

URL	Last modified (GMT)
http://365crazywebtraffic.com/sitemap-misc.xml	2014-04-02 14:11
http://365crazywebtraffic.com/sitemap-pt-post-2013-08.xml	2013-08-27 17:25
http://365crazywebtraffic.com/sitemap-pt-page-2014-04.xml	2014-04-02 14:11
http://365crazywebtraffic.com/sitemap-pt-page-2013-10.xml	2013-10-28 18:19

Generated with Google (XML) Sitemaps Generator Plugin for WordPress by Arne Brachhold. This XSLT template is released under the GPL and free to use.
If you have problems with your sitemap please visit the plugin FAQ or the support forum.

As you can see, there are only four pages on the site at this time. These are not even heavily populated. This is because I wanted to complete the book then go into the site to add support materials. These support materials will be added to revisions of the book as needed. Of course, to get the revisions, all you will need to do is visit the site often or sign up for updates and I will email you. There will be no need to acquire another copy of this book. The updates will simply be links to support materials not already in this version.

In addition, if you follow the series of books, there will be no need to purchase revised editions long into the future for by the time you get to the end of the series, you will be a webspert yourself and know how to find changes to the web.

But this does show you how to know when you are ready to add your sitemap to the search engines. From time to time, go here and check out your sitemap. Once you have around thirty pages as shown by the individual links as shown, you will be ready for submission.

Now, for the additional information I told you we would discuss shortly. It is now shortly.

Below the link to your sitemap you will notice a long listing of options. Most of these are here for advanced users of sitemaps and for the novice, I recommend simply allowing the defaults already in place to remain. However, if you want to explore these options, you can always go to the creator's website. The only exception would be where it reads, "Sitemap Content." Here you will see several boxes not checked. It never hurts to check them all. In fact, as you add more content, you certainly want the search engines to locate your archives, as these can be a considerable source of traffic. For now, you can leave them unchecked, but as you build categories and archives and if you begin to bring in guest authors, you will certainly want to have these pages indexed—especially if the author is someone known.

At the bottom of this page you will see a blue button to "Update Options." Be sure to click this anytime you make changes.

List in Footer: If you do decide to build an actual sitemap page, the best place to put it is in the Footer navigation. This is because people often turn to a sitemap page as a last resort when looking for something and they are usually at the bottom of the page when the choice is made. For those who know to look for a sitemap page, they know to head south anyway.

Send the Sitemap to Search Engines: The last thing to do is get your sitemap to the search engines. This can seem daunting to the new person, but if you follow the guidelines of whichever search engine to the letter, it is pretty simple.

The way to submit to the search engines is to go to that search engine, say Google, and type the words "sitemap submission" into their search engine. In the SERP's, there will be links to the page you need. In the case of Google, the current link to the sitemap submission information is https://support.google.com/webmasters/answer/183669?hl=en

The reason I don't provide detailed information on how to submit sitemaps to the search engines is because these methods tend to change often or without notice. I could put information here and the day I publish it becomes obsolete. I would thus make things harder on you. It is simply best to just search for the info on doing so then follow the search engine instructions.

Submitting sitemaps to the search engines is not hard, you just need to know how to find the information.

Currently, for Yahoo go to https://help.yahoo.com/kb/yahoo-merchant-solutions/submit-sitemap-file-search-engines-sln19497.html

For Bing, go to http://www.bing.com/webmaster/help/how-to-submit-sitemaps-82a15bd4

Ask no longer takes sitemap submissions.

That is all for today. By now, you have a good handle on most of what you need to know to build a website that gets crazy web traffic, but there are just a couple of details which will make doing so much easier and less time-consuming.

You have likely heard that those who fail to plan, plan to fail. The same can be said of websites. The best websites have plans for growth. Tomorrow I am going to teach you a very simple method of planning so that you can grow your website consistently and by the end of the year, have more traffic than you ever imagined possible.

Day 28: Create an Editorial Calendar

An editorial calendar is nothing more than a plan for all the pages and blogs you are going to add to your site. It is not so much a carefully thought out act than it is a guideline. An editorial calendar keeps you on course, writing regular, fresh content. It is a roadmap to be used and relied on when you don't want to get in front of the keyboard. It forces you to meet your own deadlines.

There are complex and simple ways to create and maintain an editorial calendar. I prefer the simple method. I here provide you with a simple template which we will discuss shortly.

MONTH_____

DATE	KEYWORDS/SUBJECT	ARTICLE IDEA/WORKING TITLE

Notice first that this is nothing more than a grid with the month and the dates. I recommend writing every day, so you should label the date column as starting with the 1st, 2nd, 3rd, and so on. However, your schedule may prevent daily…you may plan to write only on certain days of the week or every other day or whatever your schedule permits. Either way, this is to keep you on course.

The space for keywords/subject is so that you know what keyword combinations/subject matter you need to write on so as to continually cover all your keyword combinations. The primary keyword combination should be in virtually every page/post you create so these need not be here. This is for those keywords you said were important to defining your website, but not to the extent they were used to choose your domain.

The last column is to be filled out as ideas come to you. Ideas are a funny thing. Some days we get a ton of ideas for writing articles about our chosen topic or product and other days we may be dry. If these are written down, it makes it easier to maintain momentum once we have begun. So whenever you get an idea, jot it on your editorial calendar. When that day arrives, you will be ready.

There is not much that needs to be said of this as the concept is really very simple. But just because it is simple does not mean it is not important. It is, so use it.

On a final note, some people use a spreadsheet to create their editorial calendar. This is not a bad idea for it allows you to put more information than on a sheet of paper. Indeed, a few website owners I know even put the links they plan to build on their editorial calendar, their social media schedule, and other important elements. If you want to add a certain number of videos each month, add the ideas to your calendar. If you want to locate guest bloggers for your site, add them to the calendar. In addition, when you start a newsletter, you should add these to your calendar. Add anything that you want to do on a regular basis to build your website and traffic.

So whether you decide to use a spreadsheet, a notebook, or some other means, get started creating your editorial calendar now. It need not be perfect or fancy or overly detailed—it needs only to give you guidance and keep you going. Choose whatever method works best for you. There is no wrong way.

See you tomorrow.

Day 29: Pay Close Attention

Attention to detail is the ingredient that makes the difference between a great meal and one which is so-so or worse. If you have ever been to a restaurant that had excellent food and great atmosphere, but poor service, you understand. The food can be likened to the content you create. You can create the best content in the world, provide excellent advice, or have the best products; you can build a slick website, one which dazzles and wows; but if you have not taken the time to service your visitors properly, it will all eventually crumble.

To make my point, I will now tell you a story about my first website, jeffoakes.me, which may or may not be running by the time you read this. You will understand why in a moment.

As previously mentioned, that website has been part experiment, part promotional for me. I used it initially to test what experts were saying. I experimented with SEO, content creation, link-building, emailing, newsletters, keyword density, plugins, working in the free WP environment, then eventually moving to self-hosting, and so forth. I learned much from the several years I have been running that site. However, during the time that I have been working on this book (and my pet project, criminaljusticelaw.us), I neglected jeffoakes.me. I have not been on it in more than eight months. Why not?

To be honest, time.

More than that though, the site is primarily only there to promote myself and my consulting services. Because I was not too interested in gaining new ghostwriting or consulting clients at this time, I just left off working on the site. Before I knew it, months had passed.

I recently decided to go in and add something. I could not. Instead, I saw…

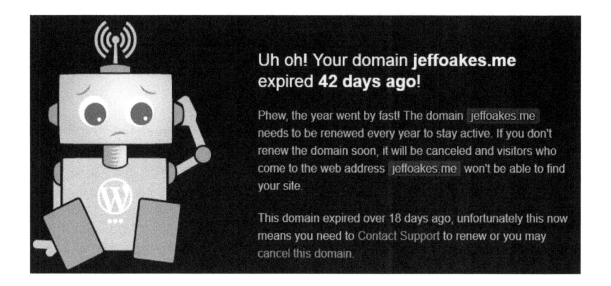

The site had been shut down by WordPress because I did not pay for the domain renewal. However, I was at first very disturbed. I set the domain renewal up for auto draft. Why was it not renewed?

I then remembered that I used my Debit Card and shortly after last years' renewal had lost it. It was replaced, but I had forgotten to add it to the account. Oops.

Now, I will have to get with WP support, which if you recall I earlier mentioned is a nightmare to deal with. This is why I am thinking of just shutting it down. I had for some time been thinking of moving the domain to HostMonster (who provides the hosting anyway), but never got around to it (again, because WP customer support is so bad). I also considered a better domain and shutting this one down anyway, but that requires rebuilding, which is time-consuming as you understand by now. So now, I am fairly forced to make a choice and as of this writing, the decision is not yet final. More than likely, after I spend all day on the phone with WildWestDomains, the company that handles domains for WP, I will transfer the domain registry to HostMonster then get the domain I want anyway. Then I can have the new domain route to my old one.

It's bad, but not the end of the world. I built traffic once (well, twice actually—I had to build again after changing to self-hosting, remember?) and I can build it again.

I tell this story for a few reasons.

First, when you are involved in the online world, things can happen pretty quick. You have to stay on top of it or face a problem like the one you see here. Because I have so many projects going at any given time and this site had ceased to be important to me, when the problem arose, I did not catch it until it had grown to serious proportions.

Second, I tell this story to remind my readers that we cannot rely on autodraft. It is a good idea to have a calendar to record certain important things like…domain renewals.

Third, I wanted everyone to know what happened so that I can hopefully help others avoid such costly mistakes themselves.

Finally, as you may have guessed, this is not the end of JeffOakes.me. I will likely get the domain transferred, but how difficult that will be remains to be seen. I believe that should I phone HostMonster, it will be a simple matter, now that the domain is completely expired. Were it not expired, WildWestDomains would have control and I would have no choice but deal with them…not something I care to do. My time is much too valuable.

So this this little story out of the way, let's review what you need to do if you are to get crazy web traffic in only 365 days.

365 Days to Crazy Web Traffic

In the first week, roughly, you learned how and why the Internet works the way it does. I told you about how you must learn to satisfy two readers—human and search engine. We discussed how search engines locate useful information and separates out the useless. You learned about the elements of SEO and why at one time they were vital, but today are less so, though still important. You also learned about keywords and Google's view of these. The number one thing you should have gotten from this section was that when you create your website, be sure to focus on a particular subject. The subject is the keyword/keyword combination. Your website needs to be clear, concise, and focused.

Moving into week two, you were focused on your subject and chose your site name, domain, hosting company, platform, and theme. We even added some plugins to prepare for going into week three. Just remember that you need to be focused on the website, which is a big reason I recommended getting a hosting company and using a platform which removes as much time-consuming details from your life as possible. That way, you can focus on the creative elements, you can focus on your position as a trusted expert in your chosen subject.

In the third week, we started adding pages to your website. Of course, recall that although we do not want to get hung up on the notion that certain pages are a must in order to get good positioning in the SERP's, there are certain pages which are necessary. Necessary simply means that we want to make the experience of our visitors as great as possible. We want people to return. If our website is user-friendly and they enjoy what we offer, they will return. Often, they will bring friends, by way of recommending us to their social media buddies. This provides what is often termed link-juice, for the search engines will read this popularity and will be more inclined to recommend us to their users.

Just remember to make the pages on your site useful, engaging, and/or entertaining and you can't go wrong.

Rounding out week three, we learned about the importance of links, not just to and from your website, but within as well. The importance of links cannot be stressed enough. The Internet developed as a direct result of the hyperlink. Links are the nerve center of the Internet. Without links, no one could find anything. When thinking of traffic, think of links as streets, roads, and highways.

It has often been said that the power of America stemmed from her infrastructure. Indeed, our incredible highway system is largely what permitted the nation to grow and become strong. Had we not had the U.S. Interstate system, imagine how difficult it would have been for farmers in Idaho to deliver their potatoes to NYC without them spoiling. Could grape and orange growers in California have delivered over the Rocky Mountains without spoilage without the Interstate? And consider how much our highway system has facilitated the transport of fuels, building materials, and other goods.

In a similar way, links allow web users the ability to travel to any website anywhere in the world. Without links, this would not be possible...or at least not with the ease we do so today. So pay very close attention to your links, in, out, and otherwise. They are ALL important.

Finally, rounding out the week we discussed the use of images and how to make sure these get noticed by search engines and our readers. If a picture is worth a thousand words, an image on the net is worth a million clicks. Not sure you agree with that statements? Type into your search engine the terms "viral images" and see what you get. You will see plenty of images that were so popular that they literally covered the earth in a matter of seconds. Manage to get one of these on your website and boom, traffic will seriously spike.

Moving into your final week, you learned an easy way to create and place video onto your website. According to some sources, video, despite the enormous popularity, is still only used by about 2-3% of all websites. Of course, given that only 2-3% of all websites ever get more traffic than one or two hits a month, this makes sense. And think too, when you begin to get just four hits a month, you will be doing better than 98% of all websites in existence. When you begin to get just 100 hits a month, you can safely assume you are in the top 1%! And really, if you apply all you have been taught in this book, you can expect far more traffic than that.

Don't forget to make navigating your website as simple as possible and when you have enough pages, submit your site to the search engines. Your goal should be to get thirty pages completed within 30 days. After that, take a breather and follow your editorial calendar. But get those pages in as soon as possible so that you can get the search engines attention. Will you fail to get listed if you do not submit your sitemap?

Of course not. The search engines will locate you eventually no matter what you do. They will index your site no matter what. But it may take some time to get noticed...or it could happen with your first blog or article. We never know, for the search crawlers, spiders they are often called, will find you when they find you. But if it hasn't happened by the time you write your 30th page, let them know where you are. They will come see you and if they like what they see, they will start making recommendations. If they do not, they will check back regularly to see if you are still adding new content to index. If you are doing so on a regular basis, they will pay more attention to your site. If you remain consistent, they will learn your patterns. Once they learn your patterns, you will get indexed quicker and subsequently receive better results on the SERP's.

I once had an article I wrote picked up in 20 minutes by Google. You may recall the story…the Miami Zombie guy. The article I wrote was called simply, "Zombies in Miami?" and within 20 minutes of posting the article, I began to get hits derived from the search engine Google. I was search the internet for stories and came across this hot bit of news. It was less than five minutes old from the timer on the page where I read it. It was one of those 24 hours news channels with a website. After writing my piece, I began to work on something else. In the middle of that something else, I happened to look at my stats bar at the top of my page. It was spiking so I went to my stats page and there it was: Google search, 2 hits. And the counter kept climbing. Later that day, the Washington Times 24/7 picked up the link and traffic soared even more (or was it the Huffington Post? I can't seem to recall now, but I had articles linked by both). What a rush that was, both times.

The point is, if you get to adding material regularly, the search spiders will learn this and check back often. The more they index your site, the better they believe your site to be. The better they believe it to be, the higher in the Search Engine Results Pages you will position. The higher you position, the more people will find you. The more people find you, the more you can make from products or ads. Traffic. That's what you want and by faithfully applying what you learn here, that is what you will get.

Happy motoring.

Day 30: Congratulations/Content/Celebrate

Remember that this book is both complete and complimentary. If anyone wants to become a webspert, then be sure to read the remaining books in the series. However, even if you simply want to have fun and build a website that generates copious levels of traffic, all you need is contained herein. The key lay in content.

Bill Gates was once quoted as saying about the Internet that "Content is King."

Of course, the Internet is changing every day. Within a year, portions of this book will be obsolete if I do not update them (and I will). What this means for the webmaster-to-be is that you must continue to read and learn all you can about the web. It's either that, or hire someone who does. In the early stages of your website, you will not likely have the cash flow to go hiring folks, so you had better do your homework.

This book can stand on its own and teach you the basics so that you get far more traffic than 99 percent of the people building on the web. If you want to supercharge your traffic, you want to follow the remaining titles.

I cannot say when each will appear. I will get them out as soon as possible, but I refuse to just churn them out with no attention to quality. I hope you enjoyed and learned much from this book so I would love to hear from you.

Email me at cjeffoakes@365crazywebtraffic.com and let me know what you thought. Also, if you want to be notified of future releases, just say so and your wish is my command. And be sure to visit 365crazywebtraffic.com often for updates. I will begin to work on that site once this book is published, so if there is little there, be sure to sign up for the updates to be notified when new pages appear.

Your Task for Today:

Pat yourself on the back and celebrate. Go have a slice of cheesecake, take a cruise, or simply drink a cool glass of water. Whatever you want…you earned it. By now, you will have a fully functioning website with a growing base of pages and blogs. You are on your way to Crazy Web Traffic. In fact, if you only do a quarter of what you read in this book (depending on which quarter, naturally), you will still get more traffic than the mass of so-called webmasters out there.

Recall back at the beginning of this book that I said that if you took just A SINGLE STEP that you would grow traffic on your website? Now I will reveal that step.

If you have been paying close attention throughout this book, you may have already guessed that the key is good content. The Internet is a content hog. Give the search engines and your visitors what they want—quality written content—and you will get traffic.

Of course, the key to Crazy Web Traffic is to do everything I have taught you here. But just the one step of creating fresh, original content will result in traffic as long as you add it consistently and don't stop. When you stop, the traffic stops. So don't stop.

I certainly hope you have found this book to be the most useful ever and if you have purchased this on Amazon, I would really, REALLY, REALLY appreciate you adding your own review. Even if you were somehow disappointed, I would like to know that because I can use your reviews to make future editions even better. I thank you in advance and will turn you over now to my marketing department. After a few words from them, you can proceed to the Glossary, Appendices, and Index.

Future Titles/Months:

Month 2: Crazy Web Traffic via Link-Building

In Month Two, you will learn in much greater detail how to build sound links which will result in greater traffic. Most websperts agree that over time, link building can easily account for 30-40% of all traffic to a website. Considering that links are the most vital element of the Internet, this makes sense. So it follows that if you are to master any element of building crazy web traffic, this is the one must have in your travel kit.

Month 3: Crazy Web Traffic through Social Media

Social Media is a form of link-building, but it is much more than that. In fact, most websperts agree that Social Media used right can easily drive between 10% and 15% of a sites traffic. In some cases, Social Media accounts for much more whereas in most, it accounts for virtually none. Many social media experts also warn that done wrong, Social Media can also cause traffic to cease. You don't want your visitors to get detoured, so this book will be a must.

Month 4: Crazy Web Traffic from Directories

Directories do not carry the weight they once did, but if you check the traffic stats for many of the older, still in use directories, you will find that millions continue to use them. This is partly because millions got used to using them in the days prior to great search engines and still rely on their recommendations. These are kind of like visiting an old friend. Others may call him a useless, old kook, but he has never failed to steer you down the right path so you continue to visit him. Directories may one day become obsolete, but for now, they can still be a substantial source of traffic. The best part is that if you know what to do, directories take very little time to get a listing in. So even if directories only return one or two percent of all your traffic, is that not worth the little bit of time required to get listed in in them?

Month 5: Use Newsletters to Drive Crazy Web Traffic

Newsletters (and email campaigns) are considered to be responsible for nearly 10% of repeat traffic to many websites. Considering that repeat traffic is so important to growing a website as well as getting the search engines to consider your site worthy of good placement in the SERP's, investing some time in building a mailing list and publishing a good newsletter is time very well spent. Learn how to use Newsletter to the greatest advantage with this book.

Month 6: Crazy Web Traffic Branding

Just as companies for the last century built brands so as to gain a strong competitive edge, so too should anyone with a website. What is an online brand? Think Google, YouTube, Amazon, Twitter, Facebook, Pinterest, Reddit, StumbleUpon, and the list could continue for some time. How often do we hear someone with an i-Phone say "I'll Google it?" The i-Phone comes pre-loaded with a Yahoo browser, so in reality they are not Googling, but more than likely using the Yahoo search engine (though technically still Google since that is who they buy their search results from). Still, the Google brand is so strong, regardless of which search engine we use, we tend to say we're "Googling." When people speak of your website though using another, you have a brand and are likely raking in a hefty amount of cash in the process. This book will teach how to build an online brand using examples from all those who have done so so far.

Month 7: Video Your Way to Crazy Web Traffic

Video is still in its infant stages on the Internet. Lest we forget, YouTube was launched just 9 years ago on February 14, 2005. That's not all that long. Most of us have socks older than that. I know I sure do. But how do you use video to your advantage? How do you use video to promote your website while at the same time creating entertaining video that can stand on its own? In this book, we will explore some of the pioneers of video today—people just like you and I who are taking video to the next level and turning the world of corporate websites into empty parking lots.

Month 8: Crazy Web Traffic by Advertising

A website is marketing, which is a form of advertising. Which is why it seems odd at times to drive down the highway and see a billboard advertising a website. Advertising your advertising? Crazy, right? At first I and many others thought so, but much depends on the type of site and the reasons it exists.

Of course, there are also those who have found ways to both advertise their websites AND in turn gain revenue from the advertising they use ON THEIR website. This is somewhat perverse, but used right, it works as a means of generating both increased traffic and revenue. In this book, you will learn both when to use advertising to advertise your website and how to do it right.

Month 9: How to Monetize Your Crazy Web Traffic

Of course, what good is traffic if you cannot use that traffic to gain a fair profit? If the purpose of your website is to be a good Samaritan and not make a dime, good for you. Very noble and I applaud you. However, for most of us, we would like to generate at least some revenue. Most of us would like to be able to quit our day jobs and live a different lifestyle, one that can be provided with our website running on auto-pilot. So in this book, you will learn all the different ways to use the traffic you are gaining so that you can see a profit. Think of it as an automatic toll booth, but a toll booth where the drivers do not pay. Rather, the tolls are paid by those placing virtual billboards along your road.

Month 10: Crazy Web Traffic with Guest Blogging

Guest blogging is another great way to increase traffic, but websperts are very divided on this topic. This is because there have been plenty of great success stories and just as many stories of horror. In this book, we will examine many examples of each and let you determine whether this strategy is for you. Indeed, guest blogging can be great, but it can also be fraught with dangerous curves and drop-offs. So as to help you navigate this winding, mountain road and make it to the top, this book will provide you with the signs to point you on the right course. If you follow the path laid out, you will have plenty of traffic following your lead. Once on top of the mountain, throw a party and watch the fireworks together with your entourage.

Month 11: The Analytics of Crazy Web Traffic

You cannot be a webspert in your own right without knowing how to analyze your website. You need to know how to use Google Analytics as well as a number of other great analytical tools available on the web. There are many and in this book, we will introduce the good, the bad, and the ugly. At this point in time, most analytic tools are limited. Each has strong suits and none can provide you with everything you need to fully capitalize on the traffic entering your site. With this book, you will be taught how to use many of these, what their strengths and weaknesses are, and how to avoid duplicating your efforts when using multiple analytics tools. We will also explore both free and paid tools so that you can know which are a good value and which are just taking you for a ride. Fasten your seat belt, this one may be bumpy.

Month 12: Advanced Crazy Web Traffic Tactics

Our final month together is going to explore not only the hottest, current tactics, but also those which are emerging as promising ways to grow traffic. Because the Internet changes so often, this book will likewise change frequently. Thus, this book will need to be updated every year or so. Therefore, I am going to let everyone know now that anyone purchasing this book directly from the publisher in electronic form will have the opportunity to receive updates free of charge for life. I figure it is the least I can do because this book will be a vital tool for advanced websperts and will have to change frequently. Books for life…isn't that exciting? Oooo, I can hardly wait. And I just love giving stuff away. It makes me all…giddy.

SPECIAL NOTE FROM THE AUTHOR

It is with great anticipation that I will soon turn my attention to the website, 365CrazyWebTraffic.com

I hope to see you all there, hear your comments, answer questions, and help you build crazy web traffic to your website. This brief journey we've taken has been a delight and I enjoyed the company of you all. I look forward to the rest of our journey together and seeing how much traffic flows to you.

I cannot wait to hear your success stories and when you send them to me at cjeffoakes@365crazywebtraffic.com I will be honored to share them on 365CrazyWebTraffic.com. When sending your success stories, let me know if I have your permission to publish with your name and website/domain. Remember, this will help grow your site and I would be delighted to do my part to help. And of course, if I like your site, rest assured that I will add you in all my social bookmarks and join you in your social media. Naturally, if you are a fan, I will be biased in your favor, of course. Wink, wink.

Thanks for riding along with me through 365 Days to Crazy Web Traffic, Month One. I have really enjoyed the ride and hope you did too.

Kindest Regards,

C. Jeff Oakes

Glossary

Adwords – (see Google Adwords)

Adsense – (see Google Adsense)

Alexa – Traffic Ranking/rating scale developed to rank all websites on the planet. After Google purchased Alexa, the site was altered to rank only sites using Google tools.

Algorithm – a computer program that performs a function. A calculator functions according to an algorithm, but in Internet terms, this generally applies to search engines.

Alt Tags – Word tags used for images to tell the search engines what appears.

Amazon – Website which developed first as a bookstore but which has since expanded into virtually any kind of product sold today online. Website owners can even build their own Amazon store right on their site for generating additional advertising revenue.

Anchor Text – text that is used to "anchor" the keywords of a website through the link represented. Though not as important in SEO as in times past, anchor text is still a great tool for helping visitors see exactly where they are going when clicking on a link. In other words, I have created anchor text by telling you to visit 365 Days to Crazy Web Traffic dot com, because I have embedded the link, which contains the keywords "365, crazy, web, and traffic" while at the same time using them in the text associated with the link. At one time, this was very important to SEO…today, not so much.

Blog/Blogging – the creation of a rolling set of posts, originally as a form of journal, used by websites to provide latest news or commentary outside the regular bounds of their pages.

Bricks and Mortar business – traditional business. Physical location.

Brin, Sergey – One of the founders of Google. Sergey Brin met Larry Page while getting his PhD in computing at Stanford University. He had developed a data mining algorithm that functioned nicely with elements Page had developed for "scoring" a website and the pages within.

Host/Hosting – a website that provides other site owners the ability to store their sites on a server.

Chrome – a free browser developed by Google.

Chrome Extensions – additional functions available at no charge for use with the Chrome browser.

Compuserve – an older, less known browser, Compuserve was the first major online service.

Content – any material created for a website including words, video, audio, tools, etc. In general, content refers most often to the written material created for a website.

Control panel – the place on a host company website where a site owner can add functionality to the basic programming of their site, create email accounts, determine the building platform, and other features.

Conversion rate – the rate at which a website achieves its purpose. Most often used to denote how many visitors translate into sales, this could also be an indicator of how many visitors provide information which can be used as leads.

Crawlers – a short term used to describe the function of the search engines as it indexes web pages and websites. Also called search crawlers, spiders, and web crawlers.

Dashboard – an admin tool on a WordPress website which allows the webmaster the ability to modify the site to his/her desire. This is the backside of the website, where building takes place.

Directories – tools for locating useful websites. Less prominent today for the rise of good search engines, at one time these were the only viable means of locating good content on the web.

Domain – the web address of a website. Also called the URL or sitename, though these are slightly different.

Engagement – the measure of how well visitors to a website stay and use other parts of the site. Is tied to how the search engines view a website in terms of usefulness to visitors.

EvoLve – a theme available on WordPress.

Facebook – the largest social media website in the world.
file-sharing platform – (See open source software)

Free hosting – a term used in conjunction with blogging tools for providing free websites/blogs to users.

Ghostwriting – writing material for other people in exchange for money. The ghostwriter generally accepts payment in exchange for copyright to the material.

Gmail – the email account provided free of charge by Google.

Google – the largest search engine in the world. Google changed the way people used the Internet by building and providing free of charge a search engine that actually did what it said it would do…provide quality search results every time. Google continues to modify and fine tune its search algorithm so as to prevent cheating by webmasters and give searchers the great results they want. As the company grows, it continues to provide tools free to anyone wanting these, in exchange for the freedom to add cookies to the user's PC. The company then uses these to target advertising.

Google Adsense – the advertising arm of Google which allows website owners to share in the revenue derived from ads placed on their website or YouTube channel.

Google Adwords – the advertising arm of Google which allows site owners to place ads and bid on the rate paid. Adwords is used to drive traffic to websites by the use of targeting cookies such that people only receive ads for things they are interested in. Such targeted ads are changing the face of Advertising today and lowering the overall cost of advertising to consumers.

Google Keyword Tool – a tool formerly provided to the general public but now restricted to Adwords account holders, which allowed webmasters the ability to determine, within certain parameters, how many people search for certain words and word combinations worldwide each month.

Google slap down – a term coined after Google made its first major algorithm changes so as to catch websites cheating the system in their eyes. When an offending site was detected by the search crawlers, the program would then penalize the site, often permanently. Thus websites which had grown in the search engine results pages (SERP's) as a result of "cheating" the system, suddenly found they no longer ranked and traffic plummeted.

Google Webmaster Tools – free tools provided to Google members for checking the parameters upon which Google makes its assessment of the site. By using these tools, a webmaster can learn how Google views their website and make adjustments to improve search traffic.

HTTP – hypertext transfer protocol. This is the term used to denote the programming developed by Tim Berners-Lee, which made the Internet as we know it today possible. The "http" which appears before "every" website today denotes the use of the language/programming developed by Berners-Lee. "Every" website is in the sense that there are still other protocols in use by Universities, Government bodies, and Researchers, which is why the http:// is still an important element of web addresses.

Hyperlink – (see also link)

Hyperlink protocol – (see also Tim Berners Lee, HTTP)

Hypertext – the text associated with the link embedded behind the text.

Hypertext Transfer Protocol – (see HTTP)

Internet – the connection of computers worldwide made possible through various protocols developed since the 1950's. When Tim Berners-Lee developed the Hypertext Transfer Protocol, which utilized the hyperlink, the Internet as we know today was born.

Internet Explorer – the web browser developed by Microsoft.

Keyword combination – the stringing together of several key words to define the content on a page.

Keyword – a word used to define content; essentially, the subject of a web page, article, or blog.

Lead Generation – a means of using the Internet and website so as to develop leads which can be used in furthering the interests of a traditional Bricks and Mortal business.

Link – a way of connecting web pages and content across the Internet in a simple way. The link makes the Internet possible by allowing webmasters the ability to instantly connect their readers to additional, useful information spanning the globe. (See also HTTP and Tim Berners-Lee)

Meta – is derived from a Greek term which means literally "About about." At one time, meta tags and descriptions held considerable weight by the search engines in locating useful information, but Google has largely eliminated these with their 2009 updates, with some minor exceptions.

Meta Descriptions – Used to describe the site. Today, these are mostly important for use in describing video, audio, and images since the search engines can neither see nor hear.

Meta Tags – single words used to describe a website. Also called keywords, but Google has largely done away with the need for these tags with the 2009 updates, which created a new indexing system, free of the need for outside tagging. However, these are still used for video, audio, and images.

MySpace – one of the first Social Media websites, today mostly relegated to music interests, eclipsed by Facebook among others.

Natural Search results – results when searching which are not paid for by others, but which are naturally generated by the search engines when indexing and locating results. These are not affected by advertisers, at least not yet.

Open source software – programming made publically available at no charge. The most popular such today is WordPress, which in a few short years has grown to be the most popular blogging/website building platform in the world, largely as a result of making their source code free to anyone willing to abide by their rules/terms of use. A key term being that modified programs must also be free, or at least have a free option alongside a paid version. (see also WordPress)

Page, Larry – one of the two founders/developers of Google, Page developed the system for ranking websites so as to provide great results. This system worked perfectly with Sergey Brin's data mining system and the two turned Google into the most dominant force on the web today.

Page rank – the name of the original ranking system developed by Larry Page, but which has been largely eliminated with the 2009 updates to the algorithm. Still, the Page rank system remains in place, so webmasters wonder what this means for the future of this system and how they build websites.

Pages – web pages. These provide the content of which people search daily.

Paid search results – these are ads generated by the search engines which reflect results which match what the searcher is seeking, but which have not naturally ranked. Instead, someone has created and paid for the results which appear. On Google, these appear first and to the right of the natural results.

Panda/Penguin updates – two separate updates by Google, but occurring so near to the other that most websperts refer to them jointly. The goal of Google with these two updates was to eliminate the "cheating" of their algorithm that had developed while creating a form of artificial intelligence, learning, by their program. This would allow the algorithm the ability to continually sort out the good from the bad and provide their users with the best search results possible.

Plagiarize, plagiarism – the stringing together of five (5) or more words which match exactly what has already been published. Thus, one can even plagiarize even their own writing. The search engines look for cases of plagiarism and websites violating this fundamental principle of publishing pay for it by losing their position in the SERP's. The extent to which the search engines tolerate plagiarism is not currently known.

Plugin – a tool used by WordPress users to add functionality to their websites.

Privacy Policy – websites today often collect information from users and because of this should have in effect a policy stating openly to users what they will and will not do with this information. Whereas a website may even tell users that they have no privacy, this should still be disclosed.

Publish – traditionally, publishing meant print, but today, if someone creates a website, it is a form of electronic publishing. Thus, with the development of the Internet has come a spike in publishing.

Sales site – a website developed to sell something. For example, eBay, Amazon, and WallysWeirdStuff are all sales sites.

Search crawlers – (see search engine)

Search engine – an algorithm developed to help searchers locate useful information. The search engine operates by use of crawlers, special programs, which search the Internet and Index information using a ranking, or scoring system.

Search Engine Optimization – fine tuning a website so that it gets the best search engine results possible. Frowned upon largely by Google, SEO is the means by which careful webmasters not only create good content for human readers, but content that pleases the search engines as well. Google has since implemented changes which prevent site owners from ONLY creating content which will please the search engines and fairly rewards those which play by their rules.

SERP's – Search Engine Results Pages – these are the results you see when entering words for a search. Based on what you enter, the search engines attempt to provide the most accurate return of results.

Self-hosting – a term used to denote leaving a freely hosted blog site so as to host with an outside company. The benefit is that with free hosting a website owner cannot derive a profit from ads or sales whereas with self-hosting, a website owner may.

Self-publishing – (see self-hosting)

SEO – (see search engine optimization)

Settings – A section of the WordPress dashboard that allows a user to adjust settings of the website.

Site – (see website)

Site building platform – the basic tool for building a website, the most popular of which today is WordPress.

Social Media – often called web 2.0, social media has become a force of its own on the Internet. Social media is so powerful, that used well a website can transform from a minor site to a major one in weeks, even days. Used wrong, however, and a website can just as quickly enter oblivion, never to return. Social Media attempts campaigns should only be attempted by those who know both how to use the particular SM site AND are willing/able to put in the time needed to do it right.

Sponsored results – (see Paid Search Results)

Subject – (see Keyword)

Support sites – websites developed to support other businesses, whether online or off. Google is a support site, hosting companies, as are websites built to further promote a traditional brick and mortar business.

Template – a structure developed to provide a guideline for building. In the case of a website, a template is often used to create a structured theme to the site. Largely unseen today for when someone creates a website using WordPress or a similar platform, the theme was built on a template, but users simply choose the preferred theme with no though to the underlying structure.

Terms and Conditions/TOC – the terms of use of the website. All websites should have a terms page to let users know what may or may not be done when using the website.

Theme – an overall appearance or style of a website, most often associated with WordPress websites.

Themeforest – an excellent source for locating themes for sale.

Tim Berners-Lee. Father of the Internet as we know it. Tim Berners-Lee created the hyperlink while working as a researcher at the supercollider facility CERN, in Switzerland. See also Hyperlink/link

Traffic – visitors to your website. Just as a store or billboard needs traffic to be successful, a website is just collecting dust unless people...traffic...arrives. With traffic then comes the ability to capitalize on the traffic and monetize the website, that is, make a living from it.

Twenty Ten – one of the most popular free themes on WordPress.
Two audiences – humans and search engines are the two audiences to which a webmaster must write if he/she is to gain traffic.

Uniform Resource Locator (URL) – also called the domain, or web address, the URL is the form the address takes on so as to direct visitors to a website or page. Just as a physical address has a standard placement of components, so too the URL, through standardization, allows anyone to located any website in the world.

URL – (see Uniform Resource Locator)

Webspert – A Web Expert; as opposed to a Webmaster, a webspert knows how to actually run a website in such a way as to develop traffic and loyal followers/readers.

Webmaster – A term coined for people who know how to build websites. While many can build, few can build in such a way as to develop traffic.

Weblife – A life or business built online.

Widget – a tool used by web builders, primarily WordPress users, to add functionality to their websites. Widgets allow a webmaster the ability to add virtually any tool desired to their website so as to further enhance the user experience.

Word – the word processor developed by Microsoft.

WordPress – open source software software provided by Automatic, Inc for use in building blog/websites. It also provides a free option for users or permits hosting companies to install this on client websites at no additional charge. As a result of the open source choice by the company, WordPress has grown to become the most popular building platform in the world, with users adding new plugins, themes, and widgets daily to the growing library of available features.

World Wide Web – the former term for the Internet, largely out of use today except among the older users, such as the writer of this book.

Yahoo – a web browser and search engine developed pre-Google. At one time the dominant force on the web with a reasonably good search engine and free email client. Yahoo has since slipped and today purchases their search results from Google. Although still a dominant force on the Internet, Yahoo is an example of how quickly things can change on the web.

Appendices

A. How to Sign Up with BlueHost and Install WordPress
B. Theme Ideas/Changing Themes on a Whim
C. Plugins
D. Widgets
E. Live Keyword Analysis

Appendix A. How to Sign Up with BlueHost and Install WordPress

Go to http://www.hostmonster.com/track/cjeffoakes

You will see a screen that looks like this...

Click on "Sign Up Now."

The next screen will look like this...

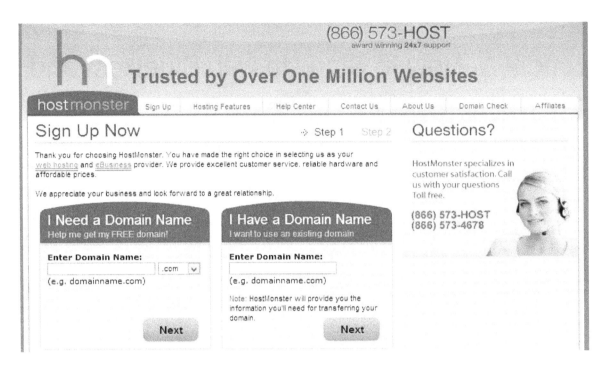

Simply enter the domain name you have chosen in the left option and choose either .com, .org, .net, etc from the dropdown menu to the right of the domain you seek. If you already own a domain, use the choice on the right. If you have a free website you are transferring to self-hosting, you will use the right option. After entering the desired domain information, click "Next."

The next screen you will go to will ask for your personal information such as name, address, email, and so forth. Scroll down and there will be a special offer. This offer chances from time to time and whether you choose it or not is up to you, but generally speaking, if you are just starting out and are uncertain whether to go with an offer or not, just refuse for you can always add it later. The only difference being that if you add it later, you will pay a little more. In some cases, the offers you may choose can be had by obtaining free or very inexpensive plugins.

For instance, the current offer is a special rate on the Power Pack, which to be honest, I am considering adding myself for the higher rate, so you may consider it. Much depends on your personal finances at this point, for this extra is not vital, but nice.

Scroll further down and you will find package choices as well as various security options. Personally, I opted out of the extra security functions for I did not feel I needed them for my kind of websites, but you can read about these by clicking "More information" and decide for yourself.

Finally, you will enter your billing information and choose "Next" at the bottom of the screen.

After choosing "Next," you will be given additional instructions and receive an email from BlueHost. When I first signed on, I had to enter the password information sent to me in an email, but a friend has informed me that he was allowed directly into the control panel. Whichever method is in operation when you sign up, just be sure to make a note of any user name and password information for you will need it for logging in to the control panel.

To log in, you will simply go to either Bluehost.com or HostMonster.com and enter your login information. You will then arrive at a screen that looks like the original screen from which you first entered the site. But at the top right-hand corner, you will notice a blue button which reads, "Control Panel Login."

Click on this blue button and you will arrive at a screen that looks like the following...

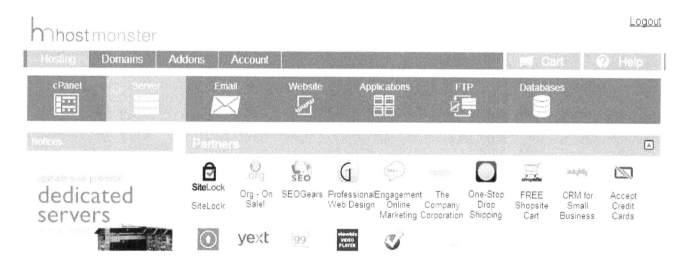

Just below the HostMonster (or BlueHost) logo, you can see a tab in green that reads "Hosting." Just to the right of that is a blue tab which reads "Domains." We are now going to assign your domain.

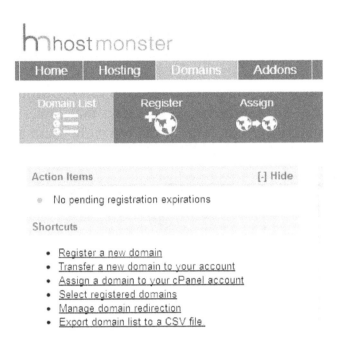

Under "Shortcuts" choose "Assign a domain to your cPanel account. The next screen will look like...

Assign Domain

This utility will help you assign a domain to your jeffoakes.me cPanel a

Step 1: Enter Domain

First, select a domain name that you would like to assign.

○ Use a domain that is already associated with your account.

Domain: [All domains assigned ▾]

OR

◉ Use a domain that is **not** already associated with your account.

Domain: [|]

There are 4 steps here. Some choices will be pre-populated so you may need to change them. In Step one as seen, choose the first option, "Use a domain already associated..."

You can likely skip step two as it relates only to websites previously owned and transferred. If your website is completely new, you should be able to just ignore this step.

Step three will ask you to choose the location of the new domain. Since you are setting up your primary web address (domain), choose the second option, "Parked domain." Later, if you add another domain to the first website and want the two linked in some way, you can connect them using the other options. I recommend phoning support if you do this so you can get it the way you want it. For now, because this is your only website and your primary one, park it.

Finally, Step four asks for the directory location. Again, as this is your primary website, you will choose the first option, "use an existing directory" and ensure that the proper site is chosen in the dropdown box (there should only be one if this is your only website—otherwise, get with support for detailed instructions).

The click the green "assign this domain" button at the bottom.

Your domain is now assigned.

Next, you are going to choose the platform in which to build your website.

Go to the tab at the top which reads, "Hosting."

Here you will face a control panel with numerous options. At first, this will seem quite intimidating, but don't worry, it is really fairly simple.

Scroll down until you see a section called "Site Builders." It will look like this...

Recall that I said you could build with a variety of site builders, depending on your own preferences and needs? If you want a strictly mobile website, which is growing in popularity, though seems counter-productive to me considering it is easy to make a standard website also mobile, you can choose the "goMobi" builder. Weebly and Simple Scripts are also here which are standard website builders, but considering that you are going to want to add a blog anyway, I recommend just starting with a blog site, WordPress. The choice is yours, but I am going to explain the WP way since that is all I use.

After choosing the site builder, you will be taken to a screen that allows you to upload this builder program into your server space. After doing this, all your building will occur from your website control panel and you will only need to come here for adding things such as email and other special features (explained in another book/month).

At the top of the screen, you will see an image/set of choices which look like this...

This is very simple. Scroll down to where you see the following "Script List."

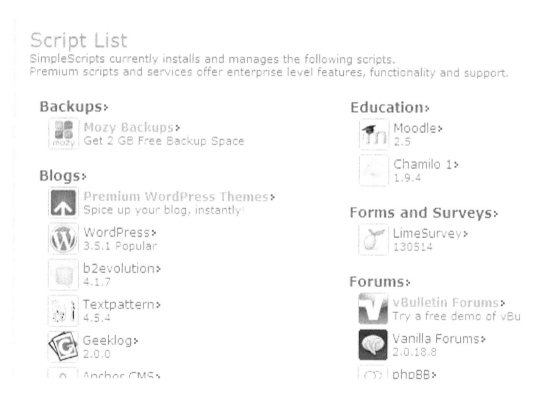

Choose the one you want, namely WordPress, and click on it.

On the next screen, scroll down until you see "Install WordPress" as follows...

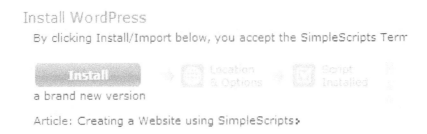

Next, you will be taken to a screen which asks you to enter location and preferences.

See the following image.

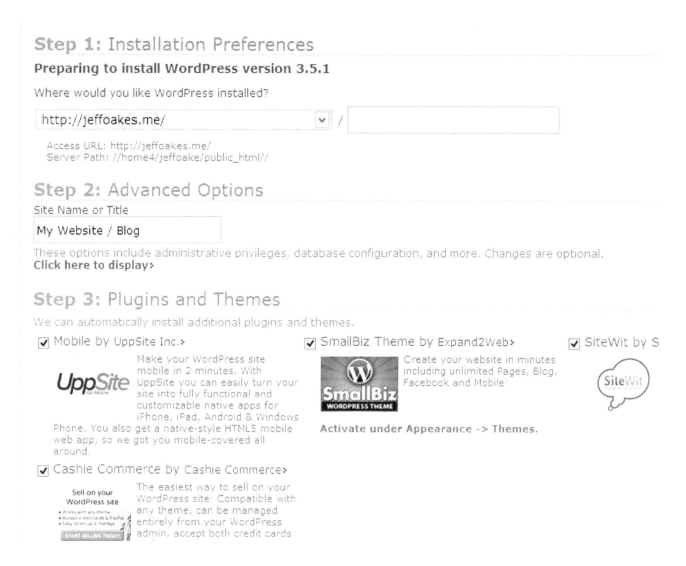

Step 1: Installation Preferences

Preparing to install WordPress version 3.5.1

Where would you like WordPress installed?

http://jeffoakes.me/   /

Access URL: http://jeffoakes.me/
Server Path: //home4/jeffoake/public_html//

Step 2: Advanced Options

Site Name or Title

My Website / Blog

These options include administrative privileges, database configuration, and more. Changes are optional.
Click here to display

Step 3: Plugins and Themes

We can automatically install additional plugins and themes.

☑ Mobile by UppSite Inc.

Make your WordPress site mobile in 2 minutes. With UppSite you can easily turn your site into fully functional and customizable native apps for iPhone, iPad, Android & Windows Phone. You also get a native-style HTML5 mobile web app, so we got you mobile-covered all around.

☑ SmallBiz Theme by Expand2Web

Create your website in minutes including unlimited Pages, Blog, Facebook and Mobile!

Activate under Appearance -> Themes.

☑ SiteWit by S

☑ Cashie Commerce by Cashie Commerce

The easiest way to sell on your WordPress site! Compatible with any theme, can be managed entirely from your WordPress admin, accept both credit cards

Step One will ask for the location. Since this is your only website/domain currently with BlueHost, there will only be a single option and it should populate. If not, just choose the domain from the dropdown menu. Later, if you add more domains, you will have to choose which to install to. This allows you to have some websites in WP, others only mobile, and others in Weebly or Simple Scripts. Or you can have them all in WP as do I. The choice is yours.

In Step two, you will change the site name from "My Website/Blog" to the actual name of your website. In the case of wallysweirdstuff.com, I entered Wallys Weird Stuff for this is the proper name of the site.

Step three allows you to automatically install certain useful plugins from the get-go. These change from time to time so just read them and if you think you may like to use them, leave them checked. If you are uncertain, just leave them checked for all this does is add them to your plugin list. To use them, you would still need to activate them later (This is discussed fully on Days 14 and 15 of this book).

Finally, Step four is the boring legal stuff. Read the Terms and Conditions, check the box, and click complete.

Now, after you have done this, you will likely be taken to a screen which informs you that you are about to overwrite your website. It will ask you to verify this choice and you want to confirm. If you'd like to understand why this is happening, simply open a new tab in your browser now, enter your domain name in the address line, then hit enter. Your website will open but you will notice the BlueHost/HostMonster logo and a bunch of links for ads. This is the default of your website until you install a script/platform and begin building. Since you don't want your website to look like this, you overwrite the script. After you do so, you will be informed of success and you are now ready to begin building your website.

If the tab with your website is still open, refresh it. If not, reopen it. You will then be taken to a fairly blank screen that looks like this (if using WordPress)...

This is the login screen for your website. To enter this whenever you want to access your site as an administrator, you will type into an address line "yourwebsitename.com/admin." Notice that I even used Admin for my username. Remember earlier I told you to keep track of your login information? If you did not choose (or were even given an option to choose) a username, enter the email address you signed up with and the password you either chose or were given. The click on the blue "Log In" button to the lower right.

From here, you will be take to your WP dashboard and this ends this tutorial. On Day 13 of this book, you learned how to explore the dashboard and choose themes and other options.

Additional Host Options

One of the most popular choices worldwide is Hostgator. Hostgator is also one of the oldest web hosting companies with millions of happy users. They have 24/7 support via chat or a toll free phone number, but bear in mind that they are located in the United States, so toll free is a relative term. As for up-time, hostgator is known for having excellent reliability and their rates are very low, starting at just under $4 USD. However, to make up for the reduced rates, the company also tends to put inline ads on your website. Some find this to be a bit of a nuisance, though others do not. One thing to consider is whether these ads will detract from your business for if they run an ad for a competitor, this may not be good. This is assuming, of course, that one of your competitors is even advertising with them. On the plus side, they offer unlimited disc space and bandwidth along with a number of other nifty perks. If you'd like to check out Hostgator, just go to hostgator.com.

Another popular option, also located in America, is Justhost. Justhost offers unlimited bandwidth and disc space along with unlimited domain hosting and email accounts. They boast one of the best money-back guarantees in the industry and have a strong, loyal following—so they must be doing something right. Their packages generally run $6.95/month USD, but they are often running great new account specials. As of this writing, new clients can get their service for $3.25 USD per month. They too have 24/7 live chat support along with a toll-free number (but remember, they are located in America). To check out Justhost, go to http://www.justhost.com/track/owe4

One of the best choices among American host companies for WordPress is Hostmonster. This company provides all of the features found with the previous mentioned companies along with a plethora of perks including bonus Google Adwords time, three free domains when siging up, a low-cost option to increase loading time for your website (available at sign-up or any time thereafter), and excellent customer service. Millions of WordPress site owners use this hosting company. They have numerous options for signing up and offer rates as low as $3.95/month USD. This is an excellent choice. If you would like to get Hostmonster, just go to hostmonster.com.

Saving the best for last, Bluehost is the old man on the field. Bluehost has been around a long time and was one of the first companies to offer self-hosted WordPress websites. They offer all of the perks mentioned in the previous companies along with very reliable service, incredible customer service and support, and a guarantee that they stand solidly behind. Of all the WordPress host companies, this one has the highest marks regardless of whom you ask. In short, Bluehost is clearly the most popular choice but also the best. Aside from Ez-web-hosting.com (which I recommend simply because they are an excellent choice AND local), Bluehost is the one you simply cannot go wrong with. They offer rates as low as $3.95/month USD and provide WordPress website owners with one-click installation when switching from the free hosting platform to self-hosting services. In other words, if you decide to build in the free platform initially and switch to self-hosting later, this is the best choice to make. To get Bluehost, simply go to http://www.bluehost.com/track/owc5

Appendix B. Theme Ideas/Changing Themes on a Whim

As mentioned earlier in this book, it is very easy to change themes in WordPress. If you keep on the lookout for great themes and learn how to adapt each to your website, you will in the course of time acquire several in your library. There are pros and cons to this.

The main pro is that it gives you options, choices.

The main con is that after some time, your library becomes cluttered and sometimes, you may inadvertently switch to a theme which messed things up a bit the last time you used it. If you ever get one of these and you know you will not use it, get it out of your library.

Now, about that library. Go to your Dashboard, then Appearance, then Themes. You will then see at the upper left, the "Manage Themes" tab. Below the theme which is currently installed on your site, you will see "Available Themes."

These are all the themes you have downloaded and either tried, or meant to try at some point. Here is my current library on 365CrazyWebTraffic.com

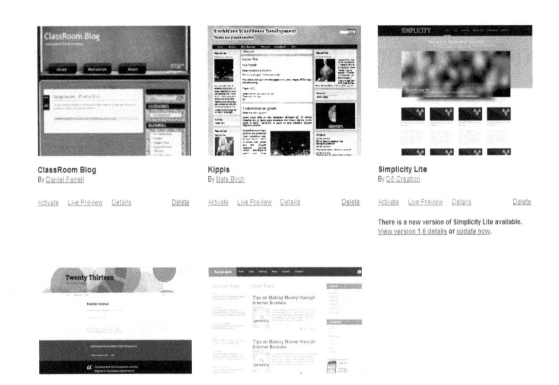

ClassRoom Blog
By Daniel Farrell

Activate   Live Preview   Details   Delete

Kippis
By Mats Birch

Activate   Live Preview   Details   Delete

Simplicity Lite
By D5 Creation

Activate   Live Preview   Details   Delete

There is a new version of Simplicity Lite available.
View version 1.6 details or update now.

So I have five themes in my library, not counting the theme I am already using. These I downloaded and considered, but some are better with little content whereas others look best when filled. Thus, I am not sure which of these, if any, will become the key theme for the site, but at least I have them.

Some things to note however.

Not all themes switch over the same. Sometimes, you may switch themes and discover that header or footer or whatever that you spent hours perfecting is now crud. And you can do a "Live Preview" of the theme before activating it, but often these do not show the whole truth and nothing but the truth. I have previewed themes, been pleased with what I saw, then cried when I activated.

The solution?

I returned to the previous theme and deleted the one that made me cry. Serves it right.

Another thing to keep in mind too.

When you get your host company, all have limits on how much storage space can be used for your website. Yes, there are limits. Themes add to this space as does anything else. That said, I cannot imagine anyone killing their storage space with themes. I have several websites running on my account with HostMonster and am coming nowhere close to filling my limit. Still, it is good to keep such things in mind.

Finally, as mentioned earlier in this book, if you don't like any of the free themes, you can always purchase them. Themeforest is the best site I have found for doing so and not only can you buy themes, you can buy them exclusive, meaning that ONLY you get to use it.

Go to http://themeforest.net/?ref=owc to check out their selection. You can search by virtually any category of website you can imagine for they have thousands of excellent themes "in stock."

Appendix C. Some Cool Plugins

This is simply a listing of plugins which you can find through WordPress to add to your website. I neither recommend nor endorse these but rather am simply providing this listing to give you some idea about what is out there.

According to WordPress, as of April 4, 2014, there are 30,308 plugins in their download center. To access this center, go to https://wordpress.org/plugins/. Here you will see plugins listed according to popular tags, as featured, most popular, and by search. Of course, you can located these from your WP dashboard as well, but sometimes browsing can be fun and enlightening.

Again, to give you an idea of what is out there, here is a short list without fluff or huff. If you want to see what it does, simply look it up using your search feature on the site dashboard or go to the WP download center listed above. Or, if reading this in ebook format, just click on the links.

WordPress Social Sharing Optimization

NextGEN Facebook Open Graph +

PurpleXMLs

Zedity™ The Easiest Way To Create Your Content!

WP GCM

Share Buttons by E-MAILiT

Convertable Contact Form Builder Analytics and Lead Management
    Dashboard

Google Analytics Dashboard for WP

CP Image Store with Slideshow

Google Universal Analytics

Free Live Support Chat

Google Captcha (reCAPTCHA)

AtContent — Grow Audience & Monetize Blog

WordPress SEO by Yoast

Easy Media Gallery

Gallery Bank

Zedity™ The Easiest Way To Create Your Content!

Share Buttons by E-MAILiT

WP Image Borders

Dreamstime Stock Photos

Media File Manager Advanced

WYSIWYG HTML Editor 3D Drag And Drop Visual Editor & Web Page
    Builder!

Landing Pages Builder

Ads Campaigns

Black Studio TinyMCE Widget

BePro Listings

Embedly

Double your Email Subscribers + Twitter Sharing by SumoMe

WordPress Social Sharing Optimization

NextGEN Facebook Open Graph +

Zedity™ The Easiest Way To Create Your Content!

Share Buttons by E-MAILiT

Microblog Poster

CP Image Store with Slideshow

ThemeLoom Widgets

Social Contact Display

PR-Gateway Connect

SocialRadios

Sticky Email Opt-in Widget

Sticky Ecommerce Targeted Offer / Discount Widget

Sexy Polling

Virtual Agent by ASKOM

TT Post Viewer

WP ban manager

CM Answers

jPages pagination for WordPress

CommentPress Core

cbnet Multi Author Comment Notification

Anti-spam by CleanTalk

SZ - Google for WordPress

Conditional CAPTCHA for WordPress

bbPress Like Button

Disable Comments

iQ Block Country

NO CAPTCHA Anti-Spam

Easy Media Gallery

Appendix D. Widgets

Once again, the list of widgets is pretty massive. WordPress lists 3,827 as of April 4, 2014. You can see these at https://wordpress.org/plugins/tags/widget or locate them in your plugin search on your dashboard.

For now, this small sampling will give you some idea of what is out there.

Easy Media Gallery

Gallery Bank

Double your Email Subscribers + Twitter Sharing by SumoMe

WordPress Social Sharing Optimization

NextGEN Facebook Open Graph +

Zedity™ The Easiest Way To Create Your Content!

Meks Easy Ads Widget

Share Buttons by E-MAILiT

JM Simple QR code Widget

Convertable Contact Form Builder Analytics and Lead Management
    Dashboard

Feedweb

Recently Edited Content Widget

Meks ThemeForest Smart Widget

Dexs Navigation Tree

Meks Simple Flickr Widget

Meks Smart Author Widget

Free Live Support Chat

Meks Smart Social Widget

Vidsy.tv video gallery and video CMS

AtContent — Grow Audience & Monetize Blog

Social Contact Display

Live Chat - Casengo

Heroic Posts Widget

Instamojo button

SocialRadios

Simple Amazon.de MP3 Widget

Sticky Email Opt-in Widget

Store Locator by Donde

Japkin

Social Contests

Ads Campaigns

Black Studio TinyMCE Widget

Rating-Widget

SMK Sidebar Generator

WebLibrarian

Simple Instagram Widget

Tumblr Widget

Music Store

Button Widget

X Forms Express

Smart Slider 2

Askupa Twitter Feed

Contact Bank

Facebook Master

Youtube Master

Vine Master

BTC Exchange Widget

IntelliWidget Per Page Featured Posts and Menus

Query Wrangler

Amazon Master

StatsFC Score Predictor

Automatic Lead Generator for WooCommerce

Wordfence Security - Live Traffic Admin Widget

Storehours

WP Product Review

Free Stock Photos Foter

Simple Amazon.de Search/Suche Widget

Twitter Widget with Styling

MailMojo Widget

World Cup Predictor

Virtual Agent by ASKOM

Agent virtuel ASKOM

WebEngage Feedback, Survey and Notification

my press articles

Benchmark Email Lite

TT Post Viewer

ExtraWatch PRO (Live Stats, Heatmap, Click tracking, Download
    Monitor and more)

ExtraWatch FREE (Live Stats, Heatmap, Click tracking, Download
    Monitor and more)

LinkedIn Master

Grand Flagallery - Photo Gallery Plugin

The Events Calendar

StatsFC Live

Basic Instagram Widget

Gravity Forms Directory

Delicious Readings

Multilingual Press

FlexyTalk - Live Chat

Hitsteps Visitor Manager

Featured Post Widget

Featured Category Widget

Category Column

Advanced Featured Post Widget

Advanced Category Column

Ads Easy

A5 Recent Post Widget

amr ical events lists

Sexy Contact Form

Floating button

Suppa Menu (Free)

bbPress Like Button

StatsFC Results

Reverbnation Master

Ceceppa Multilingua support to Customizr

ieteikt Draugiem WordPress spraudnis

Link View

Easy Instagram

Sharing Buttons & Analytics by AddShoppers

Surveymonkey Button

NO CAPTCHA Anti-Spam

AAM Animate Scroll WordPress

my beautiful tubes

Nextend Accordion Menu

Random Banner

Categorized Tag Cloud

WOW Slider

Smart AD Tags

BSK PDF Manager

Add Link Post

Welcome User Widget

Bulk Photo to Product Importer Extension for WooCommerce (Free)

Scroll Back To Top

StatsFC Fixtures

StatsFC Table

Recent Posts Video Icon

Free Quotation by KRIS_IV

Business Contact Widget

WordPress Shortcodes

Appendix E. Live Keyword Analysis

One of the best kept secrets on the Internet is a little website that does a huge job helping people perfectly optimize what they have written.

If you use Joast or any other of the excellent SEO plugins found on WordPress, you may not be inclined to use Live Keyword Analysis. But this awesome tool can be very useful if you decide to write articles and sit on them for a time before publishing. In addition, this is great for getting up to three keyword combinations perfectly optimized every time. Here is what you will see when you go to http://live-keyword-analysis.com/.

livekeyword**analysis**

Keyword Analysis is a fundamental **search engine optimization strategy.** Using the **live keyword analysis tool** below, you can simply type in your keywords and then paste in your text and your **keyword density analysis** will be done on the fly. No need to press submit, it updates automatically. This means that you can do all your editing within the text box, and receive live feedback about your **keyword density.**

Click to see how to use this tool effectively and the rules it uses.

Advice on the **best** Search Engine Optimization Resources.

Step one: Put in the keyword(s) you want to check.

Keyword One:	[ ]	Ratio: [ ] %
Keyword Two:	[ ]	Ratio: [ ] %
Keyword Three:	[ ]	Ratio: [ ] %

Step two: Paste in the text that you want to analyse.

The way to use this is simple. Step One is to enter the keywords (or exact combinations) in the spaces Keyword One, Keyword Two, and Keyword Three. Then copy and paste what you want to analyze into the box for Step Two.

Instantly, you will get a keyword ratio for what you have written. If you want a density of 3% exactly, you can make live changes to the text pasted into the box and watch the density change before your eyes.

Of course, Google stands firm in stating that they do not look at a particular density, but you can be assured that if you do this and your keywords come out at less than a percentage, you had better make you subject more clear—in other words, add your keywords, your subjects, in a few more times.

Something more to remember about this is that once you have gotten the keyword density you desire, you can then copy and paste back to your Word Document or wherever. Just bear in mind that all formatting will be stripped and you will need to reformat what you have written.

I personally recommend not getting too caught up in a particular keyword density, but many people find that having some kind of guideline helps them write content that is much clearer about the subject or subjects they want emphasized.

The Live Keyword Analysis is a great tool for this.

Index

A note on using this Index. I made this Index far more comprehensive than it needed to be. The reason for this was to provide you with yet one more example in the use of keywords. When marking most terms used commonly throughout this book, I marked EVERY occurrence. This caused the Index to list a separate page number for every time that word appeared. In other words, if the word appears six times on one page, the page is only listed once, but if it appears on subsequent pages, every page is listed rather than create a range of pages.

The reason I did it this way for this first book was to further clarify subject and keyword usage. Understanding that the subject of your site must be predominant throughout your site is key to getting plenty of traffic from the search engines. Thus, take a look at this index.

By simply scanning the index, you can see that some of the dominant subjects of this book are Content, Google, images, keywords, links, SEO, pages, traffic, Internet, plugins, website, and WordPress.

If this were a website, the search engines would likely view the site as being about "How to get website traffic using WordPress." This fairly describes this book, yes? See, the words that are used most often in your website are the ones the search engines will identify as your subject. These are the words that will bring traffic and should clearly draw those looking for what you create to your site.

Index

A note on using this Index. I made this Index far more comprehensive than it needed to be. The reason for this was to provide you with yet one more example in the use of keywords. When marking most terms used commonly throughout this book, I marked EVERY occurrence. This caused the Index to list a separate page number for every time that word appeared. In other words, if the word appears six times on one page, the page is only listed once, but if it appears on subsequent pages, every page is listed rather than create a range of pages.

The reason I did it this way for this first book was to further clarify subject and keyword usage. Understanding that the subject of your site must be predominant throughout your site is key to getting plenty of traffic from the search engines. Thus, take a look at this index.

By simply scanning the index, you can see that some of the dominant subjects of this book are Content, Google, images, keywords, links, SEO, pages, traffic, Internet, plugins, website, and WordPress.

If this were a website, the search engines would likely view the site as being about "How to get website traffic using WordPress." This fairly describes this book, yes? See, the words that are used most often in your website are the ones the search engines will identify as your subject. These are the words that will bring traffic and should clearly draw those looking for what you create to your site.